IMAGES
of America

WESTBROOK

On the Cover: These unidentified girls on the float for Westbrook Greenhouses appear to be having a grand time. This float was part of the centennial celebration in 1914. (Westbrook Historical Society collection.)

IMAGES
of America

WESTBROOK

Mike Sanphy with the
Westbrook Historical Society

ARCADIA
PUBLISHING

ISBN 978-1-4671-2119-4

Published by Arcadia Publishing
Charleston, South Carolina

Printed in the United States of America

Library of Congress Control Number: 2013946727

For all general information, please contact Arcadia Publishing:
Telephone 843-853-2070
Fax 843-853-0044
E-mail sales@arcadiapublishing.com
For customer service and orders:
Toll-Free 1-888-313-2665

Visit us on the Internet at www.arcadiapublishing.com

This book is dedicated to Eleanor "Ellie" Conant Saunders, local historian and direct descendant of Samuel Conant, brother of Joseph Conant. Joseph is recognized as the first settler of Westbrook.

Contents

ACKNOWLEDGMENTS

A big thank-you goes to Suzan Roberts Norton for being a driving force in putting this material together. The majority of photographs in this book are from the Mike Sanphy collection and the Berg family collection along with other sources as noted. Thank-you also goes to the Westbrook Historical Society and the Walker Memorial Library for providing information and materials for completion of this book and to Eugene Berg for his many hours of editing.

All of the photographs in chapter nine were taken by Ernest Gerhardts and appear courtesy of the Berg family collection (EG/BFC) unless otherwise noted.

Introduction

Westbrook was incorporated as a town in 1814 after separating from Falmouth. This occurred while the area was still under the commonwealth of Massachusetts as the District of Maine. In 1820, the District of Maine separated from Massachusetts and became the state of Maine.

The original town of Westbrook was much bigger in size when it was incorporated and encompassed a large tract of land that is now a part of the city of Portland. It was in 1871 that the town of Deering was organized and annexed a large section of land that was originally a part of Westbrook. Deering later became a part of Portland. In 1891, the town of Westbrook changed its form of government to become the city of Westbrook, with Leander Valentine as its first mayor.

Evergreen Cemetery is Portland's largest and was actually founded in 1855 while the area was a part of Westbrook. Several prominent Westbrook citizens are buried there. The group Friends of Evergreen Cemetery is active in preserving the history of the cemetery and offers different programs and tours.

In 1976, the Westbrook Historical Society was founded with the purpose of collecting and preserving the town's history for future generations. It is unfortunate that many of its old buildings and landmarks in the downtown area were destroyed by urban renewal, and all that is left are photographs and memories. We have tried to include some images of the more important locations that were prominent in Westbrook's history as a town (and later, a city). There is a time capsule in Riverbank Park that was placed in 1914, and according to the plaque, it is to be opened on June 9, 2014. This capsule contains memorabilia from the 1914 centennial celebration.

In 2014, the same year this book will be published, Westbrook will celebrate the bicentennial of its incorporation as a town, and we have put this book together to capture some of Westbrook's earlier years for this event. It is interesting to look back and realize the advances that have been made over the years. Since 1914, Westbrook has changed from a mill town to a home for technology-based companies that employ hundreds of people. There has been a large increase in population, and the downtown has almost completely changed. After urban renewal, there was a period when the downtown area seemed to falter, as new businesses would come in but never last. In the last few years, we started to see some indication that the town was about to change. Now as Westbrook moves ahead, there are several exciting things happening, such as the recreational use of the river, a Westbrook Campus for Husson College, and new businesses in the city that are growing and investing money in the community. Westbrook is a great city and has great potential ahead; one cannot even imagine what Westbrook will be like in 2114. It is hoped that the Westbrook Historical Society, Walker Library History Room, and Friends of Evergreen Cemetery continue to attract people interested in preserving Westbrook's past for future generations.

The early history of Westbrook could only be told through spoken or written accounts as photography was nonexistent. We must rely on old documents, diaries, and stories passed down from generation to generation.

When first incorporated in 1814, the name Stroudwater was chosen but changed to Westbrook within six months by the citizens. The name Westbrook was chosen to honor Col. Thomas

Westbrook, a local businessman, and mast agent for King George III of England. Sadly, Colonel Westbrook died a debtor, and his body had to be secretly buried so that it could not be claimed by people he was indebted to, as was the custom of the time. In 1976, the final resting place of Colonel Westbrook was disclosed by Roger Knight, a direct descendant. The grave is located on the Knight Farm (also known as Smiling Hill Farm) on County Road in Westbrook. With permission of the Knight family, an archeological dig took place that included members of the Knight family, Westbrook Historical Society, and professional archeologists. The remains were determined to be that of Colonel Westbrook, and he was entombed back in the same spot with a marker stone. The gravesite is available for public viewing through the Knight family.

The Presumpscot River runs through Westbrook, and in the early years, hostilities with the local Indians developed when dams were placed at different locations in the river to harness the water for sawmills and other local commerce. In 1847, the Grant & Lyon Paper Mill was established on the north side of the river in the area known today as Cumberland Mills. In 1854, Samuel D. Warren of Grant, Daniel & Company of Boston purchased this mill. The mill expanded under this ownership, and Warren later became the sole owner of the company. The S.D. Warren Company became one of the largest paper mills in the world. The mill is presently owned by SAPPI and has been downsized considerably due to increasing foreign competition and a general decline in the industry. There was a time when the S.D. Warren Company was Westbrook's largest employer, and it was believed that it would always be here to provide jobs and tax revenue to Westbrook. In 1914, the people of Westbrook most likely looked at the progress that was made since 1814 and were secure in the knowledge that things were getting better; we look at things since that time and see changes but often question if they are for the better. We can only hope that they are.

The photographs in this book represent a small part of our town's history, and we invite people to visit the Westbrook Historical Society or the Walker Memorial Library History Room, where many more photographs and artifacts can be seen. We also encourage people to bring in old images and other items to add to these collections for present and future generations to enjoy.

One

Street Scenes

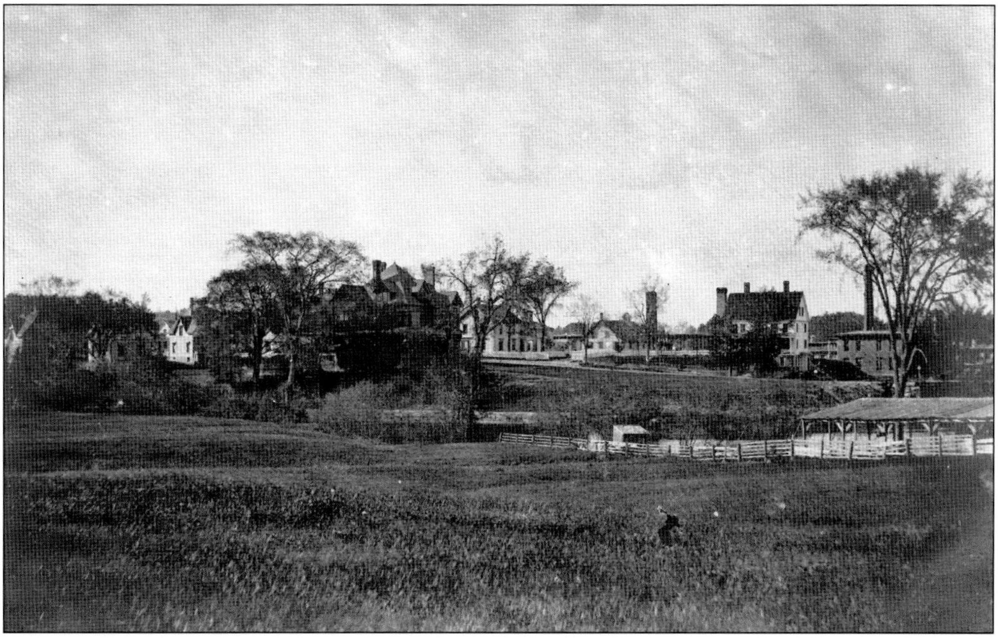

This photograph was taken in the early 1900s. This view looks north across the Presumpscot River from the rear of the Warren Library. The large building near the center of the photograph is the William L. Longley House, built in 1882 for the mill agent. This house later became the S.D. Warren Company guesthouse and was eventually renamed the Elms. The building to the right is often referred to as the White House by the millworkers. This was the main office building for the S.D. Warren Company. (Warren Library collection.)

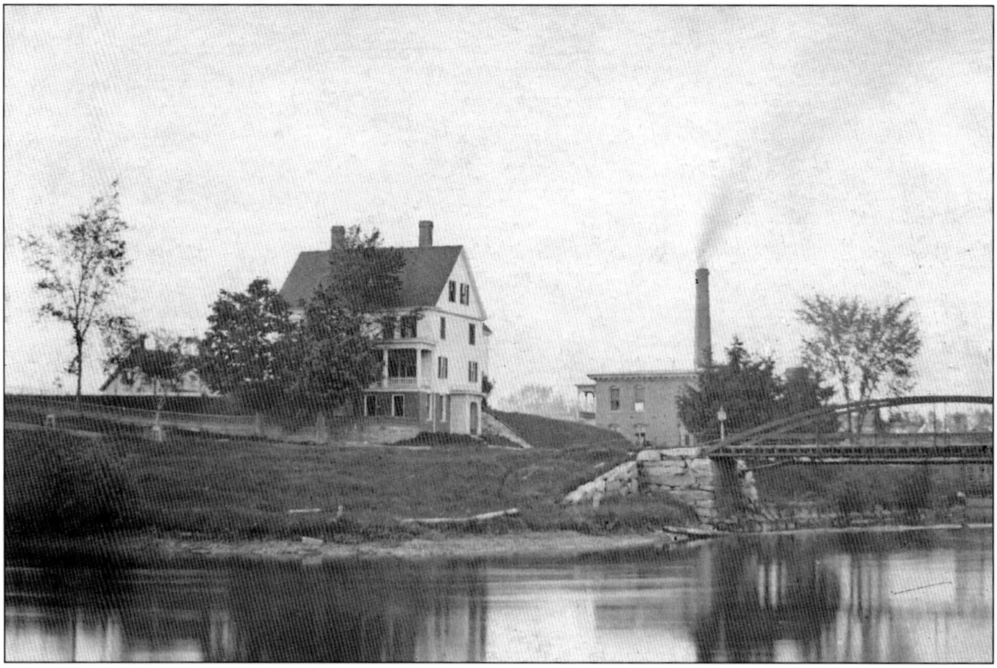

Seen north across the river, this building was the main office for the S.D. Warren Company. The office later relocated, and it was replaced by a structure to hold a new paper machine. (Warren Library collection.)

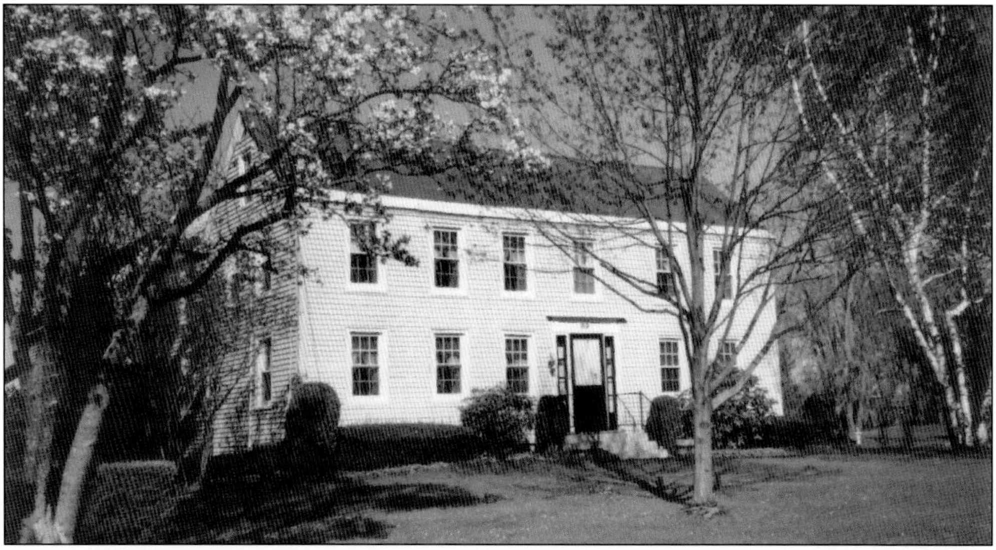

The Conant Homestead, located at 89 Conant Street, was built by Solomon Conant, son of Samuel who, with his brother Joseph, were the first permanent settlers in Westbrook. A captain in the militia, Solomon built the main house in 1774, two years before entering the Revolutionary War. The house once contained a tavern run by Solomon, and the land was farmed by generations of the Conant family. This house continues to be occupied by a descendant of its original builder. (Mike Sanphy collection.)

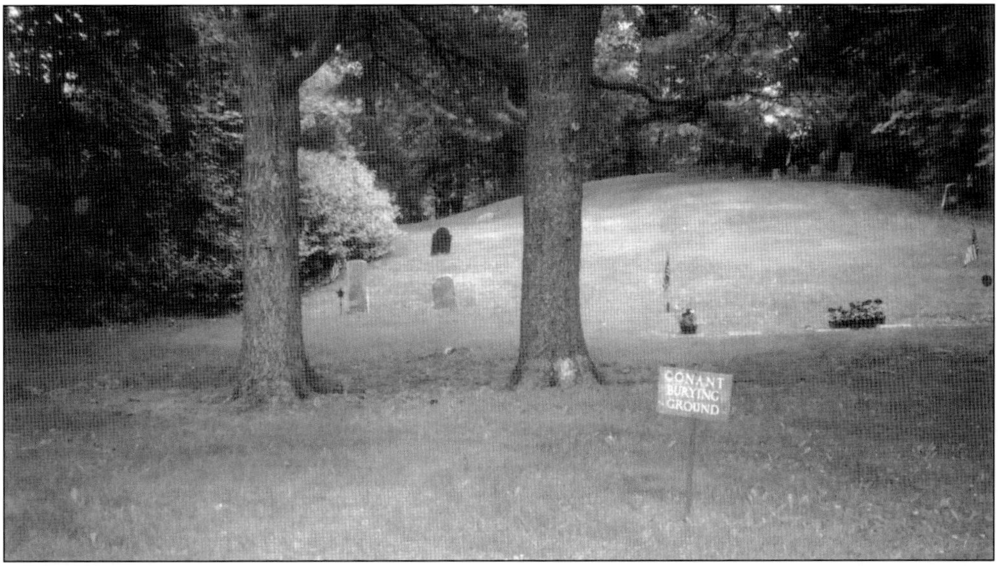

Conant Burying Ground is perhaps one of the oldest private cemeteries in Westbrook. Here lies the remains of many generations of Conants, including Joseph Conant, who was the first permanent settler of Westbrook, and his brother Samuel Conant. It has also been said that 12 Civil War veterans were interred here. (Mike Sanphy Collection.)

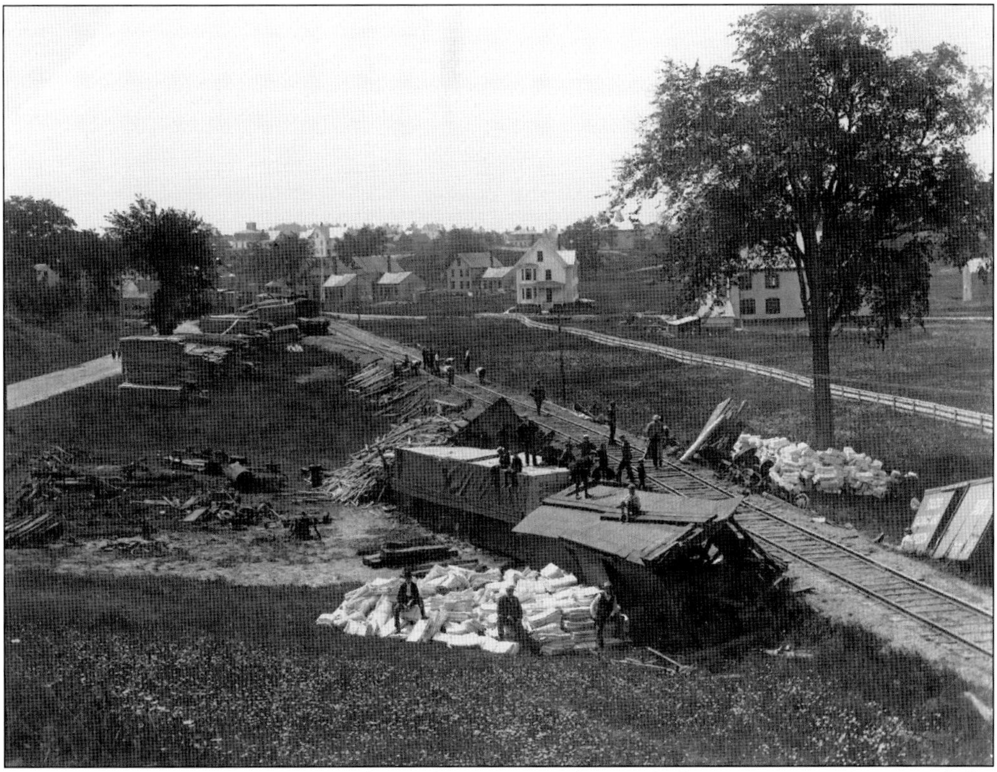

Pictured is a train derailment in the early 1900s on the tracks between Main Street and the Gorham line. Conant Street, on the left, was part of Route 25. Today, the railroad tracks are gone, and Route 25 now occupies the old railroad bed. (Warren Library collection.)

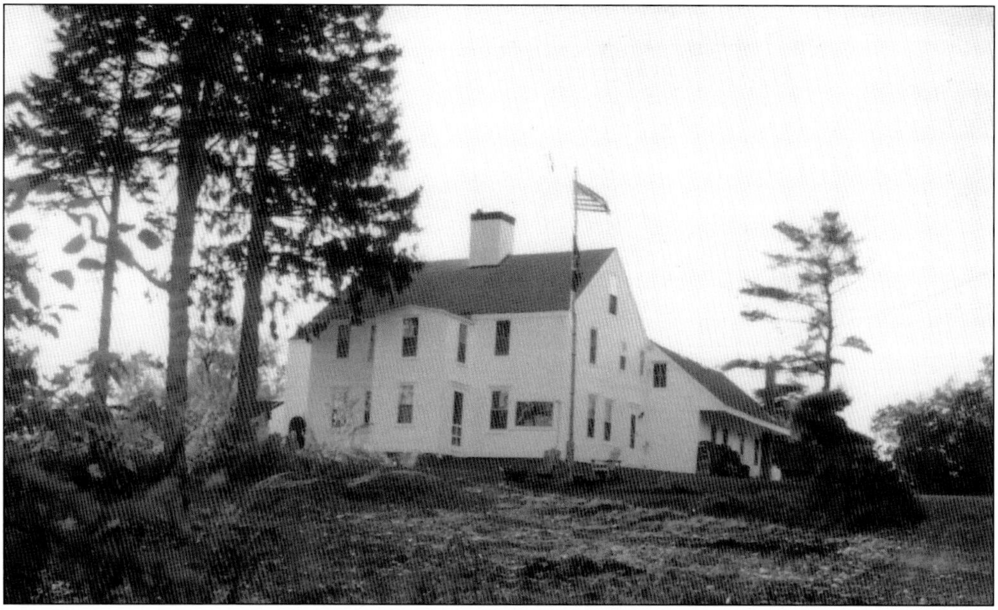

This house at 473 East Bridge Street was built around 1748 by James Winslow. Early Quaker meetings were held there, as were sessions of the first school in the area, of which there is any record. Meetings took place off the kitchen, which had deep windows and a great fireplace. In 1830, Sarah Jane Winslow, great-granddaughter of James, married Benjamin Boody, and the property remained in the Boody family until 1909. A succession of owners occupied the property thereafter. Dr. and Mrs. Ira Stockwell currently own and occupy the building. (Mike Sanphy collection.)

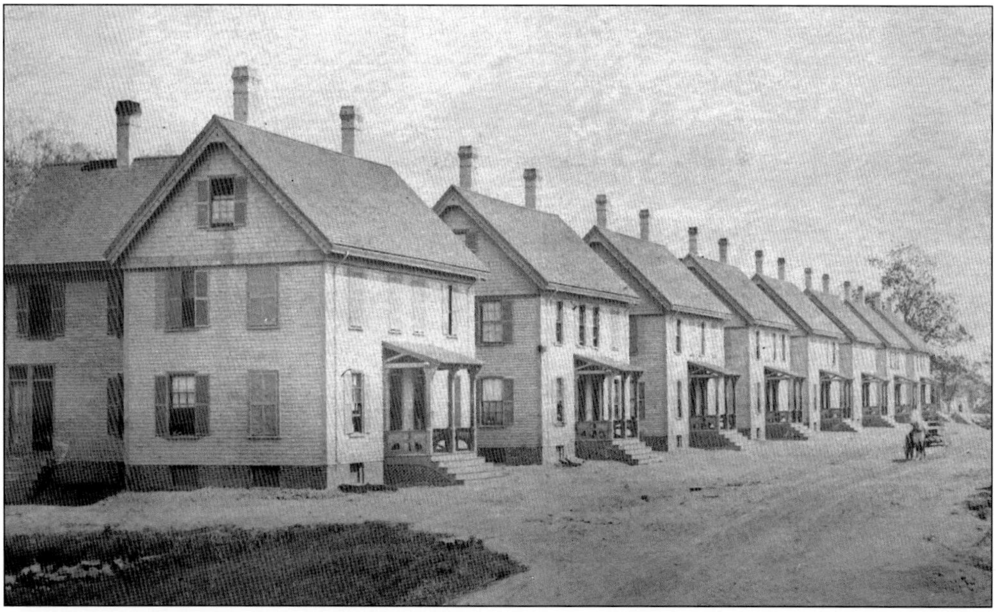

This photograph shows tenement houses under construction on Walker Street in 1881 for employees of the Westbrook Manufacturing Company. Many of the workers emigrated from Scotland, and the area became known as Scotch Hill. Many of the immigrants were skilled weavers. Most of these buildings are still standing as apartment houses and have been renovated several times. The area is still referred to as Scotch Hill. (Warren Library collection.)

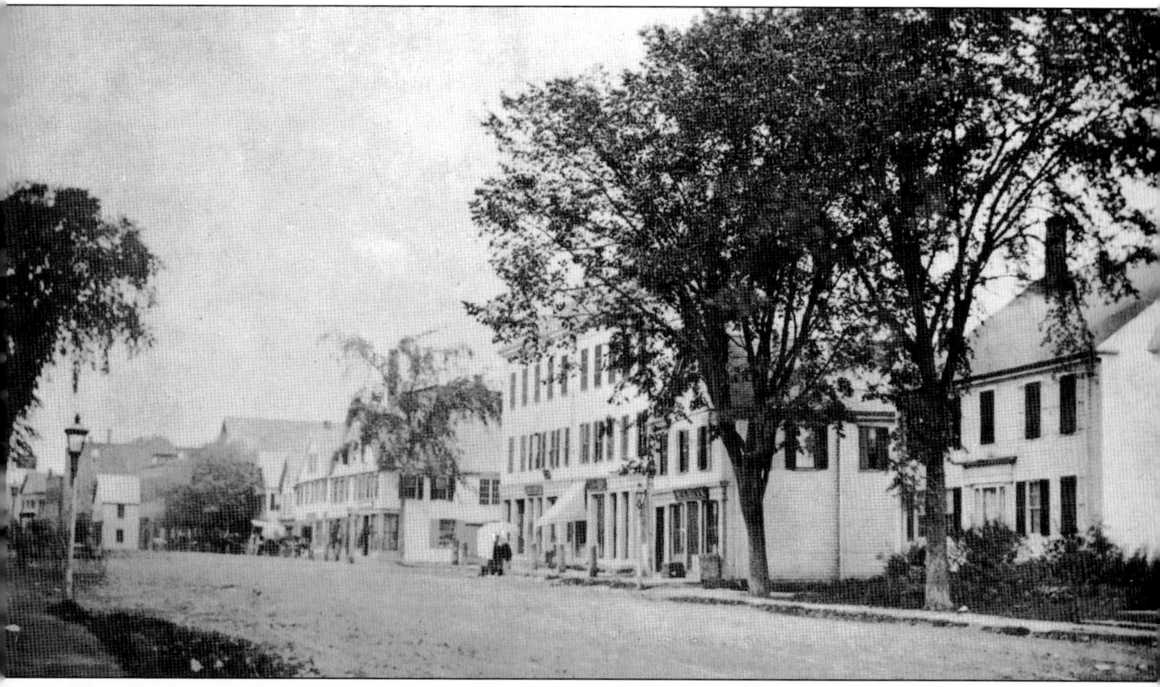

This photograph shows a view of Main Street looking west from Church Street. The large three-story building, on the corner of Bridge and Main Streets, was constructed in 1849 by Capt. John Warren, father of George and Lewis P. Warren, who were both prominent lumbermen. The building was known as the Warren Block for many years. Charles Vallee, father of famous entertainer Rudy Vallee, purchased the Woodman Drug Store on the first floor of this structure and changed the name to the Vallee Drug Store. The building eventually became known as the Vallee Block. The upper floors of the structure were destroyed by a spectacular fire in February 1942. The first floor was renovated, and several of the businesses reopened, including the Vallee Drug Store. The building still stands and is occupied by various businesses. (Mike Sanphy collection.)

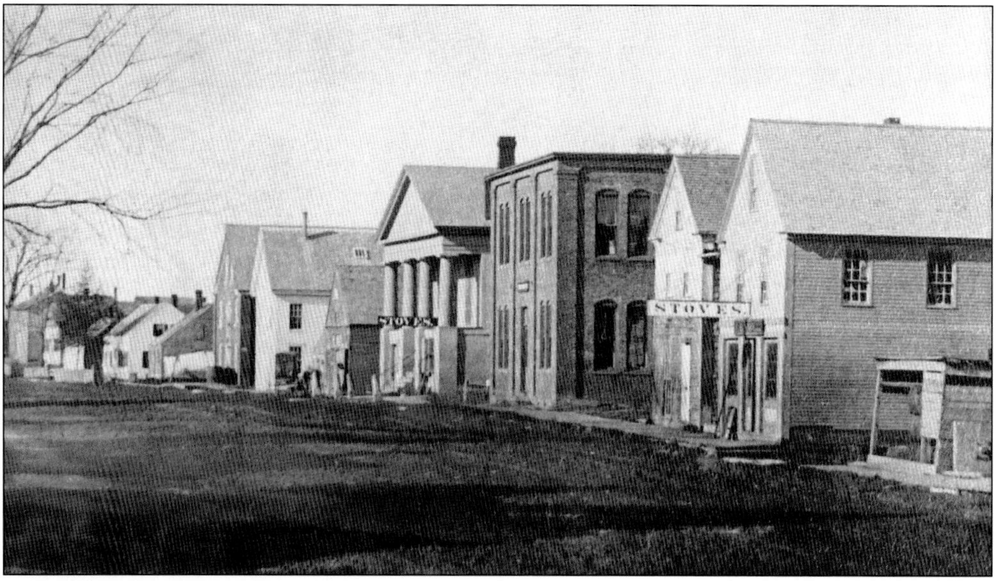

This picture was taken from the north side of Main Street and faces west from Central Street in the 1870s. The building with the pillars was the Universalist church, built in 1840. A new church was erected further down on Main Street, and this building housed several different businesses over the years. The structure was demolished several years ago. The two-story building's address next to it is 907 Main Street, and it still stands today. (Mike Sanphy collection.)

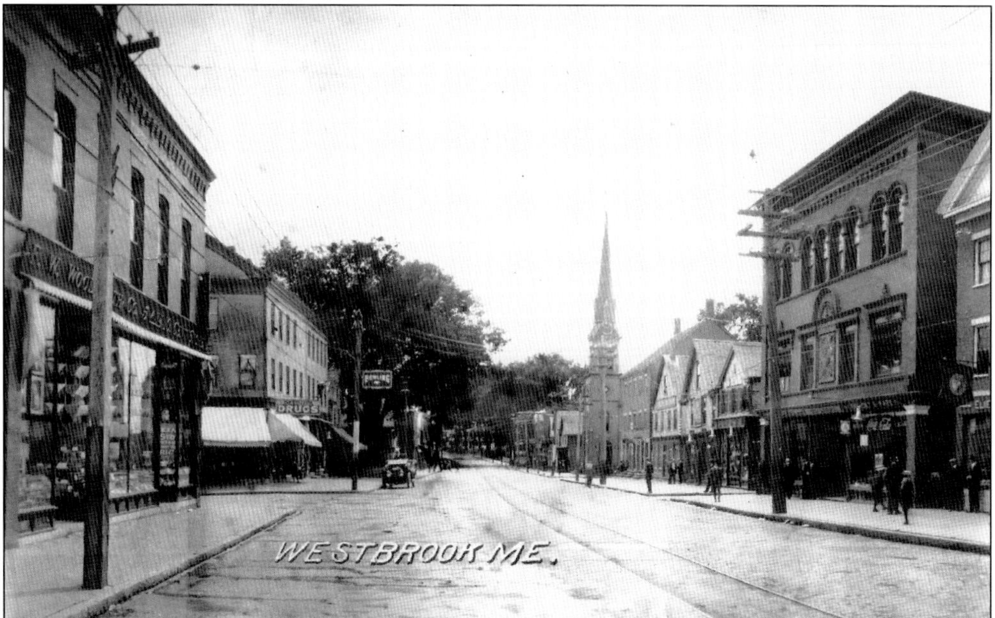

This view of Main Street looking east from Central Street was taken around 1905. At left is the Edwards Block, constructed in 1890 on the corner of Bridge and Main Streets. F.W. Woolworth occupied the first floor when the photograph was taken. Warren Furniture later occupied this space for many years, and Portland Pie Company is the present occupant. The three-story structure across the street is the Scates Building, constructed in 1903. (Mike Sanphy collection.)

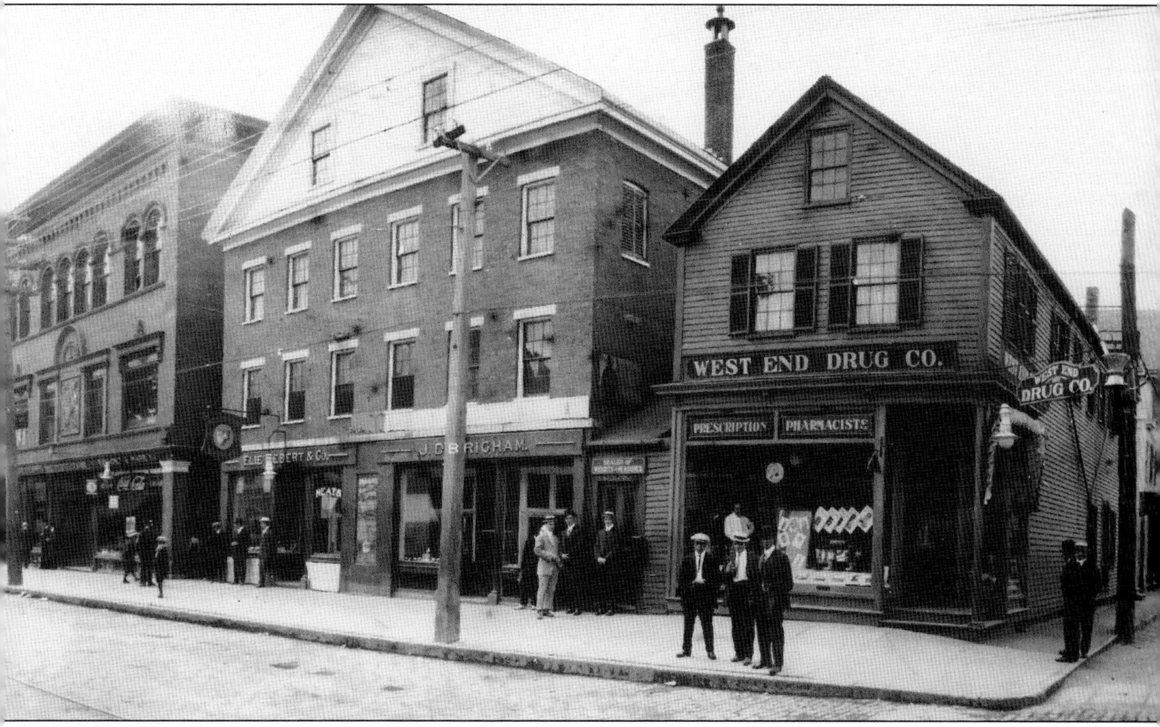

This view of Main Street at Fitch Street was taken in the early 1900s. The large building in the center of the photograph is the Brigham Block, constructed in 1844 by Dana Brigham and Henry Walker with bricks from Walker's brickyard at Prides Corner. The top floor of this structure was leased in 1873 by members of St. Hyacinth Parish and used as a church until a new church building was opened on Brown Street in 1879. The late Ernest Porell, a former mayor, opened and maintained a retail business in this building for many years. The Men's Shop opened here and later took over the entire first floor. The West End Drug Company was located on the corner of Fitch and Main Streets. As part of Westbrook's urban renewal project, these buildings were purchased and demolished in 1977. On January 8, 1978, a spectacular fire destroyed the structures before demolition. (Mike Sanphy collection.)

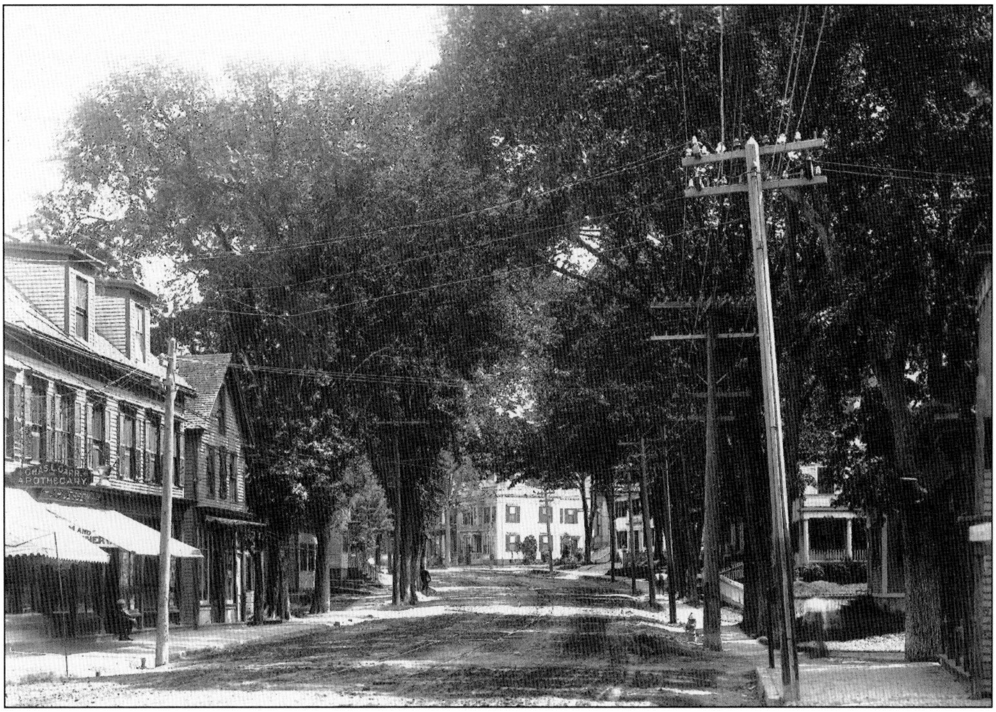

This view shows Main Street looking east from Church Street in the early 1900s. The building on the left had the Charles Carr Apothecary on the first floor with apartments on the second and third floors. In later years, Westbrook Hardware took over the first floor of this building. The large structure in the center of the photograph is the Lewis W. Edward family mansion on Main Street near Spring Street. (Mike Sanphy collection.)

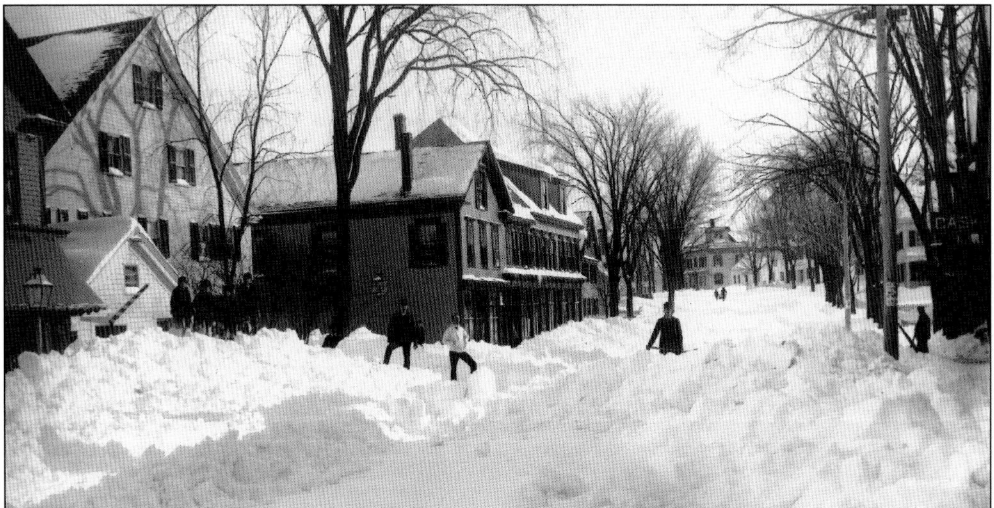

This view looks east along Main Street from the corner of Church Street after a heavy snowfall in the early 1900s. Snow had to be shoveled or rolled to make streets and walkways passable. The large wooden rollers measured 12 feet wide and 8 or 9 feet tall. The rollers were pulled by horses. The packed snow made a solid sleighing surface, but it was also the last to melt in the spring. (Westbrook Historical Society collection.)

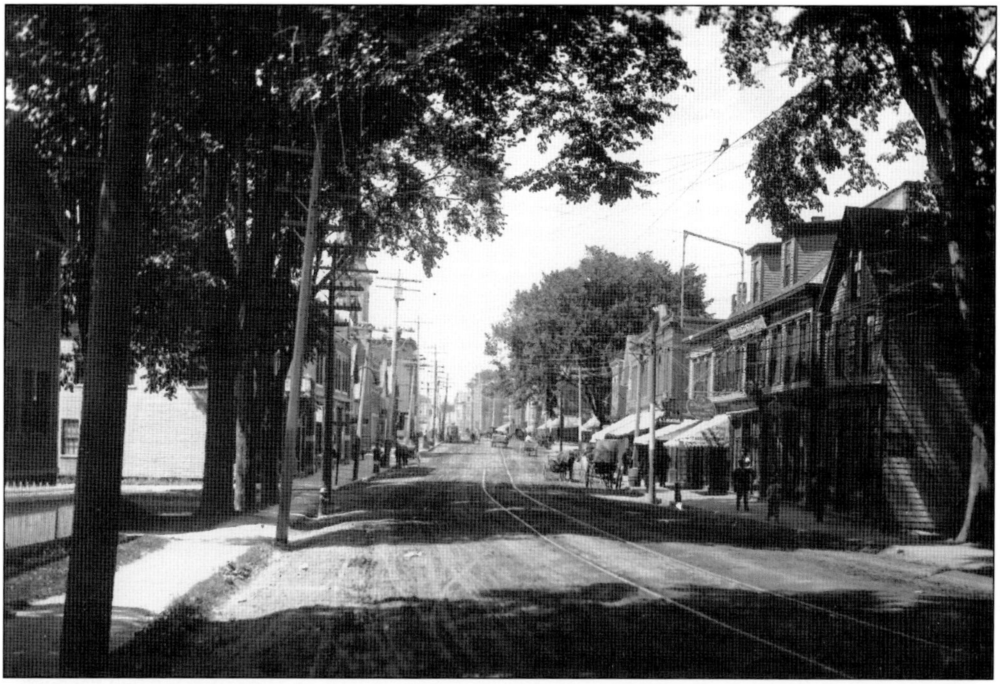

This view of Main Street looks west from the area of Spring Street around 1905. Trolley car tracks can be seen on the dirt street. (Mike Sanphy collection.)

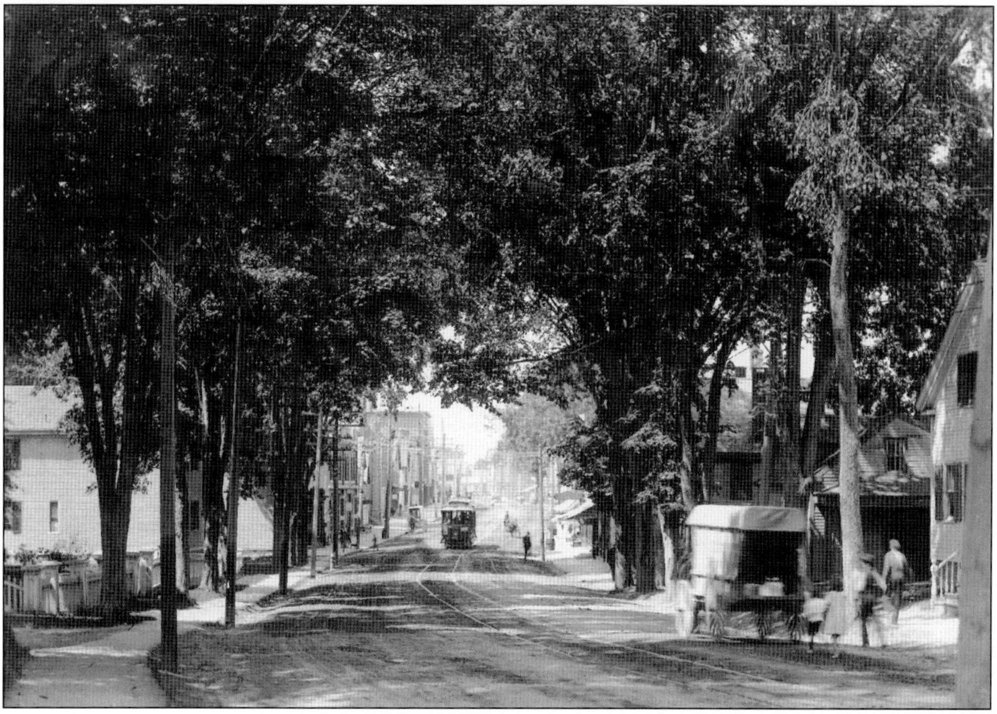

This photograph looks west along Main Street from the area of Spring Street as a trolley car approaches. Many of the beautiful trees seen in the image had to be destroyed in later years when they became infected by Dutch elm disease. (Mike Sanphy collection.)

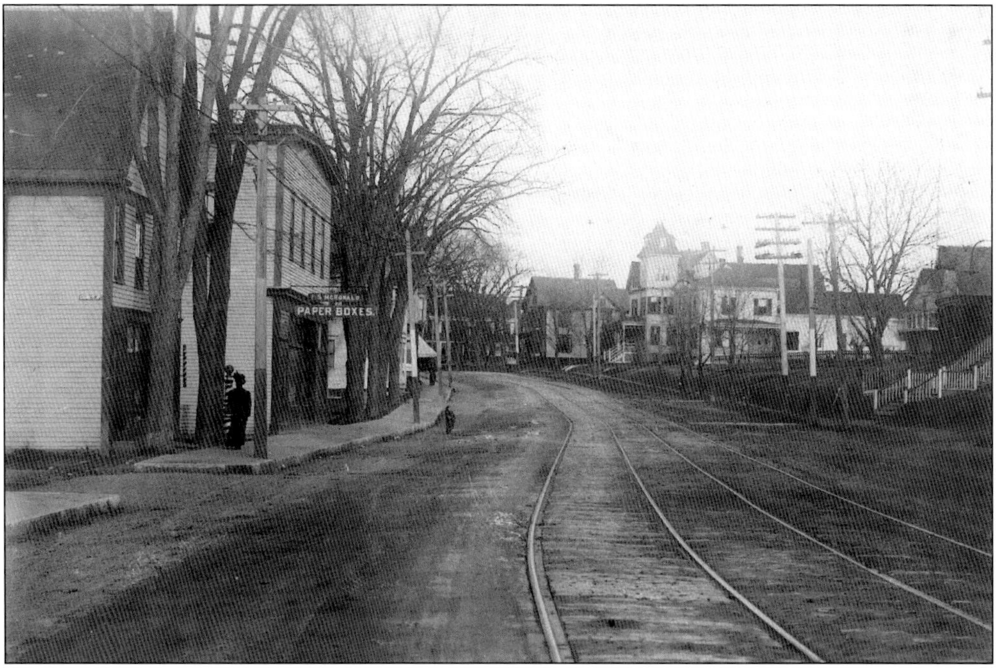

This photograph shows Main Street looking east from the area of Stevens Avenue. The large house with the tower in the center of this scene is situated at the approximate location where the Westbrook Arterial presently connects to Main Street. The building to the left of that structure is the approximate site of the Westbrook Public Safety Building. (Mike Sanphy collection.)

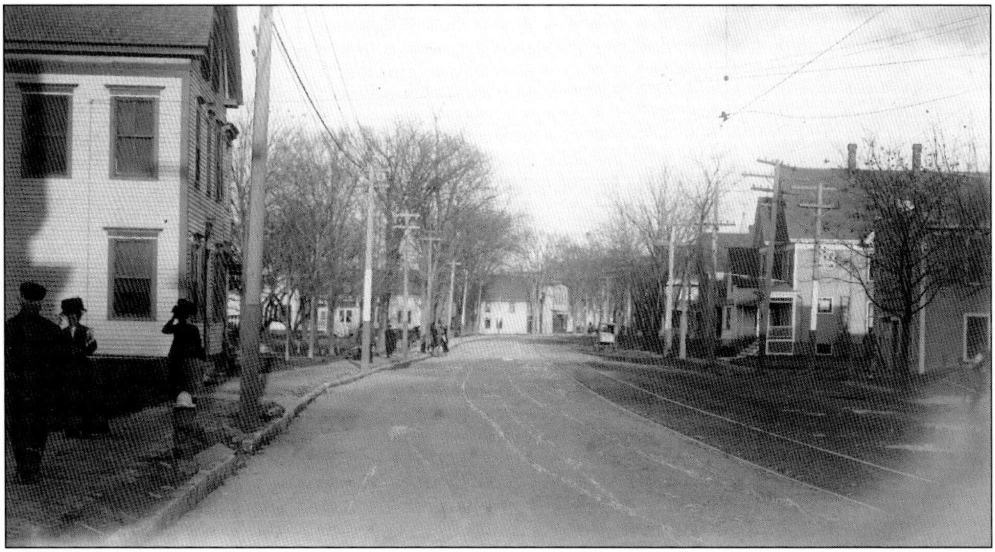

This photograph focuses on Main Street, looking east from Dunn Street. Riverbank Park can be seen to the left. Ladies with large bonnets can be seen walking on the sidewalk at left. (Mike Sanphy collection.)

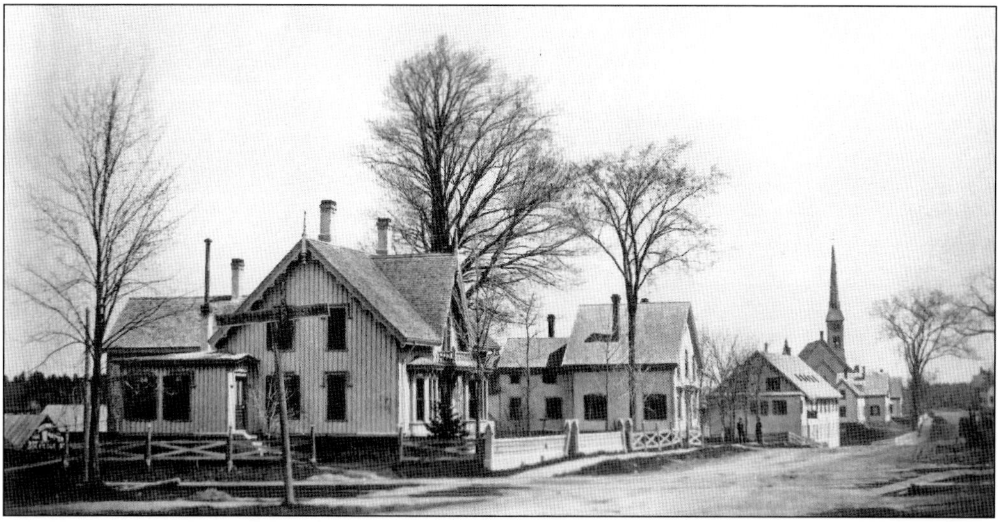

This is a view of Main Street, looking east from Rochester Street. Railroad tracks crossed Main Street at this location. The church seen in the distance is the Warren Congregational Church, at the corner of Warren Avenue and Cumberland Street. (Mike Sanphy collection.)

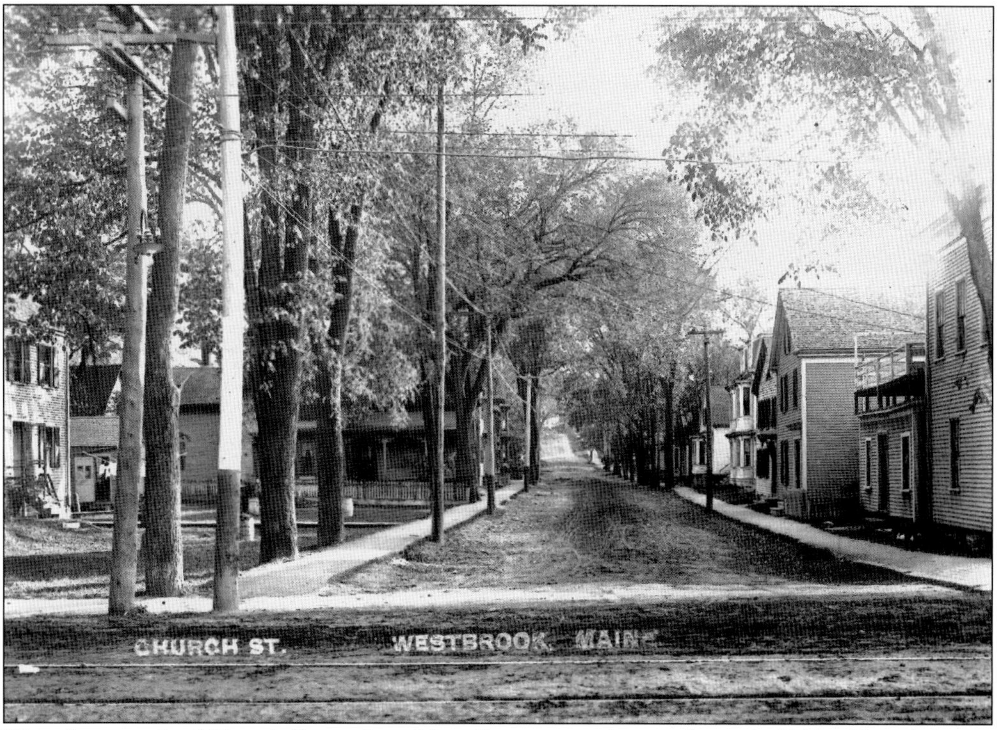

This photograph of Church Street from Main Street was taken in the early 1900s. Church Street connected Main Street to the Saccarappa Cemetery, which was located at the top of the hill at the end of the street. Saccarappa Cemetery is the oldest public cemetery in Westbrook. (Mike Sanphy collection.)

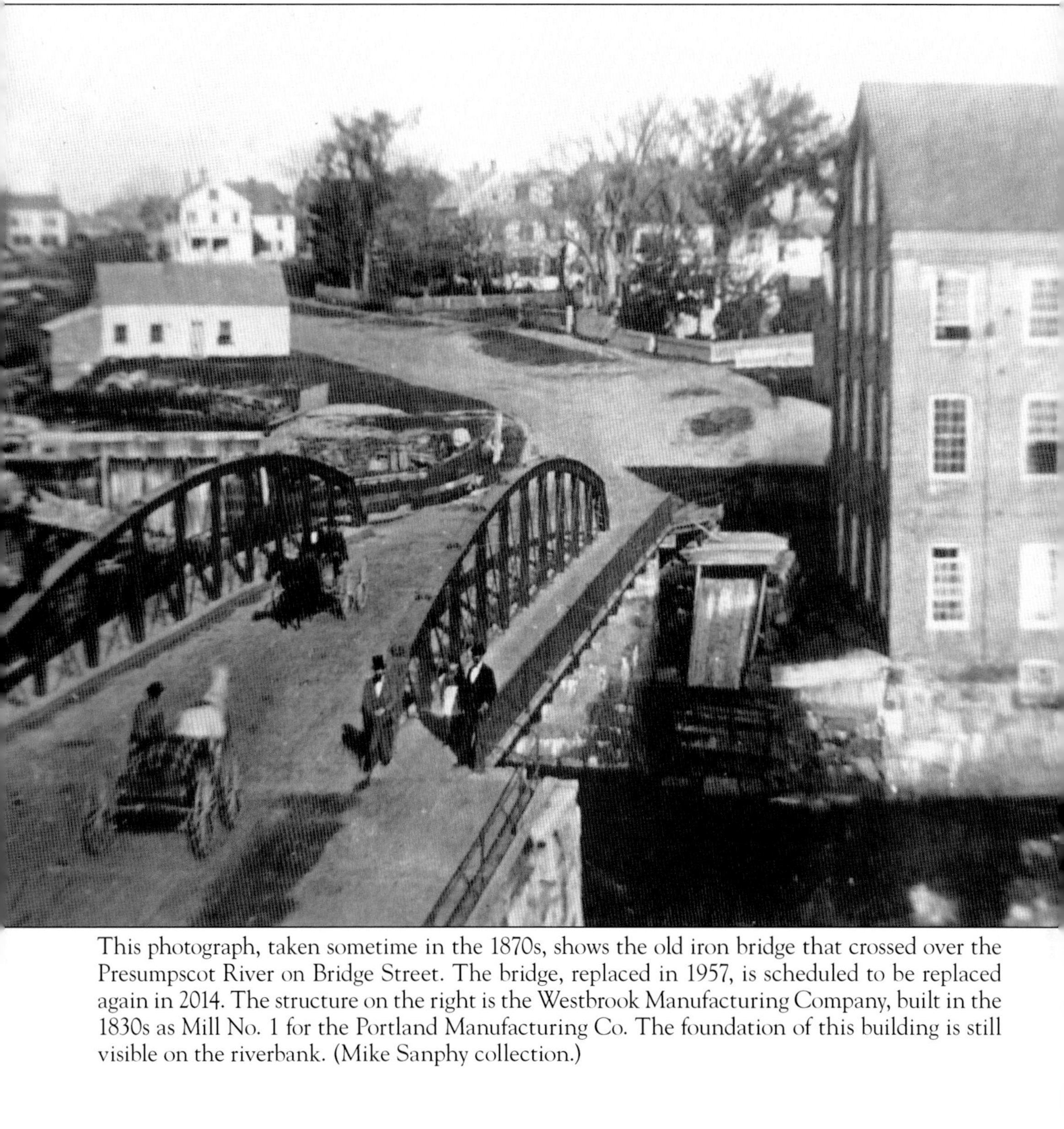

This photograph, taken sometime in the 1870s, shows the old iron bridge that crossed over the Presumpscot River on Bridge Street. The bridge, replaced in 1957, is scheduled to be replaced again in 2014. The structure on the right is the Westbrook Manufacturing Company, built in the 1830s as Mill No. 1 for the Portland Manufacturing Co. The foundation of this building is still visible on the riverbank. (Mike Sanphy collection.)

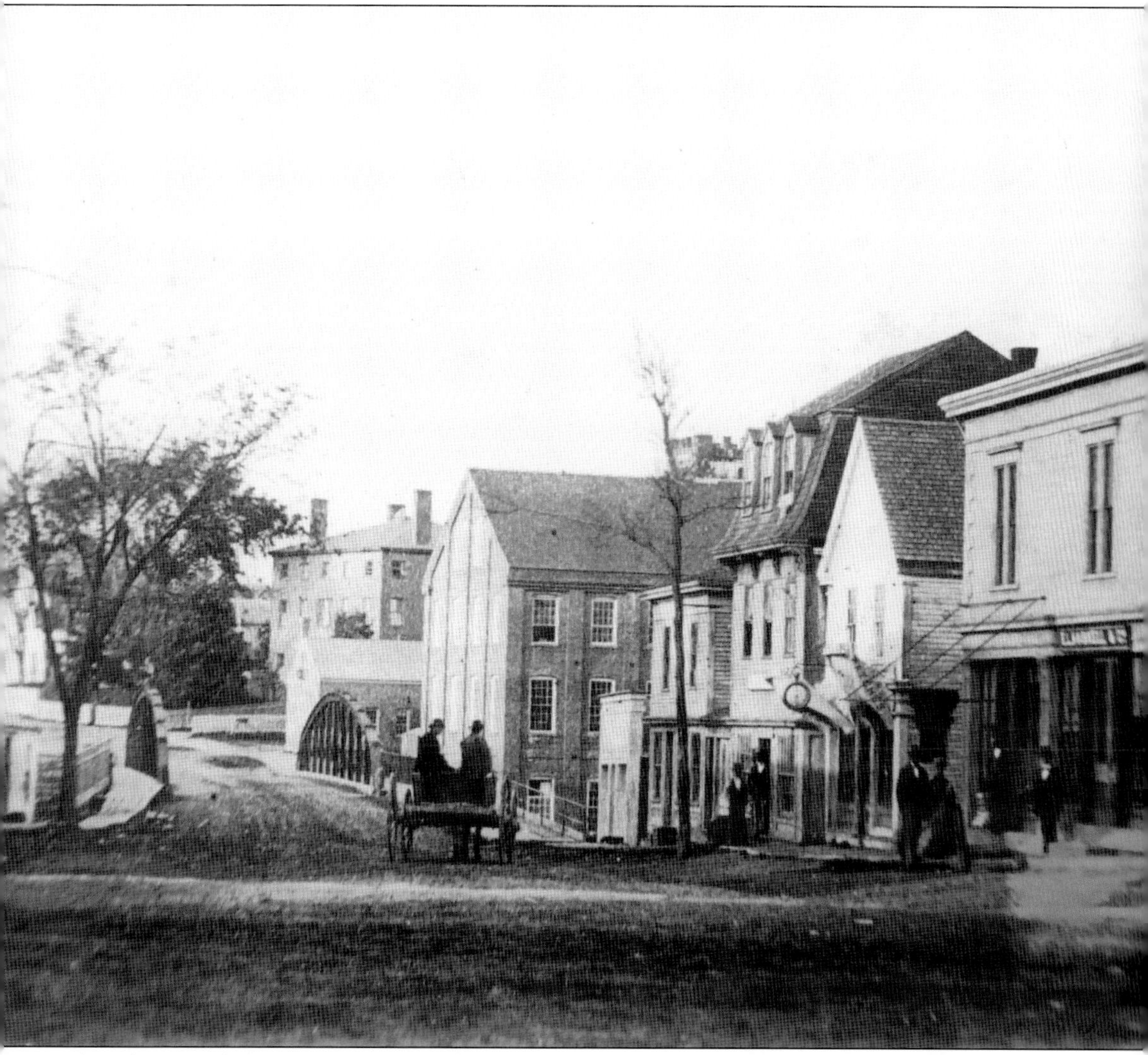

This photograph shows a view from Main Street looking down Bridge Street. The building on the extreme right was destroyed in February 1942 when fire swept through the adjoining Vallee Block. The Frog & Turtle Restaurant presently occupies this site. The old iron bridge can be seen in the distance. All of the other buildings in the photograph are gone. (Mike Sanphy collection.)

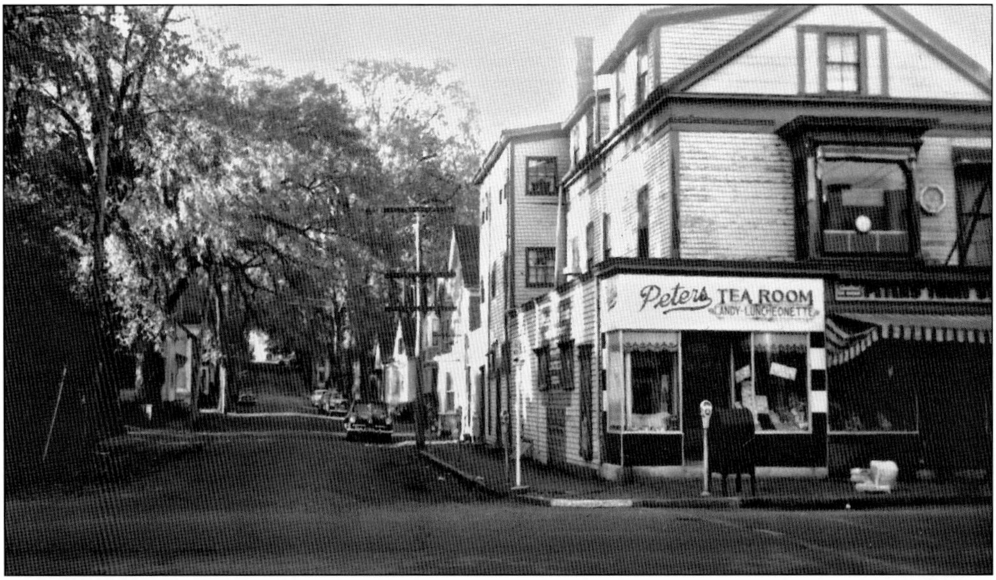

Peter's Tea Room and Fruit Store was located on Main Street at Church Street for many years. Prior to Peter's Tea Room and Fruit Store, this building was occupied by Harry F.G. Hay. Hay began operating a funeral parlor in 1903 and later moved to 795 Main Street. Harry's son John W. Hay later took over the business. It is now the Blais & Hay Funeral Home at 35 Church Street. This building was demolished during urban renewal. (Mike Sanphy collection.)

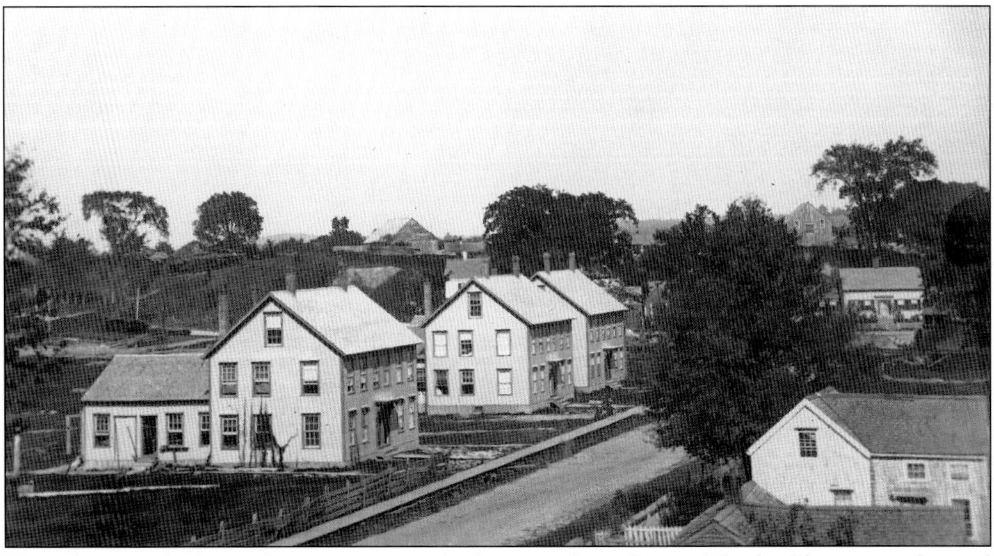

This photograph shows three apartment duplexes on Saco Street. The buildings were located opposite of where Quimby Avenue connects with Saco Street. (Warren Library collection.)

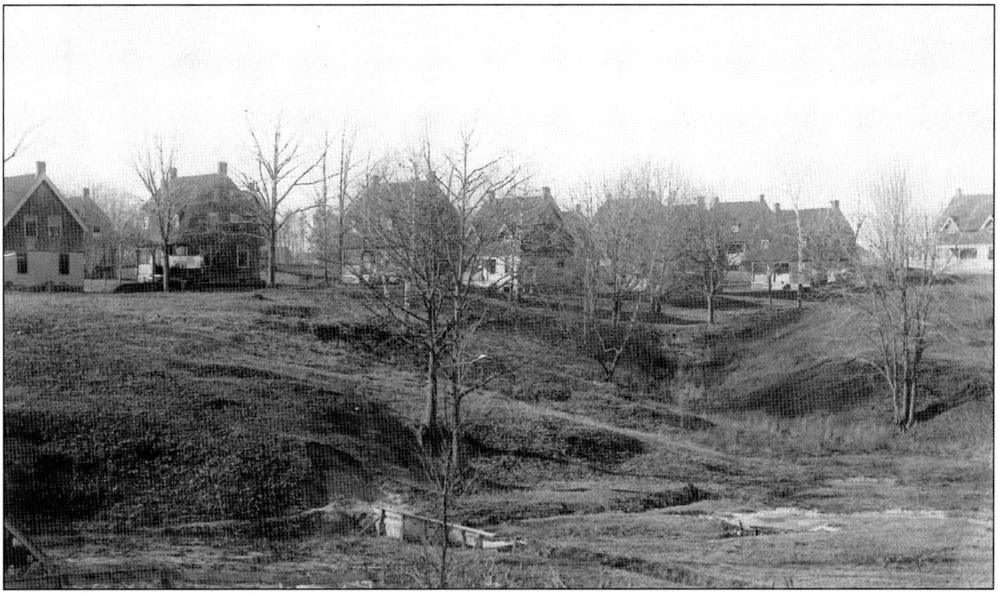

This view shows Cottage Place and the mill houses that were built by the S.D. Warren Company for its employees. (Warren Library collection.)

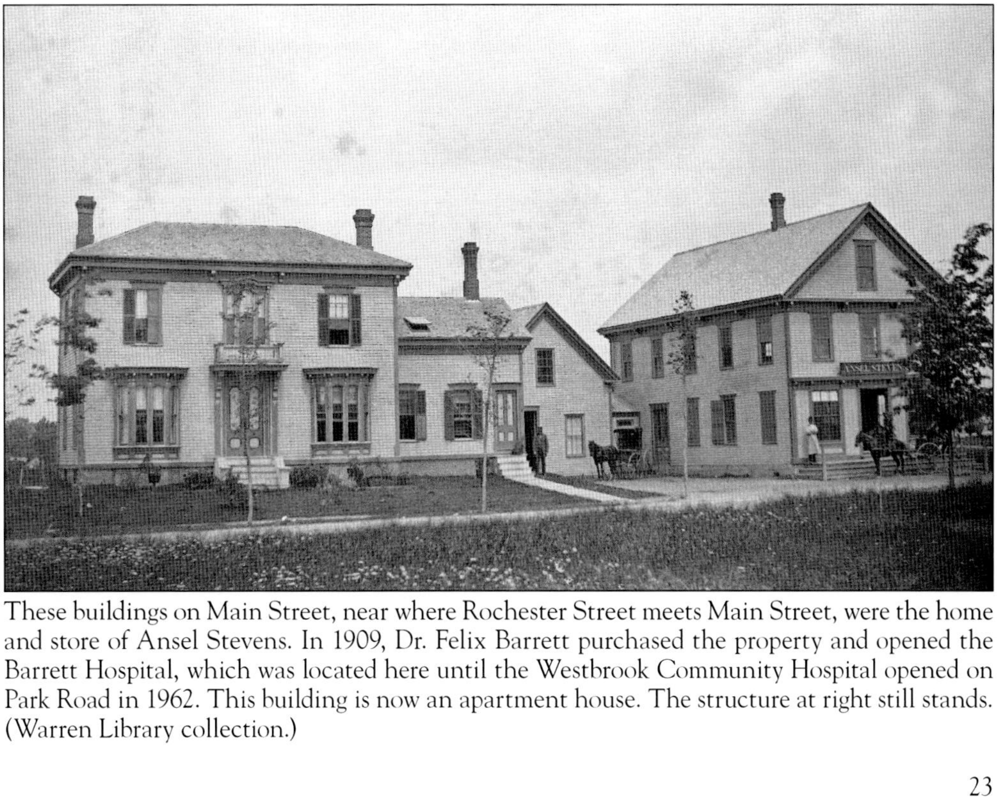

These buildings on Main Street, near where Rochester Street meets Main Street, were the home and store of Ansel Stevens. In 1909, Dr. Felix Barrett purchased the property and opened the Barrett Hospital, which was located here until the Westbrook Community Hospital opened on Park Road in 1962. This building is now an apartment house. The structure at right still stands. (Warren Library collection.)

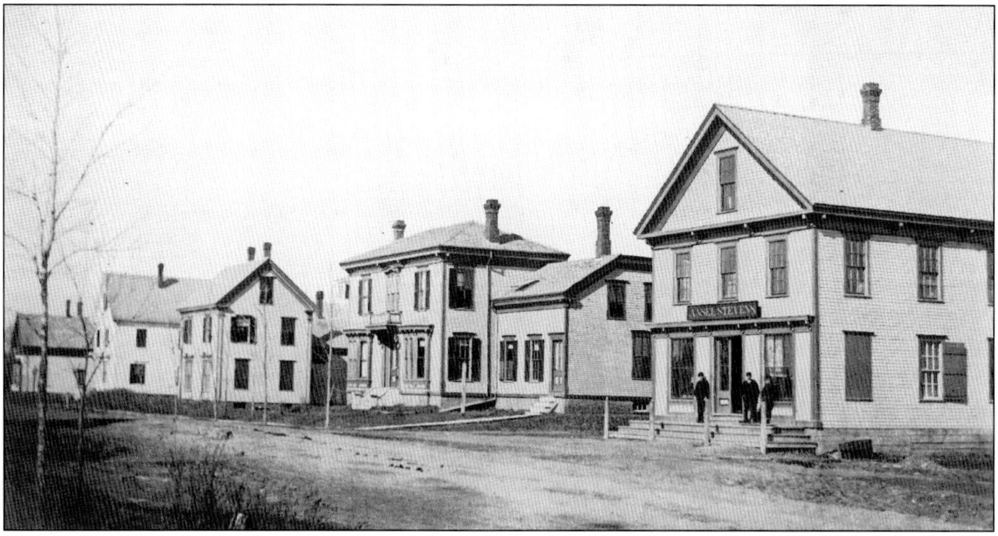

This photograph shows the north side of Main Street, near where Rochester Street meets Main Street. The building at far right was the store of Ansel Stevens. Medeo European Food and Deli presently occupies this structure, with apartments on the upper floors. The building in the center was Stevens's home, and it later became the Barrett Hospital. Presently, it is an apartment house. (Warren Library collection.)

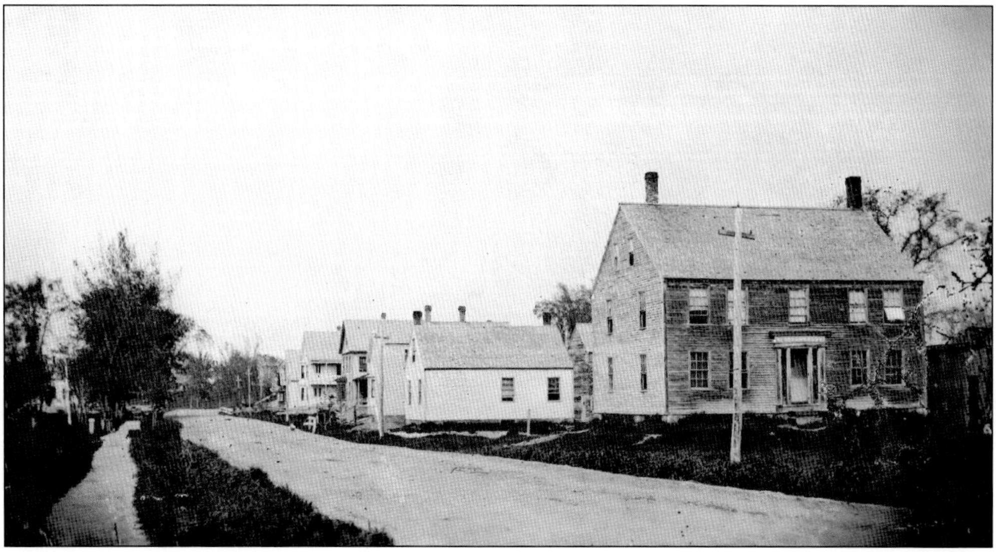

This view looking east from Dunn Street shows the south side of Main Street. This photograph was taken in the 1870s. Today, most of these buildings are gone. (Warren Library collection.)

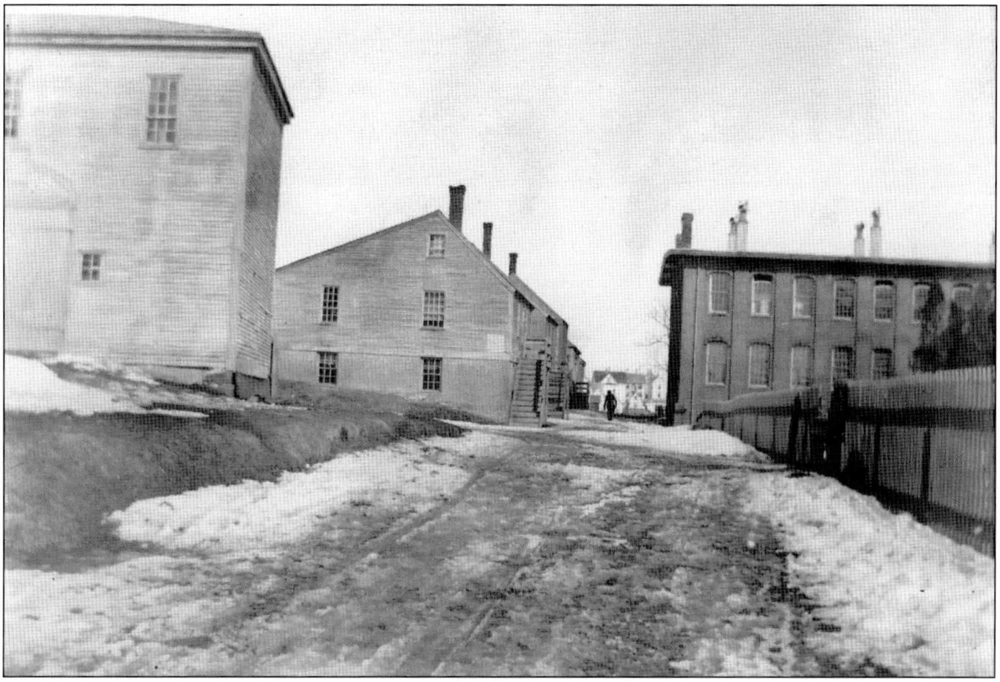

Pictured is a view of Dana Court from Bridge Street. The building at far left is the carriage house of what was called the "old Bean Mansion" because of the family that resided there. It stood on Bridge Street at the corner of Dana Court. The other structures on the left are mill houses for the Westbrook Manufacturing Company. The building on the right was erected in 1850 as a warehouse for the Westbrook Manufacturing Company. C.E. Noyes Tire Company later occupied this structure. (Mike Sanphy collection.)

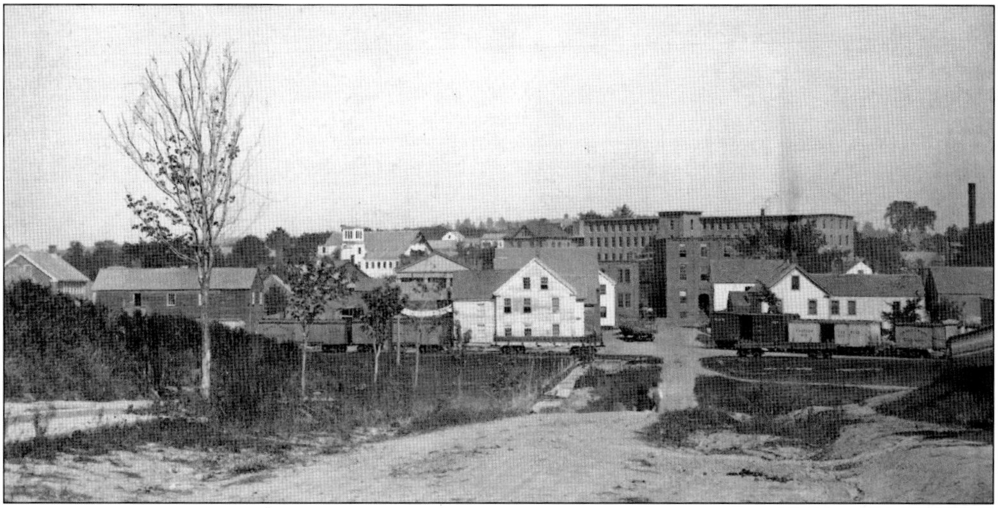

This photograph was taken from Mechanic Street looking down toward Main Street. The Dana Warp Mills can be seen in the distance. Train cars are on a siding that crossed over Main Street, between 901 and 907 Main Street, and then crossed the river on a bridge to Dana Court. The flood of 1896 destroyed this railroad bridge, which serviced the Westbrook Manufacturing Company, and it was never rebuilt. Because of the flood, the company sustained much damage and was forced to close. (Mike Sanphy collection.)

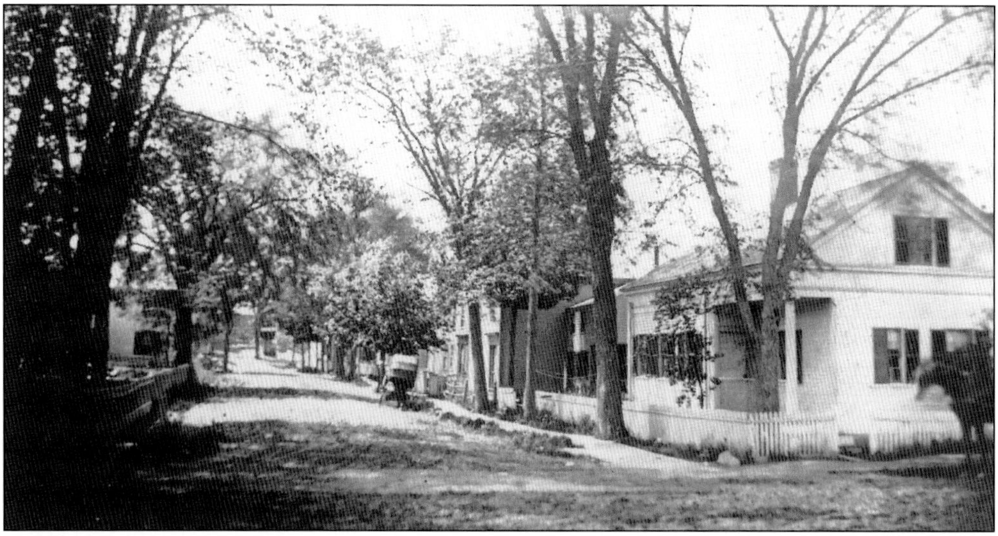

This view is looking up Spring Street from Main Street. The house at right was moved to a location down Main Street opposite the Universalist Church to make way for a larger building. In the 1950s, First Portland National Bank purchased the property, demolished the house, and built a bank, which later became city hall. Today, the structure is once again home to a bank. (Mike Sanphy collection.)

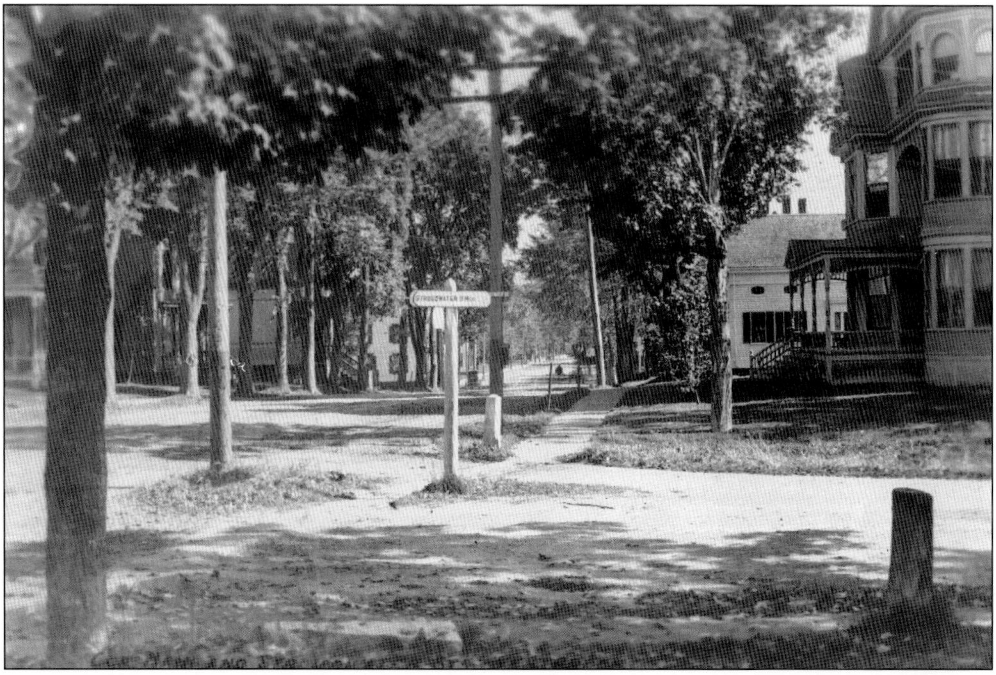

Pictured is Main Street from Stroudwater Street. The large house at right was the home of Mayor William Bragdon in 1919. It was purchased by Esso Oil Company and demolished to make way for an Esso filling station. Cumberland Farms presently occupies the site of this old house. The wooden sign in photograph reads, "Stroudwater 5 Mls." (Mike Sanphy collection.)

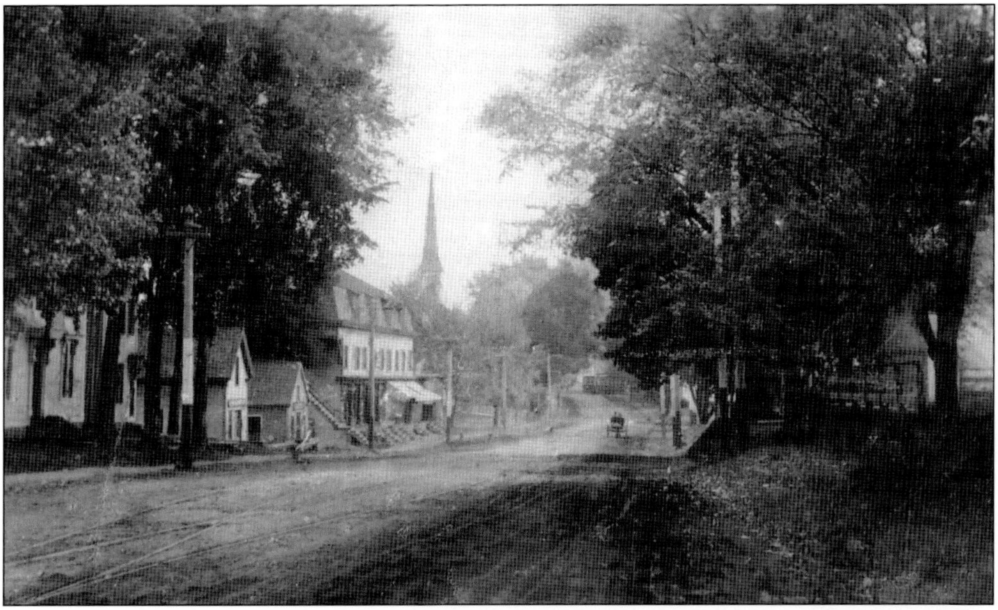

This is a view of Main Street looking east from the area of Rochester Street. The large building at left is the Brown Block, which later became the Warren Library. The church steeple seen is of the Warren Congregational Church, built in 1869 on Cumberland Street at Warren Avenue. A horse-drawn buggy can be seen in the distance, and a trolley car rounds the corner from Cumberland Street onto Warren Avenue. (Mike Sanphy collection.)

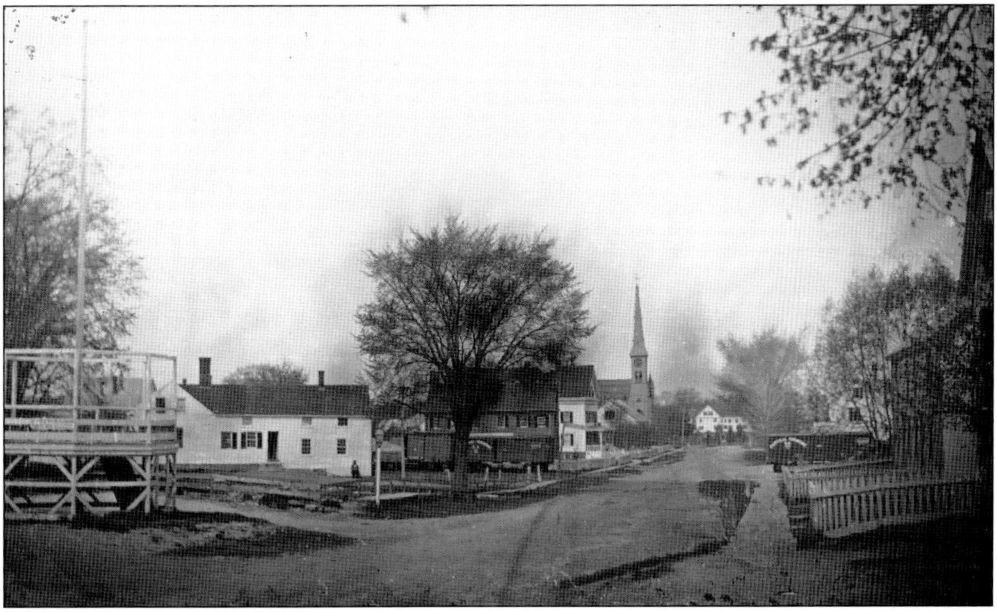

This photograph was taken from Main Street looking down Cumberland Street. A bandstand and flagpole can be seen to the left. The Warren Block was built at that location in 1883. The white house at left is presently the office of attorney Ray Pallas. The church pictured is the Warren Congregational Church, built in 1869. The white building beyond the church is the S.D. Warren Company office, situated on the other side of the Presumpscot River. (Mike Sanphy collection.)

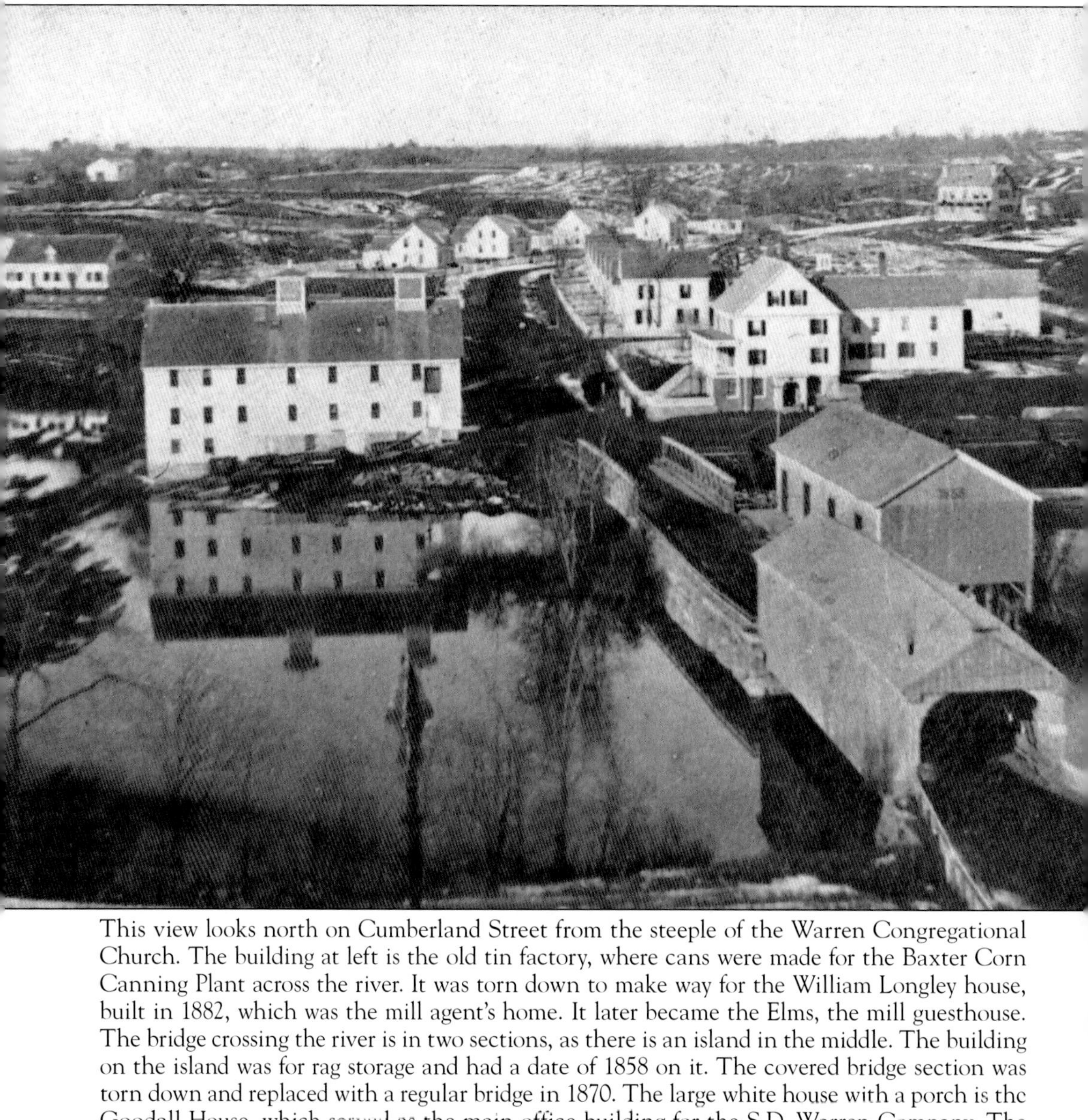

This view looks north on Cumberland Street from the steeple of the Warren Congregational Church. The building at left is the old tin factory, where cans were made for the Baxter Corn Canning Plant across the river. It was torn down to make way for the William Longley house, built in 1882, which was the mill agent's home. It later became the Elms, the mill guesthouse. The bridge crossing the river is in two sections, as there is an island in the middle. The building on the island was for rag storage and had a date of 1858 on it. The covered bridge section was torn down and replaced with a regular bridge in 1870. The large white house with a porch is the Goodall House, which served as the main office building for the S.D. Warren Company. The office later relocated, and this structure was torn down. (Mike Sanphy collection.)

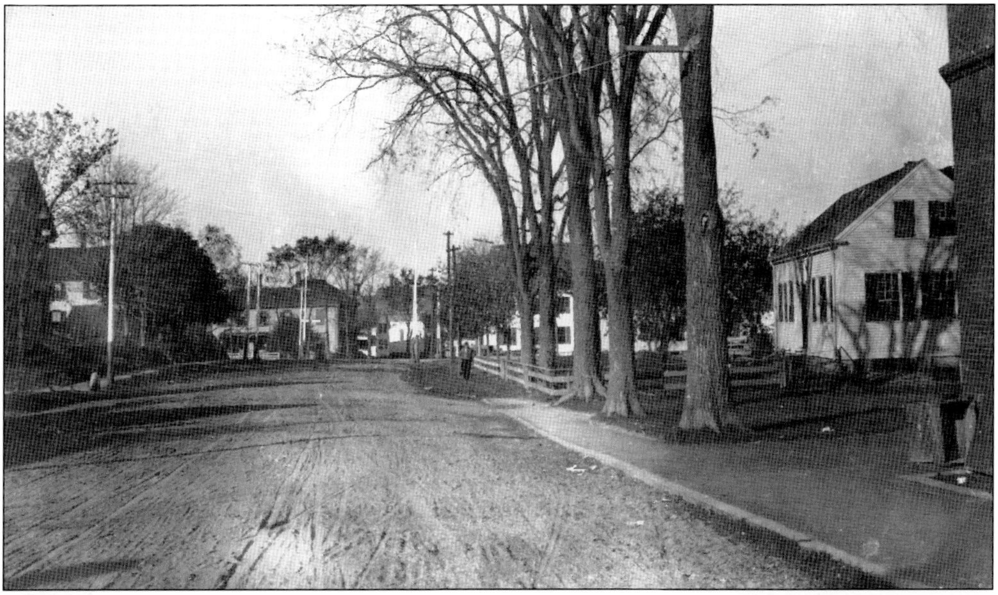

This photograph, taken from the intersection of Main and Cumberland Streets, shows a view down Main Street. (Mike Sanphy collection.)

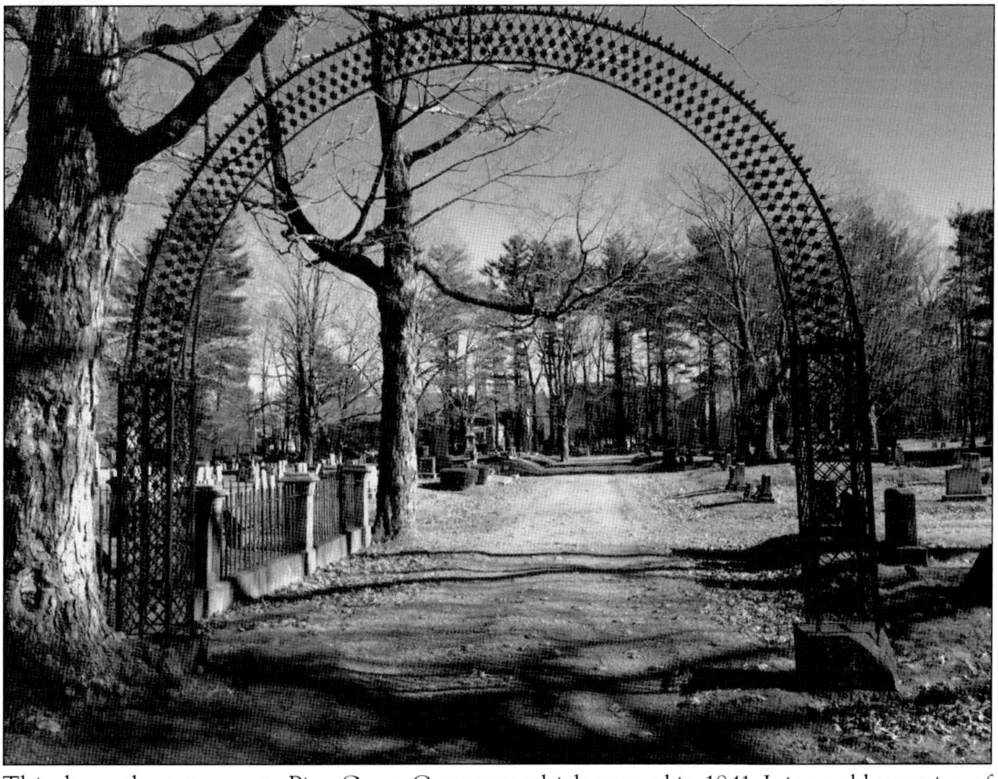

This shows the entrance to Pine Grove Cemetery, which opened in 1841. It is an older section of the cemetery within Evergreen Cemetery, which opened in 1855 when that area of Portland was part of Westbrook. Evergreen is presently Portland's (as well as Maine's) largest cemetery. It is in the National Register of Historic Places. (Jessica Siraco and Friends of Evergreen Cemetery.)

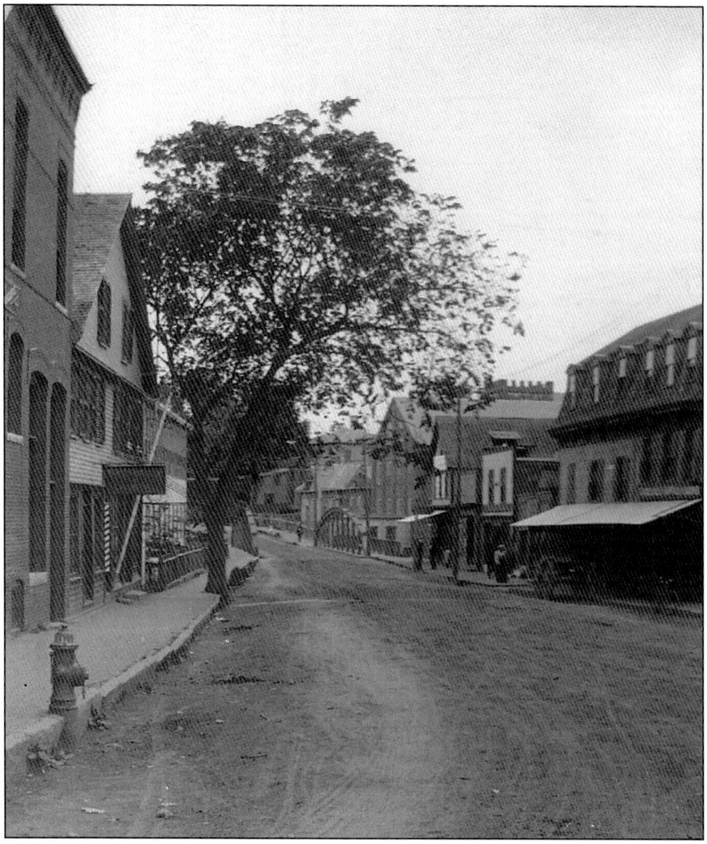

This is a c. 1895 view down Bridge Street from Main Street, many years before that intersection became known as Vallee Square. Despite the gravel road, a brick sidewalk leads past a modern fire hydrant and the Westbrook Laundry to the iron bridge. (EG/BFC.)

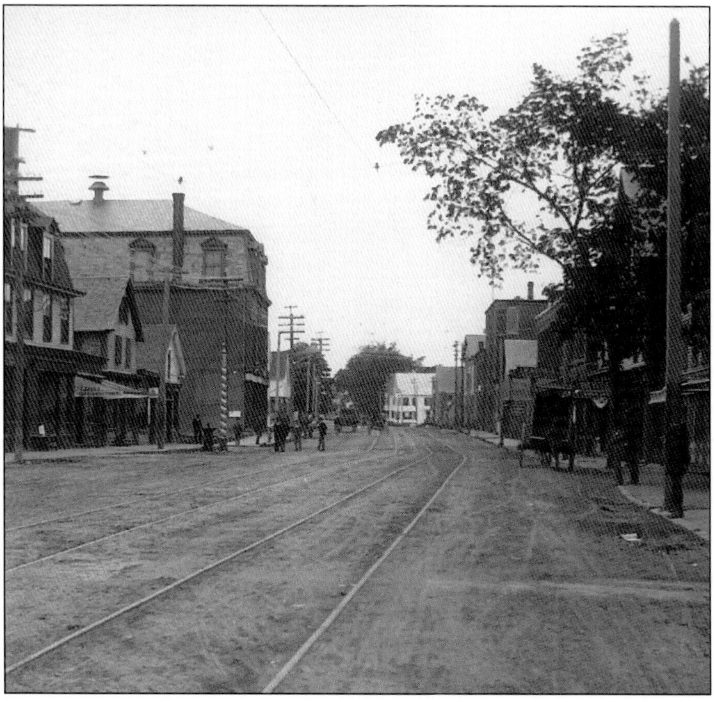

This photograph looks west on Main Street. Trolley tracks run along the road. On the left, just before the imposing Odd Fellows Hall building, is a railroad-crossing gate. Train tracks ran across Main Street here and crossed the river to Dana Court for the Westbrook Manufacturing Company. The railroad bridge washed out in the flood of 1896 and was never replaced. (EG/BFC.)

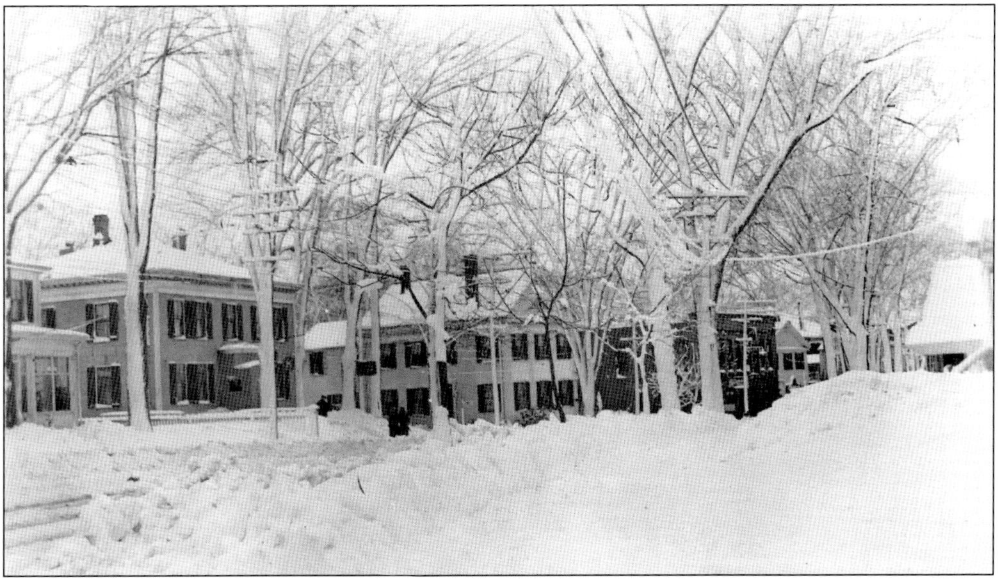

This winter 1927 picture of Main Street is from a postcard that had handwritten on the back, "left to right—Westbrook Tavern—Dr. Hill's—Tel. Exchange—Dr. Woodman." The note added that the postcard was "Bot [*sic*] from Miss Lowell—Grade 1 Valentine St. School to help get piano." (EG/BFC.)

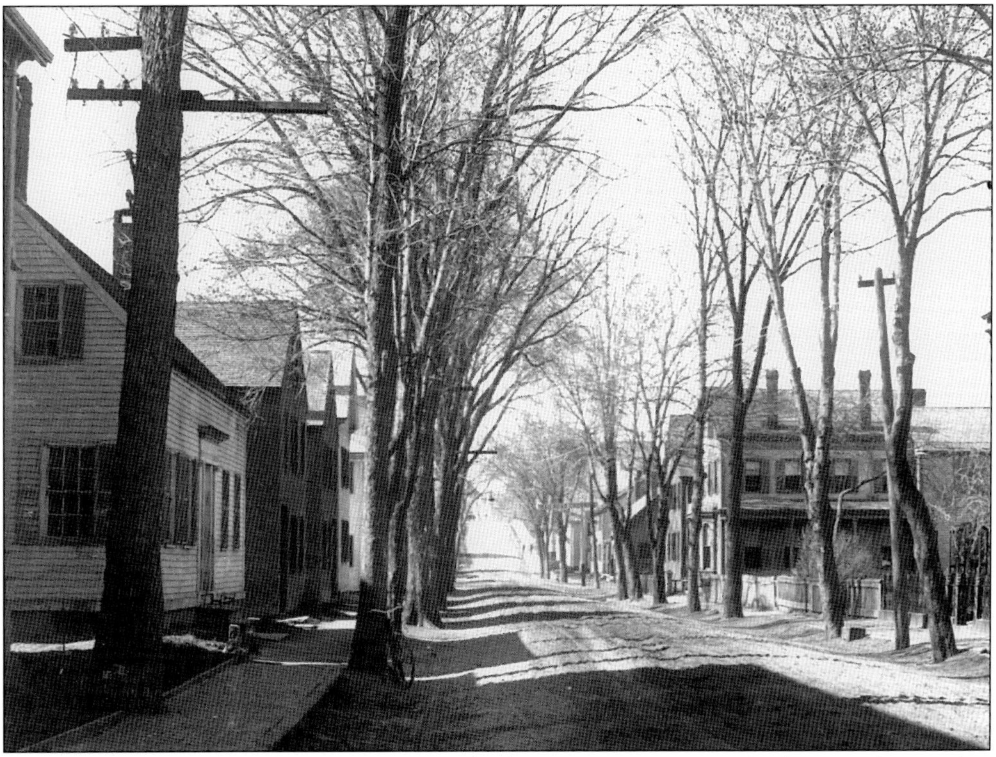

This photograph, taken from Main Street, looks up Spring Street, which was a dirt road at the time. Note the bicycle against the tree as well as the fencing on the right. (Walker Library collection.)

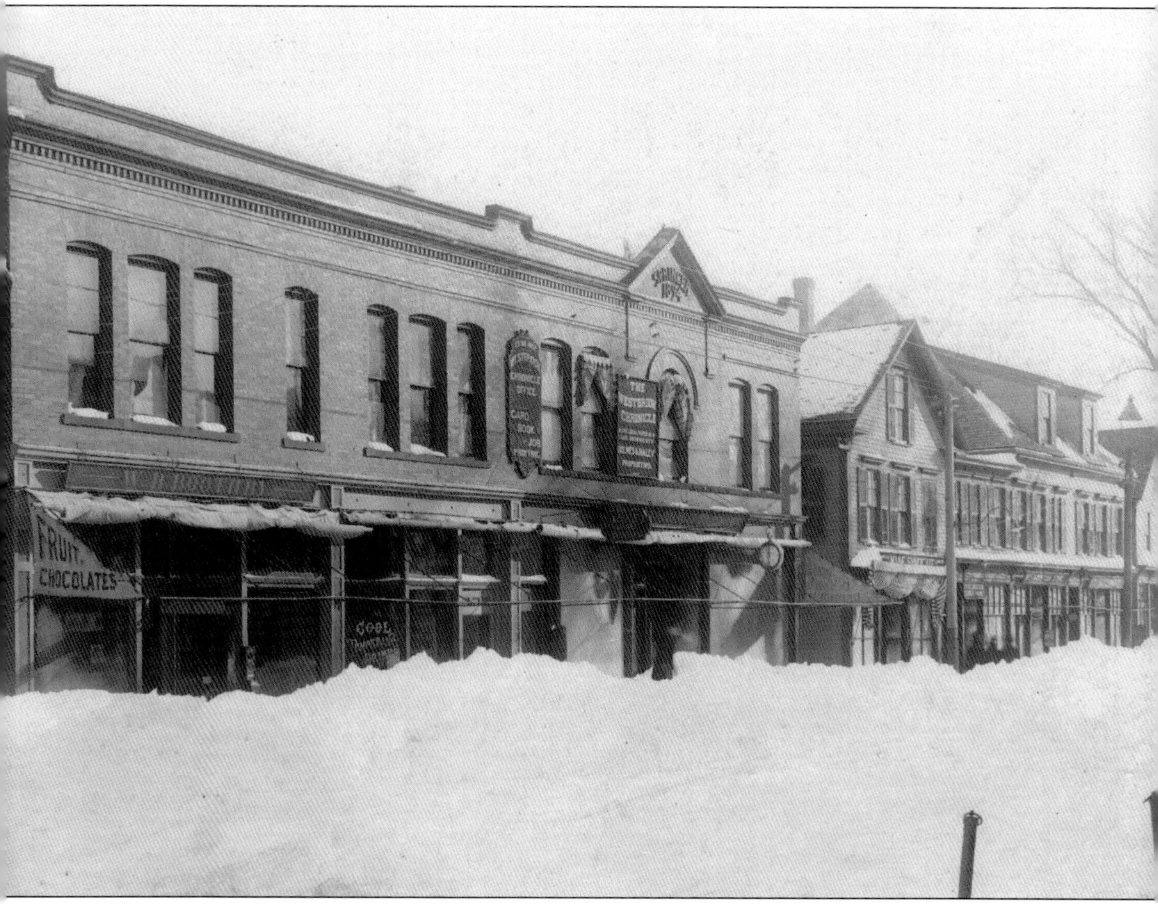

This image of the Springer building surrounded by snow reveals a variety of business tenants. On the first floor, W.B. Boothby offered fruit, chocolates, and "COOL Temperance Drinks." To the right are Casket Ware Rooms and what appear to be a watch shop and a bicycle shop. The second floor housed offices for the *Westbrook Chronicle*, "A live local paper in a live growing city." The next block included the Maine Syndicate and H.B. Jackson Central Market. (EG/BFC.)

Two

Buildings

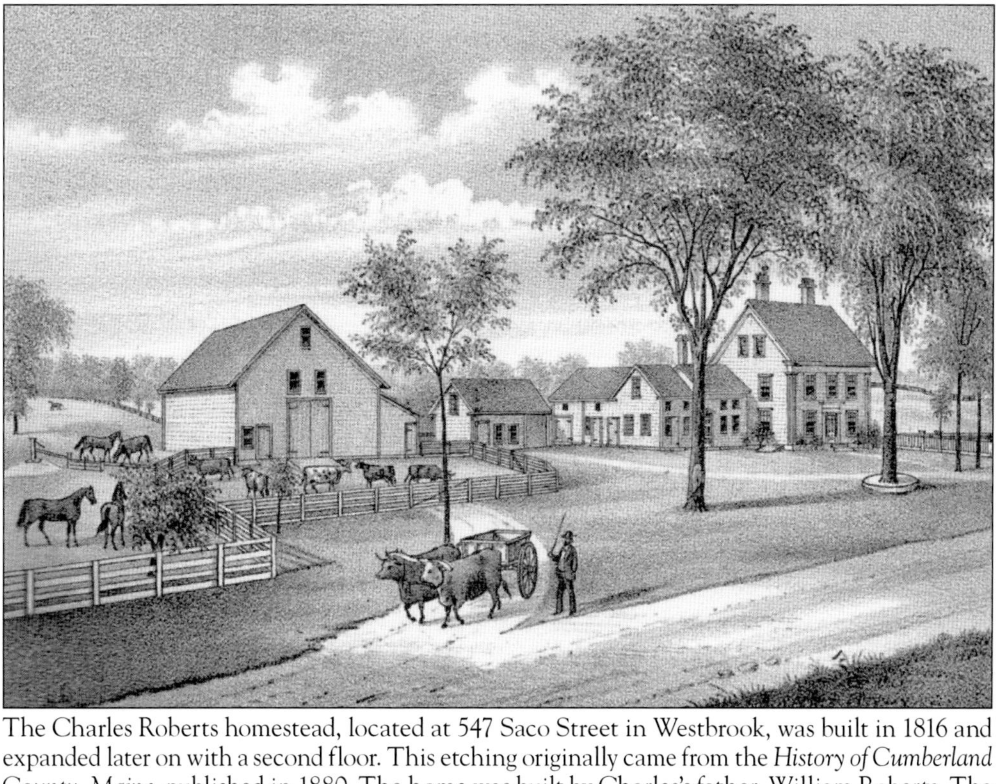

The Charles Roberts homestead, located at 547 Saco Street in Westbrook, was built in 1816 and expanded later on with a second floor. This etching originally came from the *History of Cumberland County, Maine*, published in 1880. The home was built by Charles's father, William Roberts. The family originally owned 300 acres of land. The home is still owned by a fifth-generation descendant of the Roberts family. (Suzan Roberts Norton.)

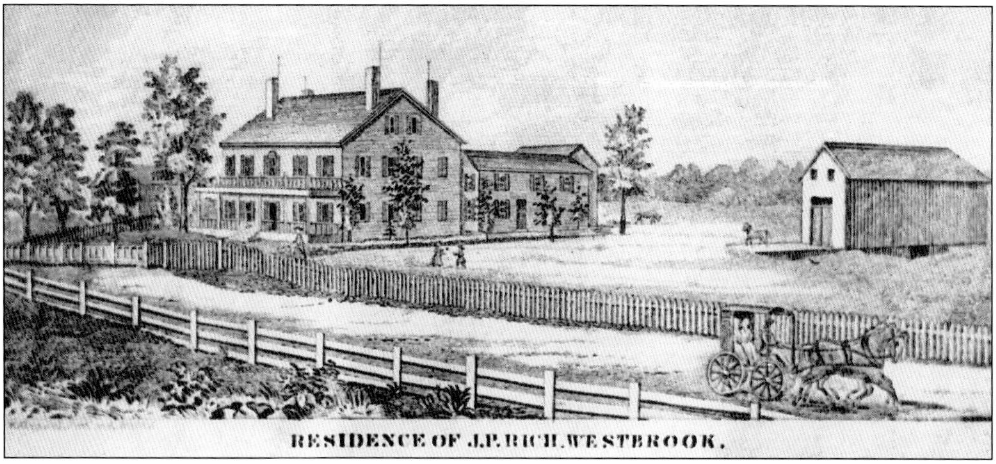

This house, located at 234 Bridge Street, was built by Daniel Pierce, a lumber merchant. When Pierce left Westbrook, he sold the house, and after several owners, it was occupied by John P. Rich, superintendent of the York & Cumberland Railroad. In 1880, Frank Haskell, an agent for the Westbrook Manufacturing Company, purchased the property, and it remained in the Haskell family into the 1960s. The house is now comprised of rental apartments. (Westbrook Historical Society collection.)

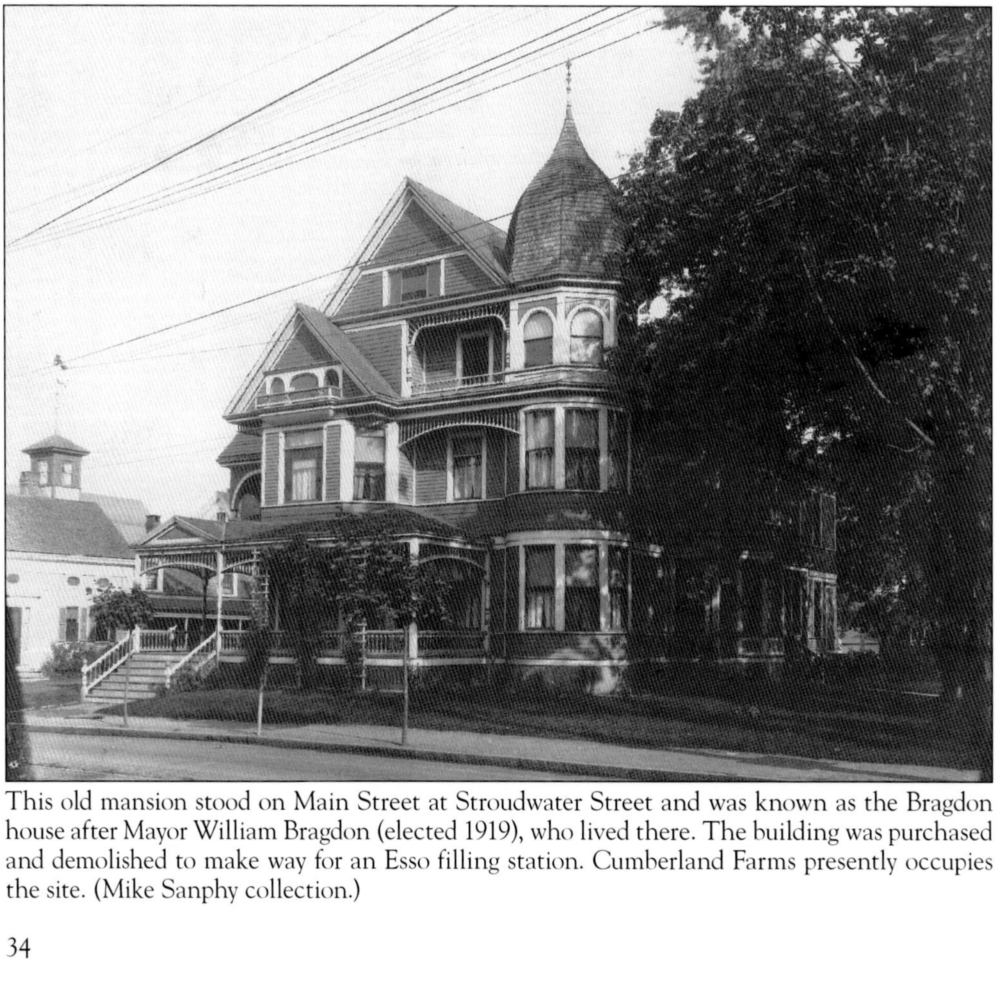

This old mansion stood on Main Street at Stroudwater Street and was known as the Bragdon house after Mayor William Bragdon (elected 1919), who lived there. The building was purchased and demolished to make way for an Esso filling station. Cumberland Farms presently occupies the site. (Mike Sanphy collection.)

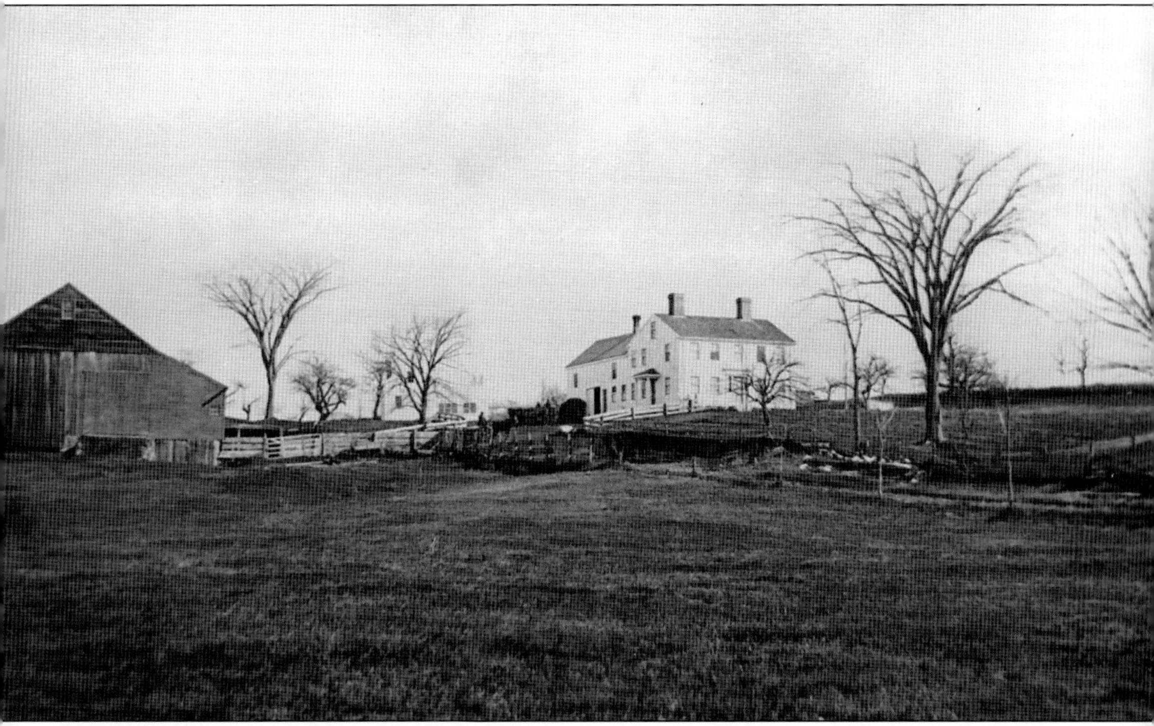

This view shows Lamb's Hill with the old farm occupied by the Lamb and Larrabee families. The location is now known as Deer Hill, and this old home still stands on Deer Hill. In later years, the house was occupied by local physician and French consulate Paul O. Proudian. (Mike Sanphy collection.)

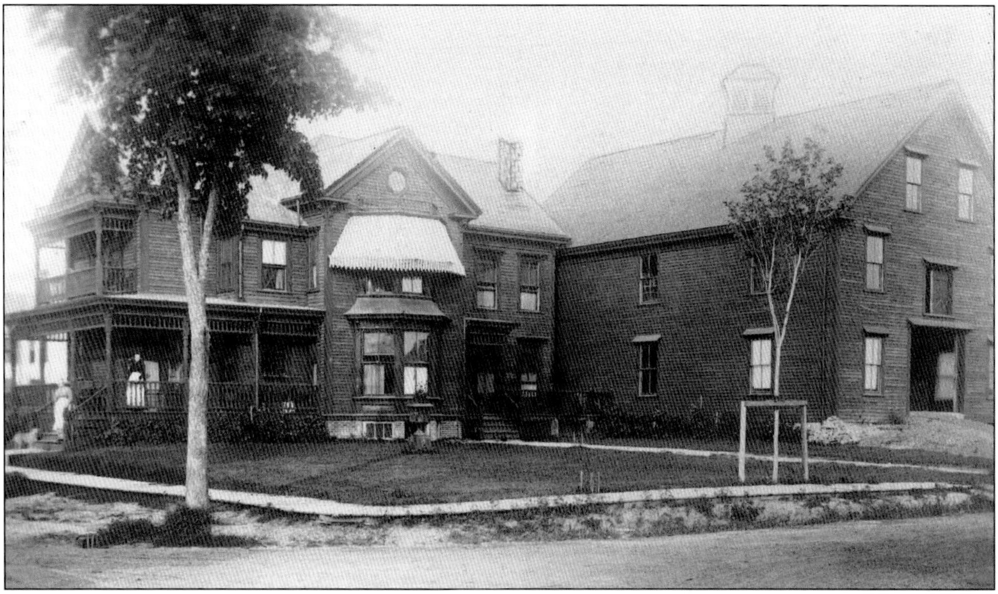

This is the home of John W. Wheeler on Main Street at Haskell Street. Wheeler owned a wood and coal business on the opposite corner of Main and Haskell Streets. The Hercules windmill, which used wind power to power the saws in his wood yard, was a longtime landmark. The Wheeler house still stands today. An apartment house and the Westbrook Public Safety Facility now occupy the windmill and wood yard site. (Mike Sanphy collection.)

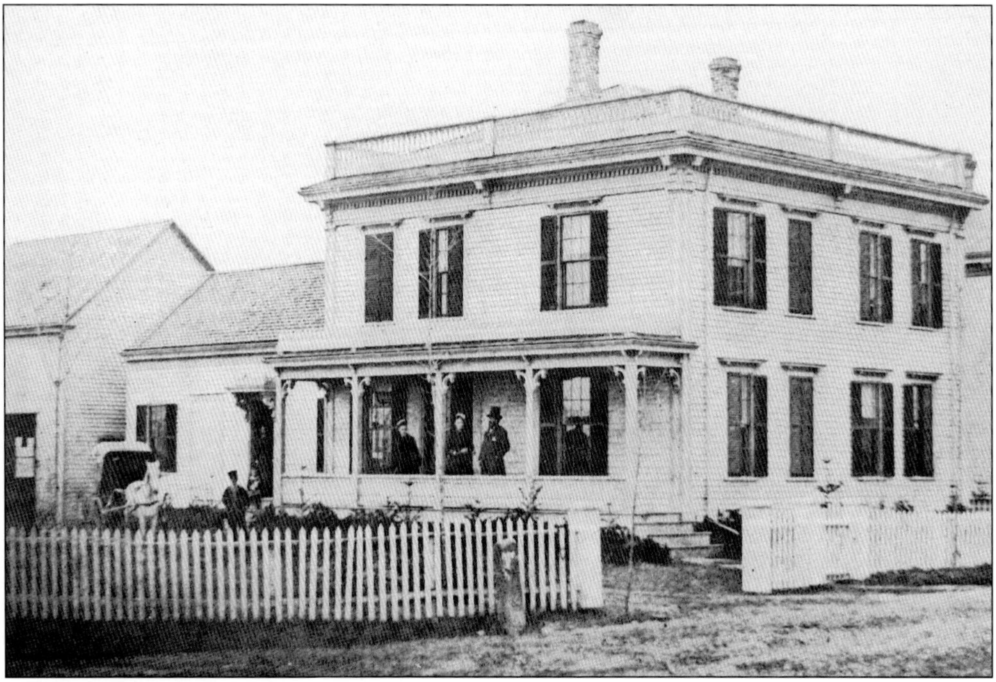

This house, located on Main Street at Stroudwater Street, was occupied by Dr. Thomas P. Smith and, later, Dr. A.H. Burroughs. In later years, the building became an apartment house, and it was demolished in the late 1960s to make way for a Dunkin' Donuts restaurant. (Mike Sanphy collection.)

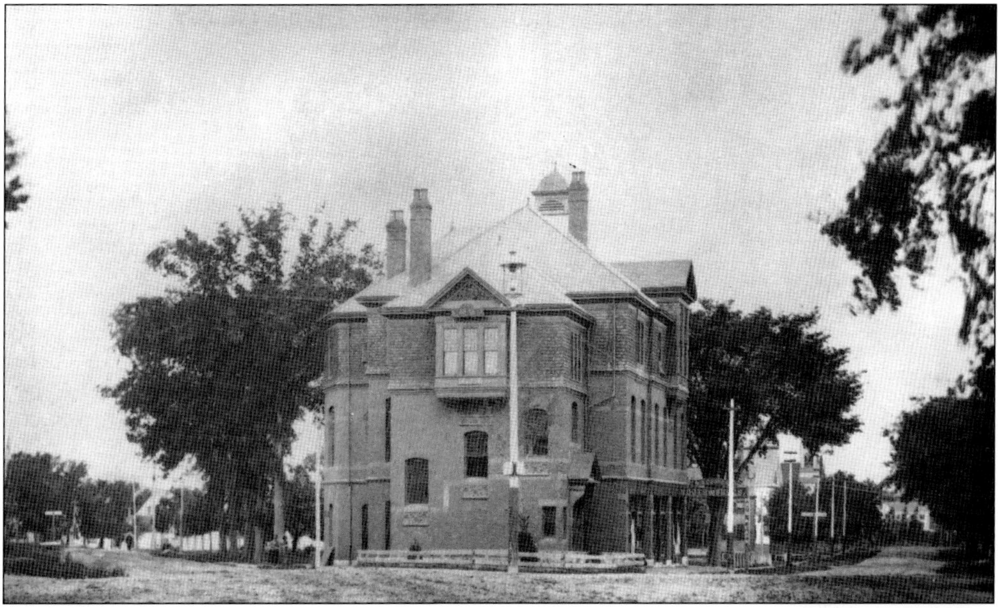

The Warren Block, at the intersection of Main and Cumberland Streets, was commissioned in 1883 by S.D. Warren as a multipurpose community center with spaces for stores, offices, meeting halls, and recreation for company employees. In later years, the post office, Paine Drug Store, Cobb Printing, and Westbrook Trust Company were tenants. The building, with stores, offices, and apartments, is currently owned by the Coyne family. (Westbrook Historical Society collection.)

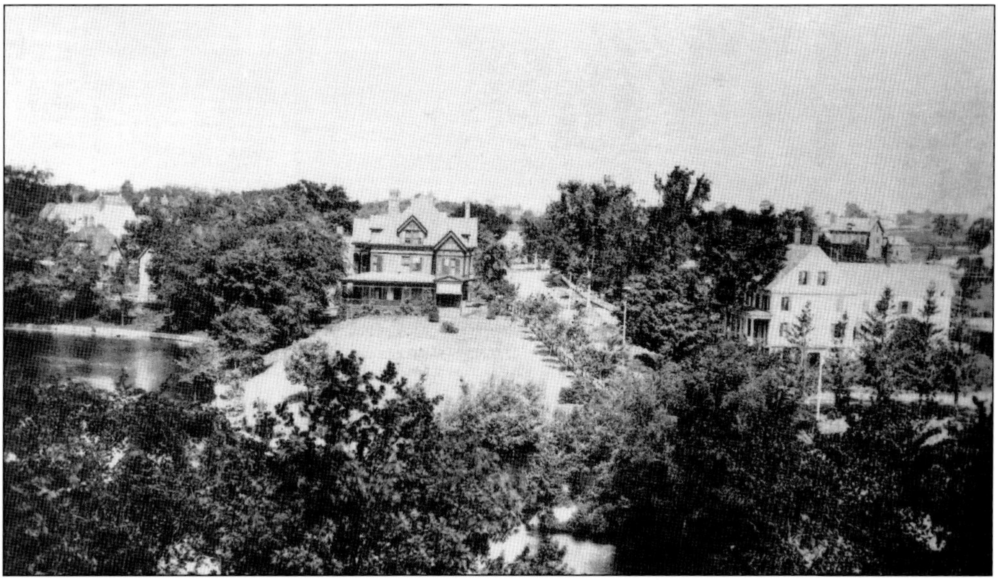

This photograph looks north on Cumberland Street from the steeple of the Warren Congregational Church. The large house in the center was built for mill agent William Longley in 1882. The house later became the S.D. Warren guesthouse. The house was sold several years ago and is now the privately owned Elms Bed & Breakfast. (Westbrook Historical Society collection.)

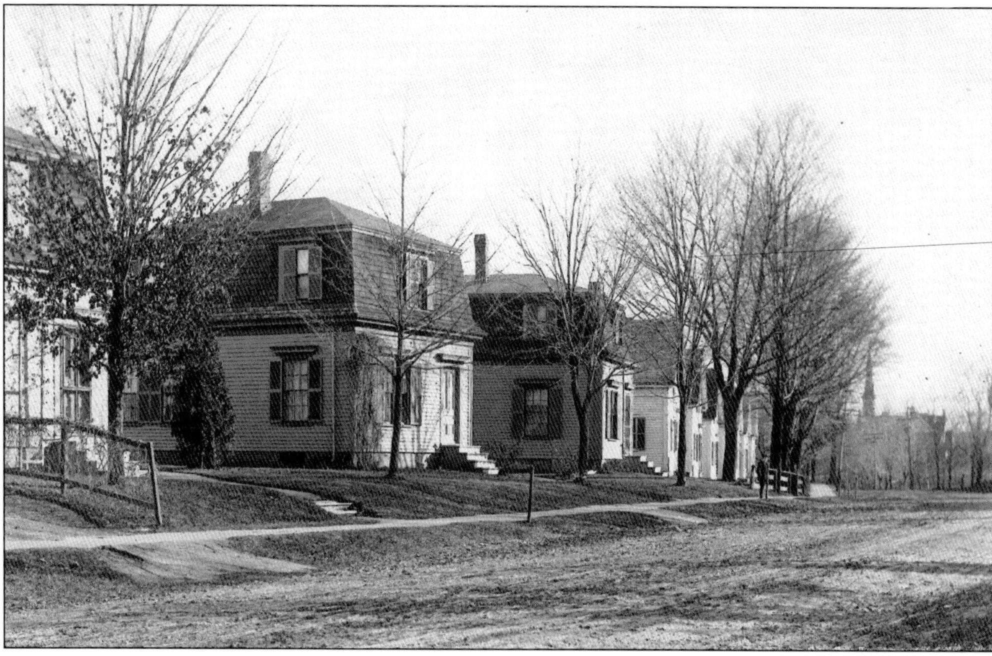

This photograph shows the S.D. Warren Company mill houses on Cumberland Street. These buildings were demolished in the 1950s to make way for the expansion of the mill with a new paper machine and parking lots. The church steeple in the distance is on the Warren Congregational Church. (Mike Sanphy collection.)

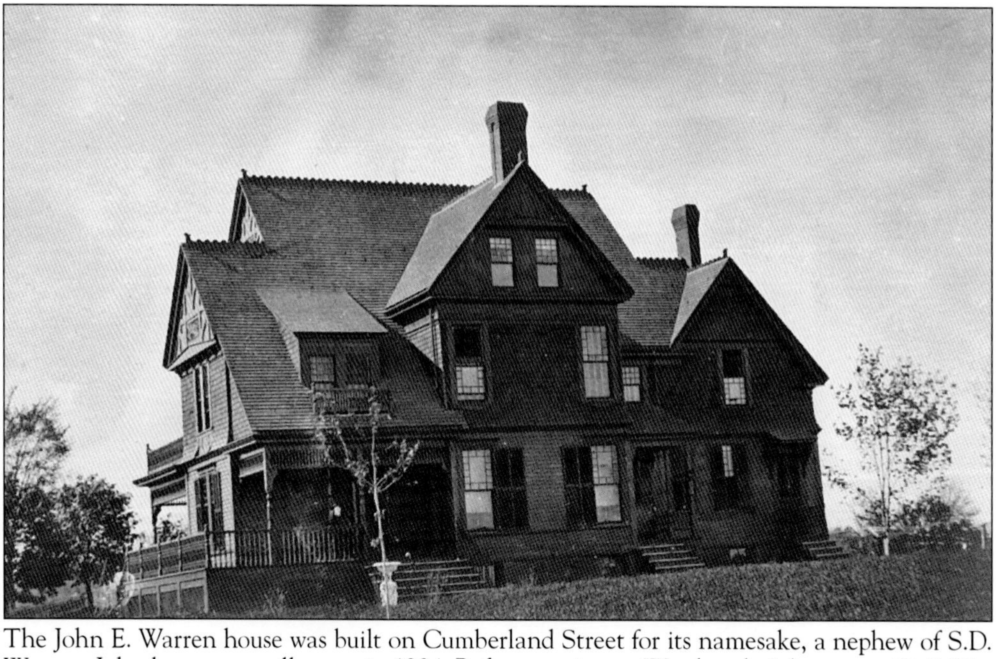

The John E. Warren house was built on Cumberland Street for its namesake, a nephew of S.D. Warren. John became a mill agent in 1884. Before coming to Westbrook, John was a Civil War veteran and a prisoner at Andersonville. John was also one of the most prominent mill agents. This house later became a senior citizen club and was then sold and moved to Cottage Place, where it still stands. (Mike Sanphy collection.)

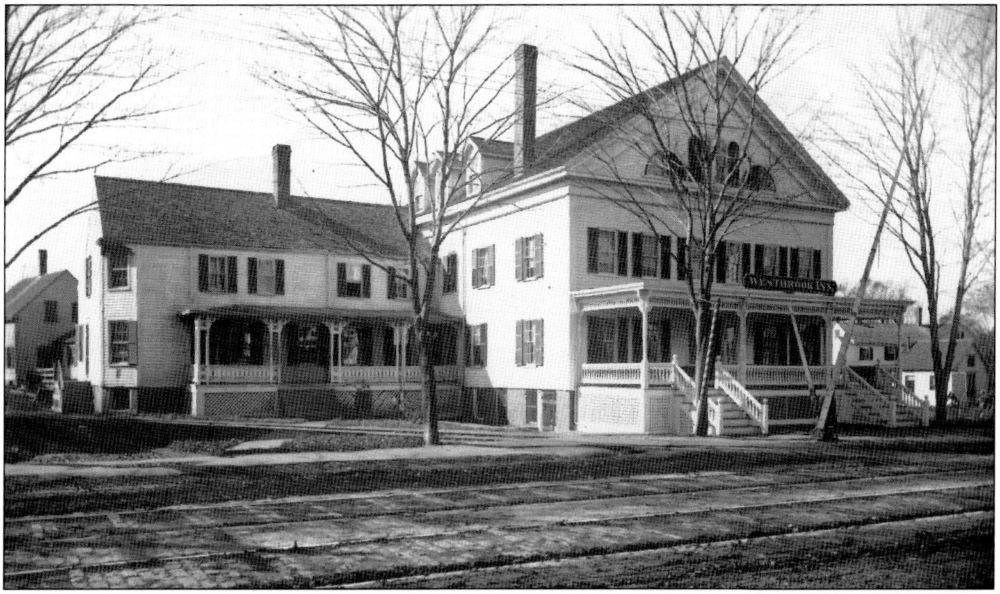

This building was constructed on lower Main Street and was later moved to its present location on Cumberland Street, opposite where Warren Avenue meets Cumberland Street. At one time, the house served as a S.D. Warren Company boardinghouse and was often called the White House. In later years, it became the Westbrook Inn. The building serves today as an apartment house. (Mike Sanphy collection.)

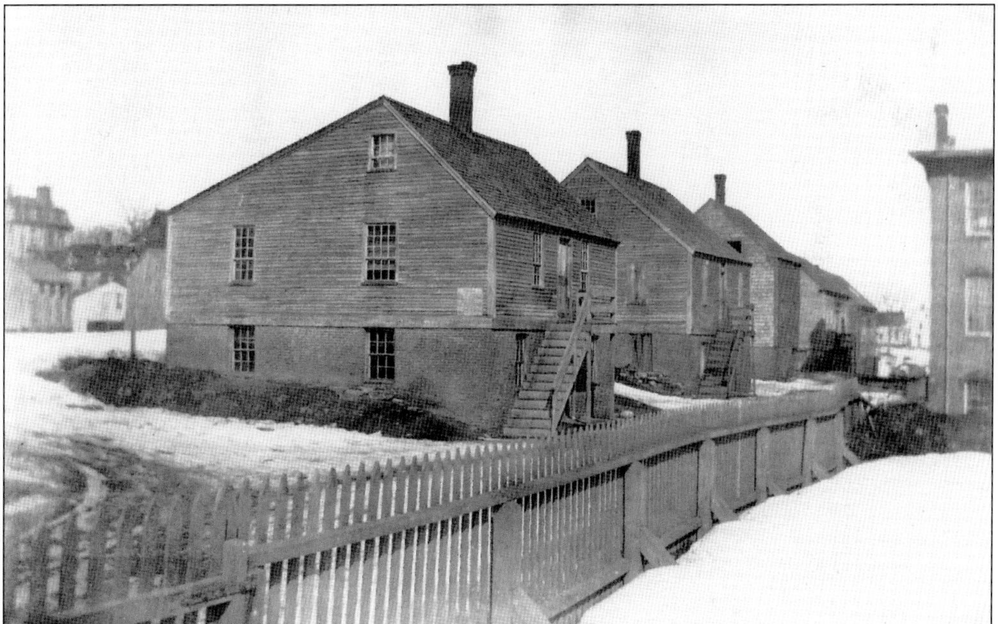

Mill houses on Dana Court were constructed for employees of the Westbrook Manufacturing Company. The building at right is the warehouse, erected in 1850 for the Westbrook Manufacturing Company. The company went out of business after the flood of 1896, and the property was sold. These buildings were eventually replaced, and the warehouse served several different functions before it became vacant and was destroyed by fire in 1996. (Mike Sanphy collection.)

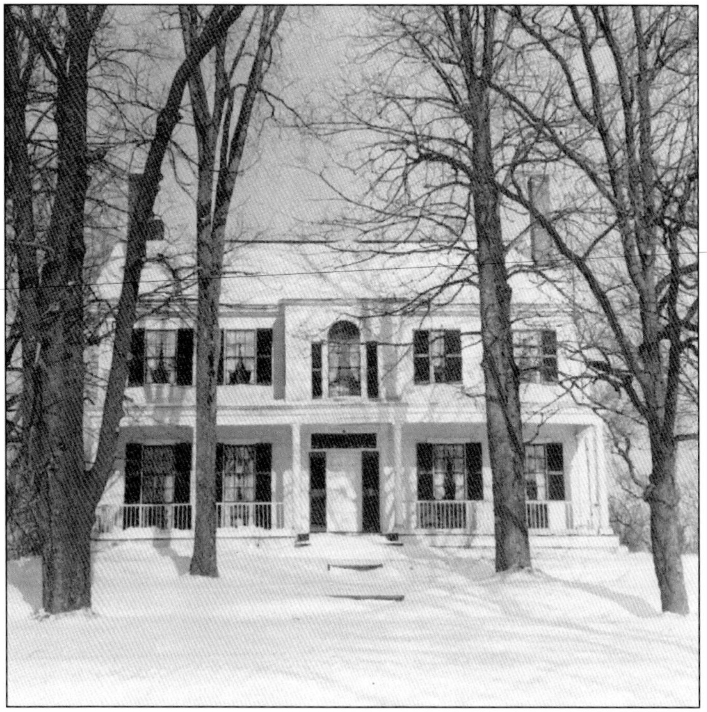

This house at 234 Bridge Street had several owners before being purchased by Frank Haskell, the agent of the Westbrook Manufacturing Company. The house remained in the Haskell family into the 1960s and was a group home of the Little Brothers of Portland. Apartments now occupy this building. (Mike Sanphy collection.)

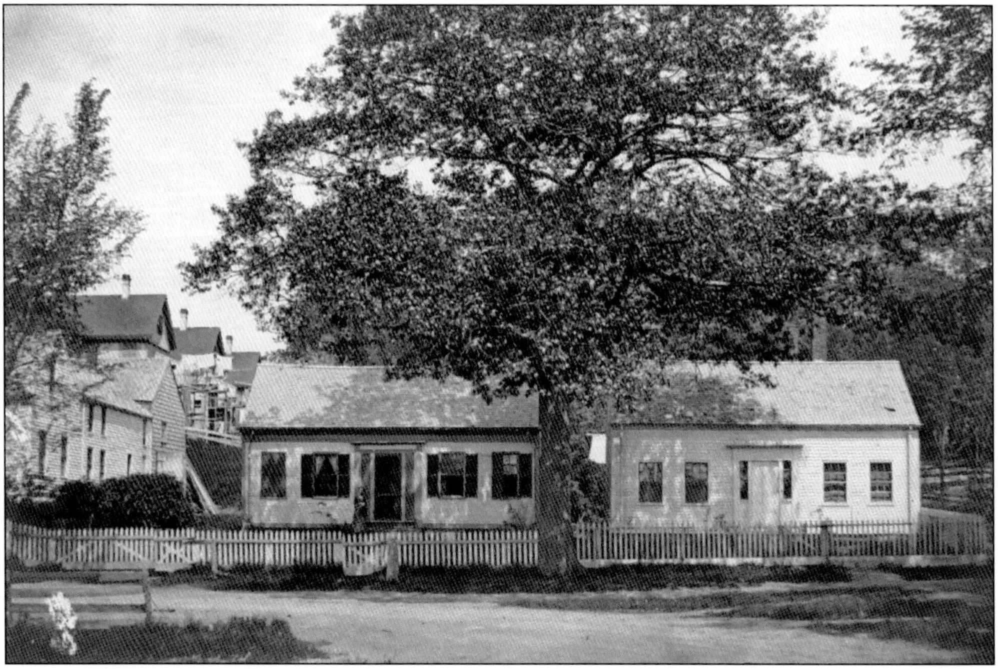

These buildings are on Brown Street. The house on left was once the residence of Woodbury K. Dana. (Walker Memorial Library collection.)

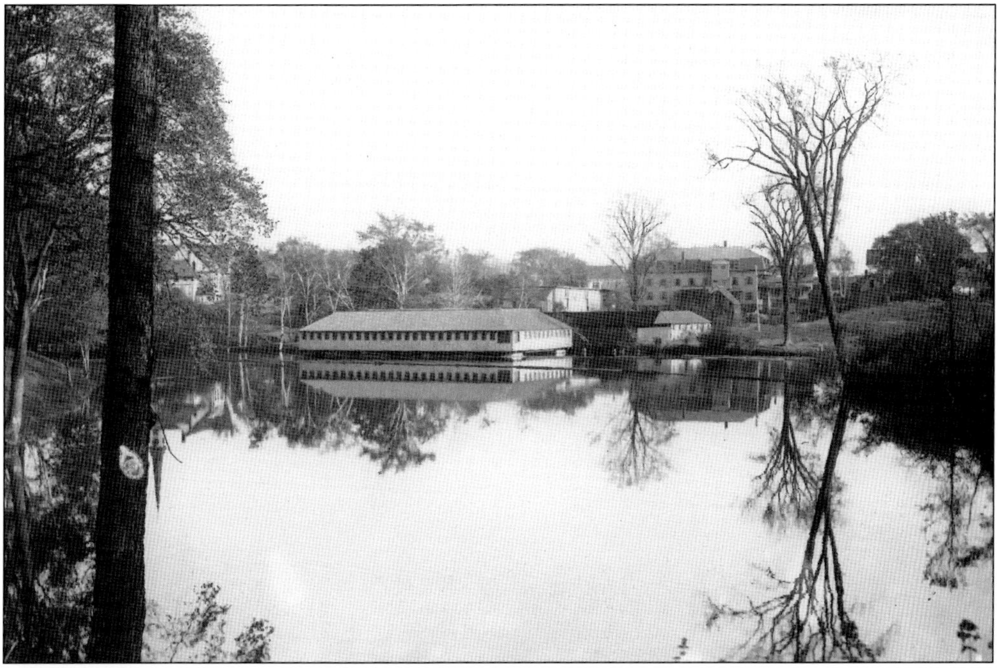

The swimming tank in the photograph was built in the early 1900s over the Presumpscot River (behind the present-day Cornelia Warren Pool). This building gave the young people of Westbrook a place for organized swimming lessons in the Presumpscot River. A large sewer was just upstream of the swimming tank, and the increasing awareness of pollution forced the demolition of the swimming tank in 1947. (Mike Sanphy collection.)

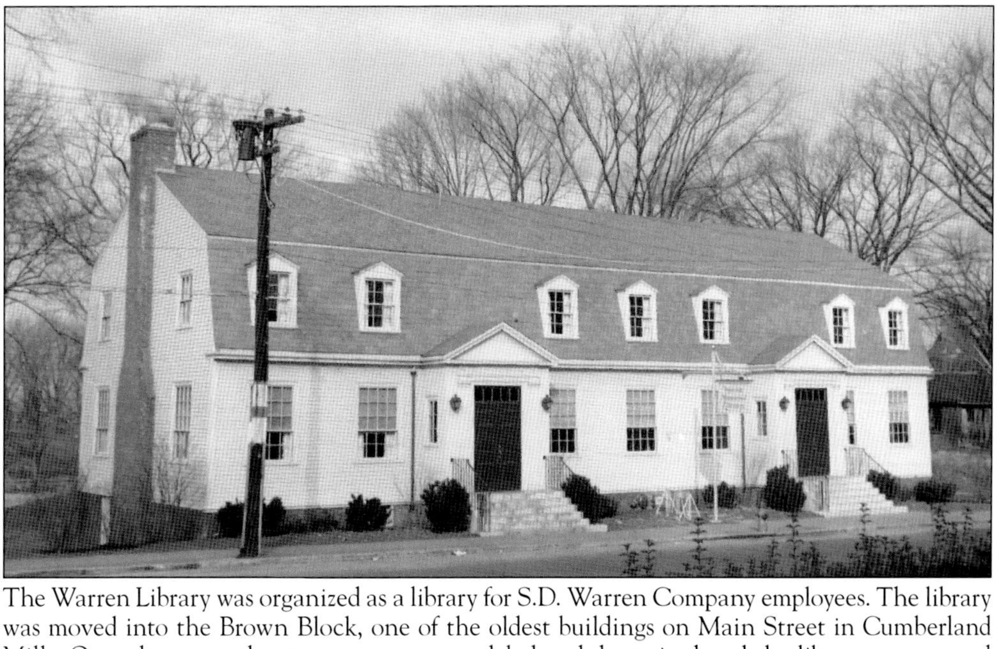

The Warren Library was organized as a library for S.D. Warren Company employees. The library was moved into the Brown Block, one of the oldest buildings on Main Street in Cumberland Mills. Over the years, the structure was remodeled and downsized and the library was opened to the public. Several years ago, the library closed and the building was sold. The Seventh-day Adventist Church purchased and remodeled the structure. (Mike Sanphy collection.)

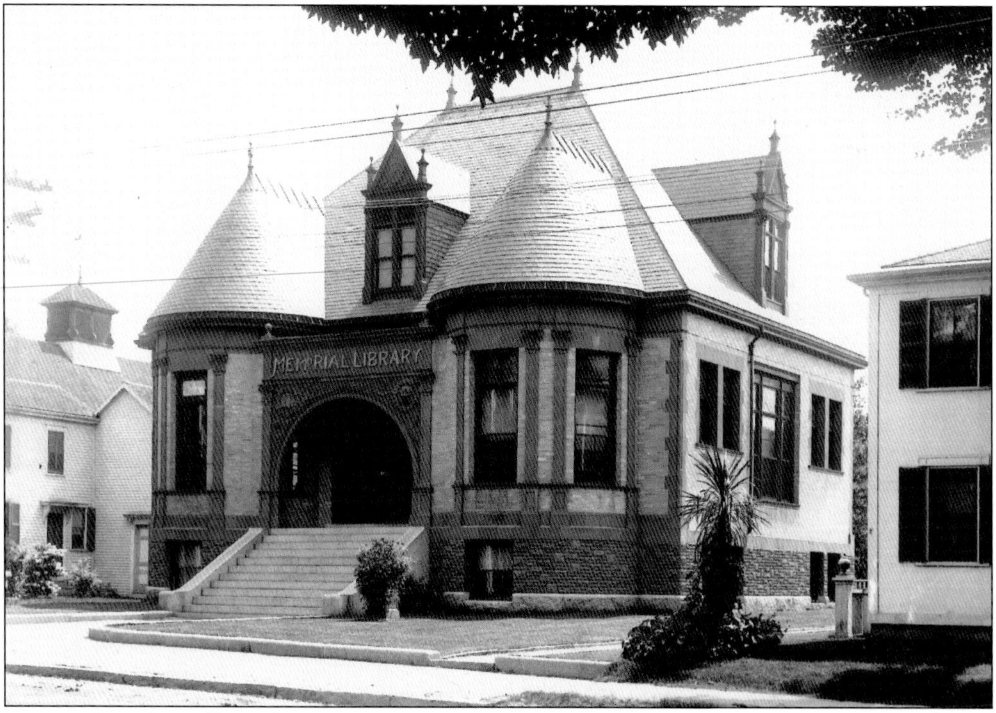

In 1891, Joseph Walker of Portland, a former Westbrook resident, died and left money for the construction of a library. On May 26, 1894, the Walker Memorial Library was dedicated by the city. The building is now in the National Register of Historic Places and continues to serve the citizens of Westbrook as the only public library in the city. (Walker Memorial Library collection.)

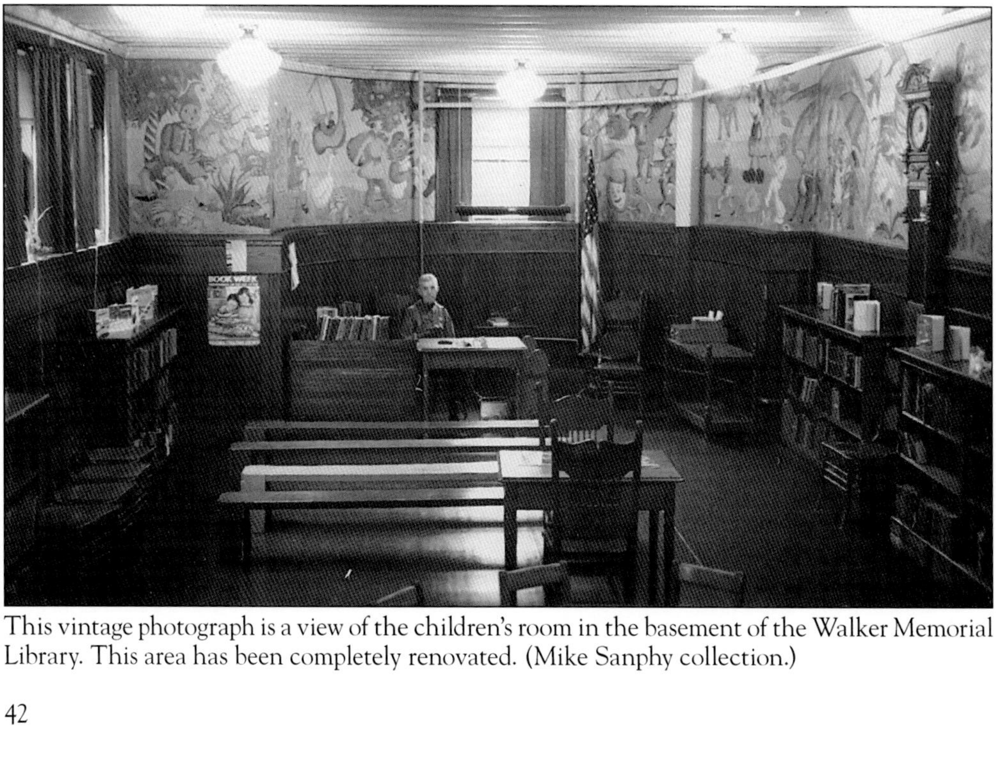

This vintage photograph is a view of the children's room in the basement of the Walker Memorial Library. This area has been completely renovated. (Mike Sanphy collection.)

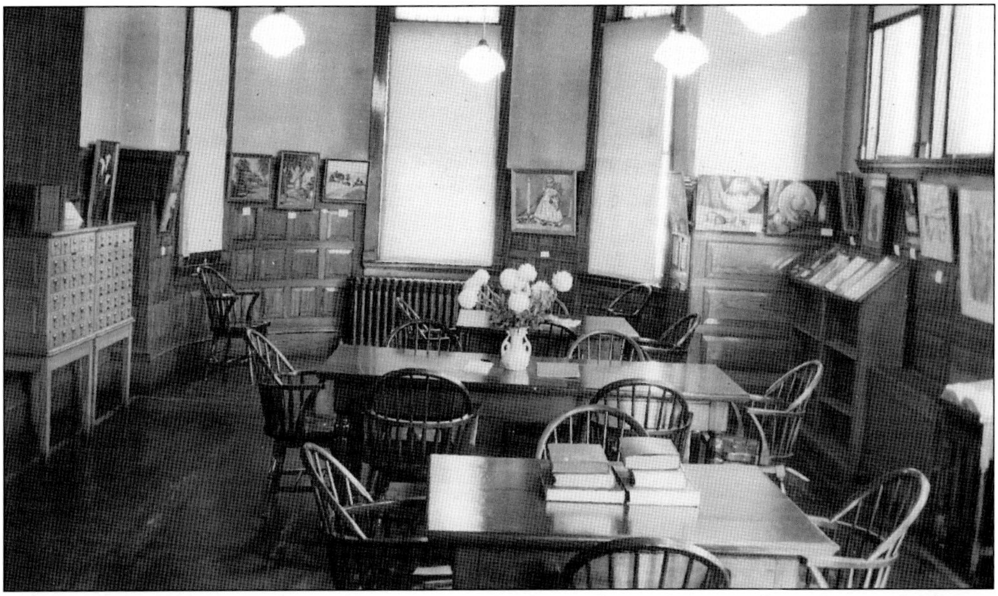

This is a photograph of the reading room on the main floor of the Walker Memorial Library. This area has been renovated, and the reading room was relocated to the newer addition of the library. (Mike Sanphy collection.)

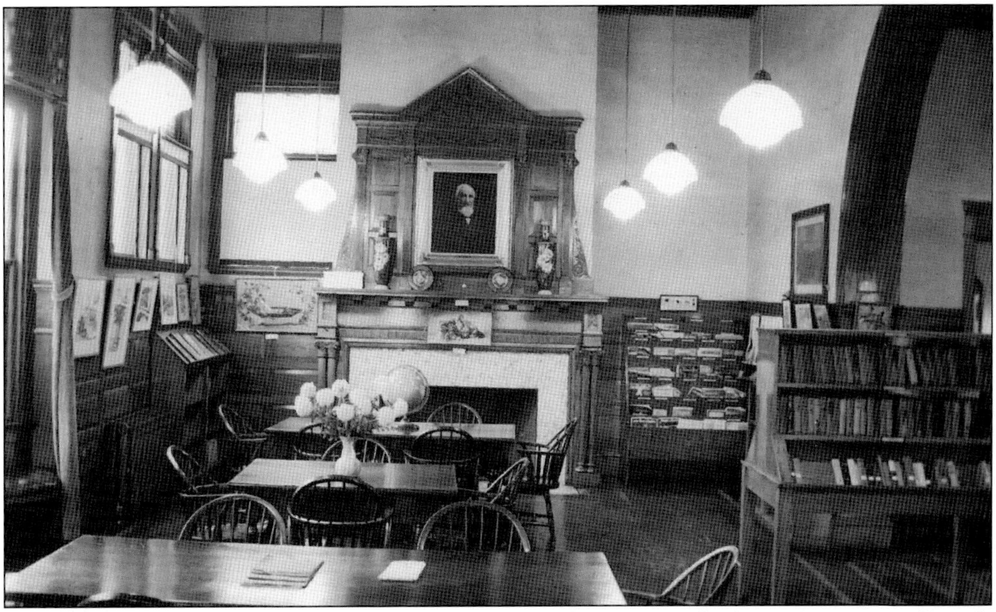

This photograph shows the old reading room in the Walker Memorial Library. A portrait of Joseph Walker, whose generosity built the library, hangs over the fireplace mantel. The reading room has been relocated to the newer addition on the library, and this space is now used for meetings. (Mike Sanphy collection.)

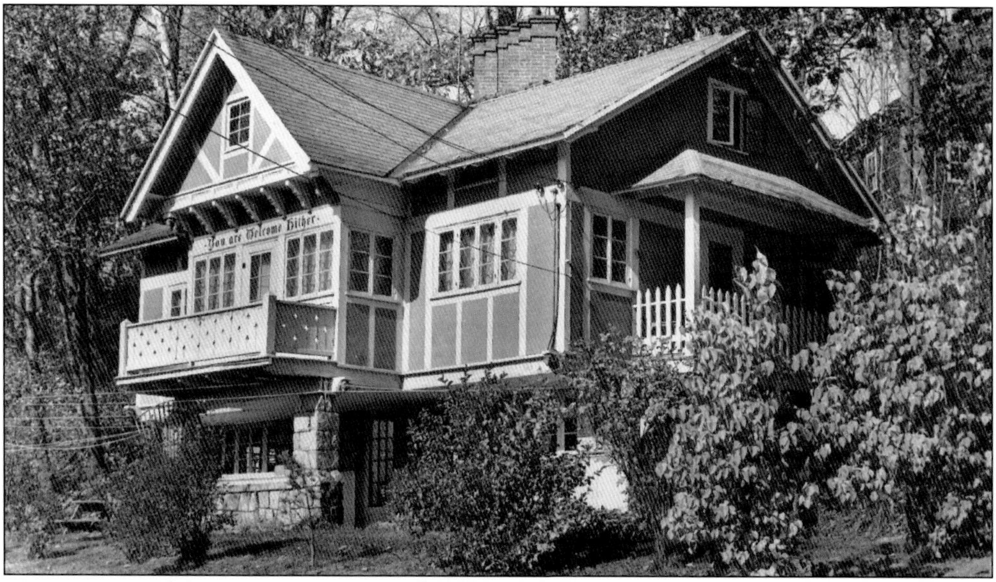

The Inn at Halidon served the village of Halidon, a single-tax colony established by Fiske Warren of the S.D. Warren family. The single-tax colony dissolved in 1952, and this house is now a private residence on Hillside Road. A sign on the building proclaims, "You are Welcome Hither." Halidon Road, off East Bridge Street, and Hillside Road, running from Halidon Road, are the two roads of this former single-tax colony. (Courtesy of Paul St. Cyr.)

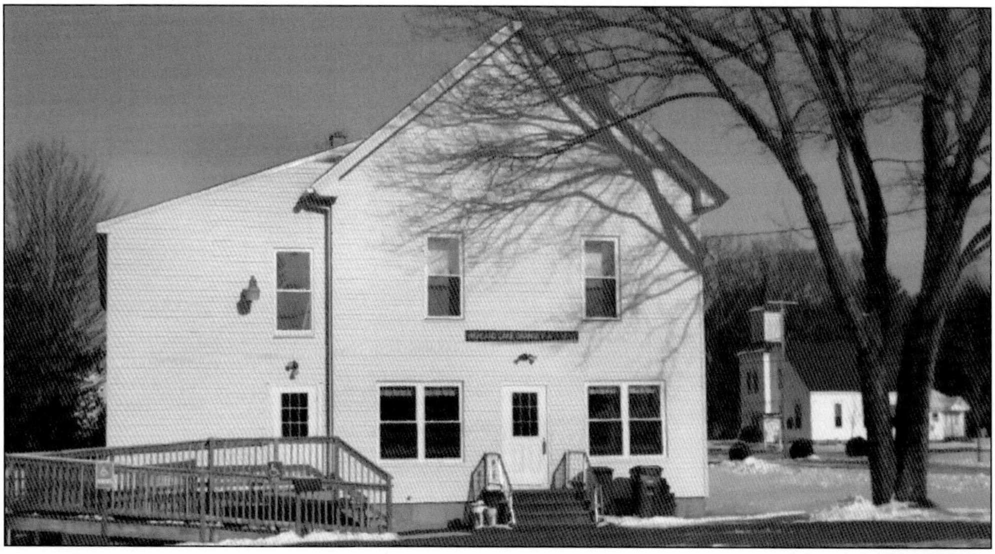

The Westbrook Lake Grange, Patrons of Husbandry, No. 87 was organized January 11, 1875. In 1934, the name was changed to Highland Lake Grange No. 87. Meetings were held in the upper room of the Duck Pond school until 1889 when this building was erected on the corner of Hardy Road and Bridgton Road (Route 302). In the 1960s, the Grange was moved from its original location and placed on a new foundation, with an addition. In the early 2000s, the building underwent further improvements. The Grange continues to be a vital part of the community, from its founding to the present in the 21st century. In recent years, public suppers are held to support various causes, and the Grange hall is used by other groups, such as 4-H, Boy Scouts, and Girl Scouts. (Mike Sanphy collection.)

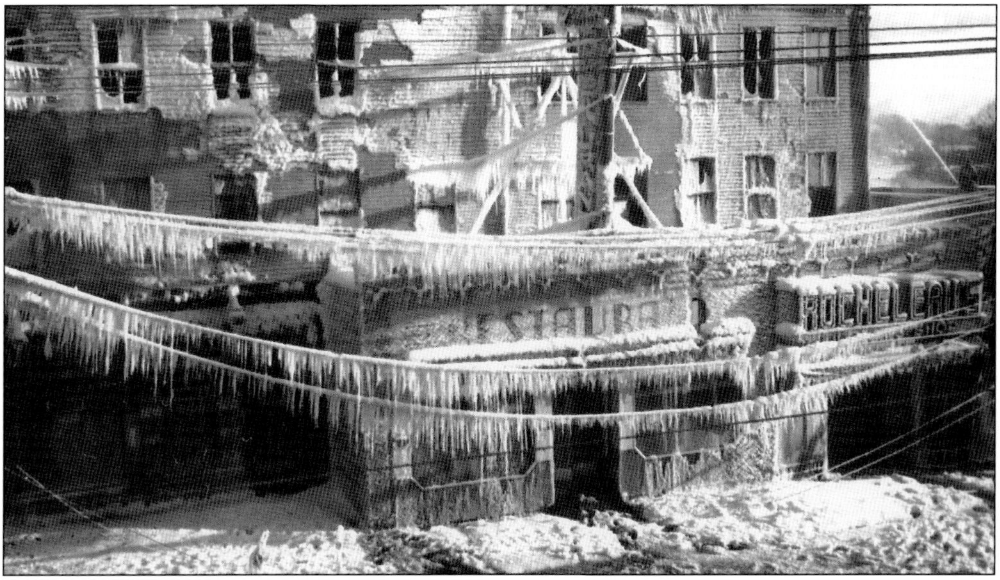

The front of the Vallee Block, at Main and Bridge Streets, is pictured here on the morning of February 13, 1942, after fire swept through the building. Firefighters endured below-freezing temperatures to battle this blaze. The first floor of the building housed businesses; Tom's Restaurant and Rocheleau, Cash Clothier are visible. Offices, meeting rooms, and apartments occupied the upper floors. The upper floors were demolished after the fire, and the first floor was renovated. (Mike Sanphy collection.)

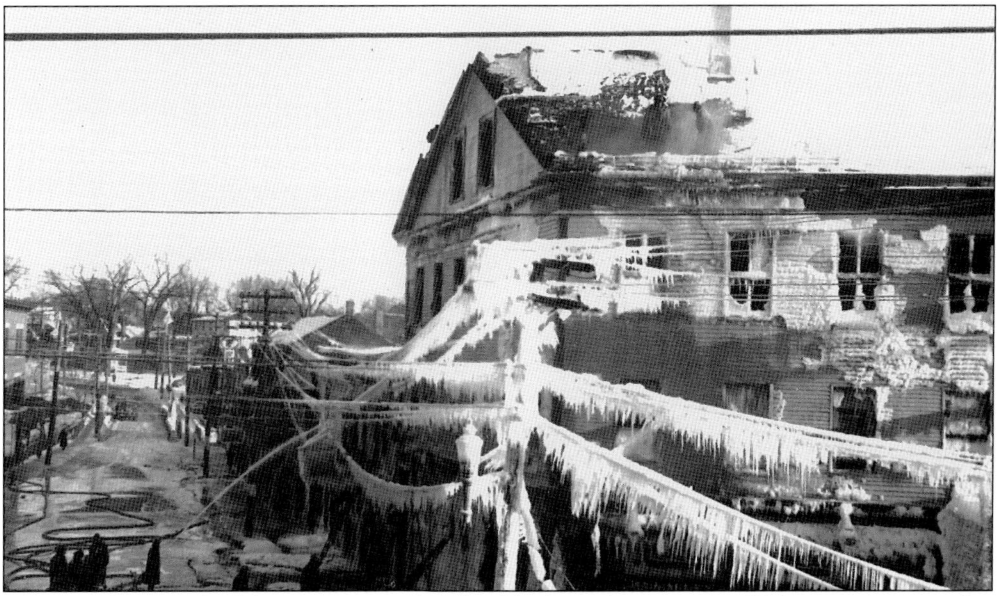

This is a photograph of the ice-encrusted Vallee Block on the morning of February 13, 1942, after fire swept through the building. The below-freezing temperatures covered the building, streets, and utility poles with ice. Upper floors of the structure were demolished, and the first floor was renovated. First-floor tenants Vallee Drug Store, Tom's Restaurant, and Rocheleau, Cash Clothier reopened and stayed in business for many more years. (Mike Sanphy collection.)

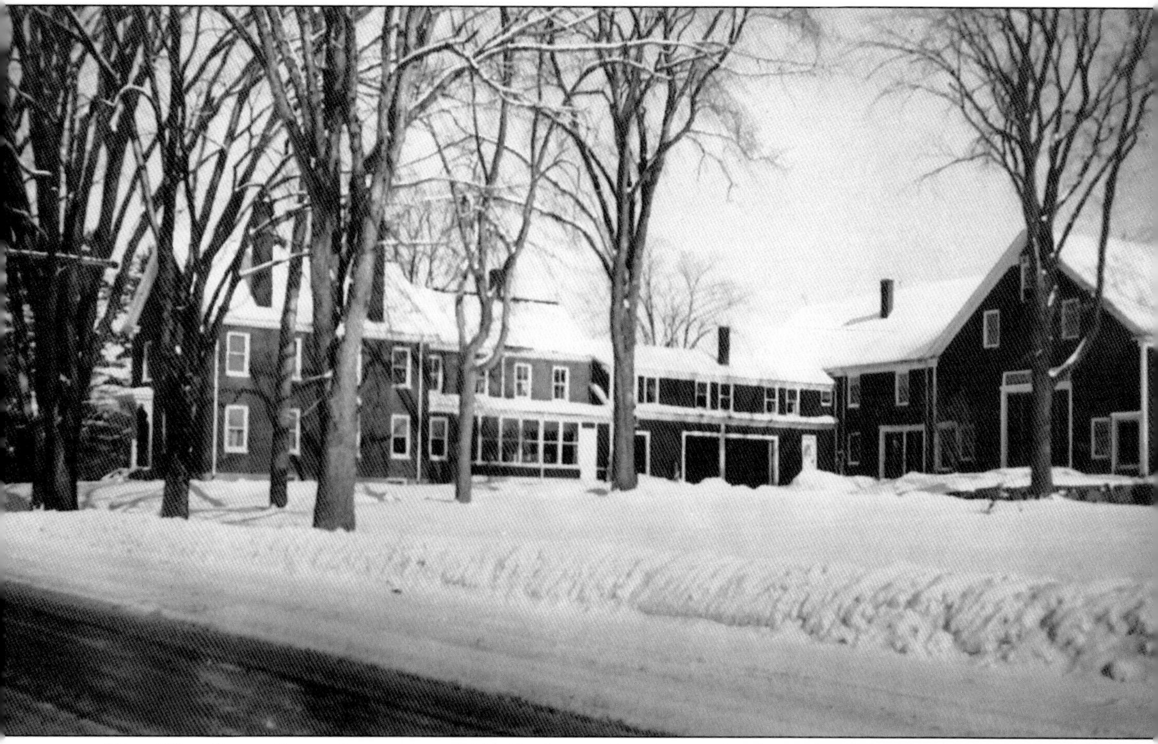

The Woodbury Farm, located at 1219 Bridgton Road, was built in 1867 by Daniel Woodbury. Stagecoaches travelling through the area stopped here for a change of horses. In the 1950s and 1960s, this farm served as the city of Westbrook school bus compound. The buses were owned by the late Lyman Woodbury, a direct descendant of Daniel Woodbury. The Highland Lake Cemetery is located behind this farm. (Mike Sanphy collection.)

Three

Businesses

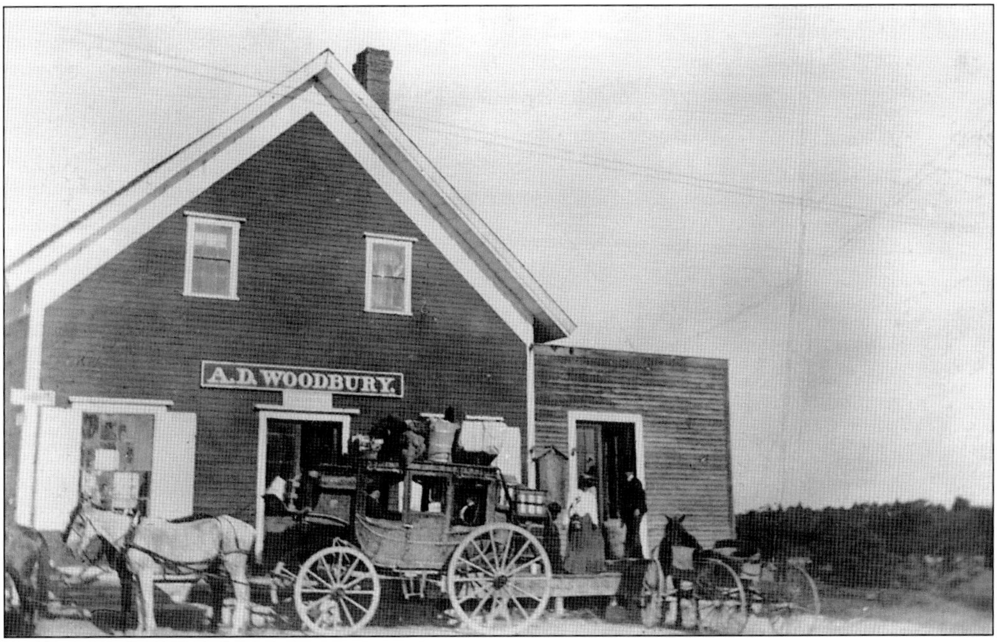

The A.D. Woodbury Store, located on Bridgton Road at Duck Pond Road, also served as a post office and stagecoach stop. This building was destroyed by fire in 1926 when P.D. Burns was the owner. An old stable building next to the Highland Lake Grange on the opposite corner of Bridgton Road and Hardy Road was hauled across the street and remodeled into a store. Highland Variety now occupies it. (Mike Sanphy collection.)

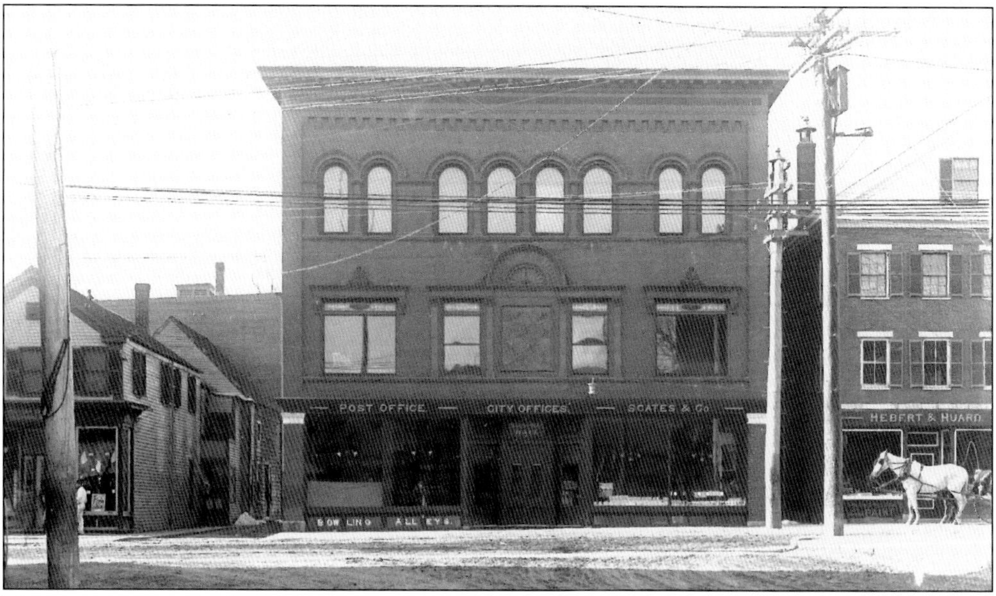

This structure was built on Main Street, opposite where Bridge Street meets Main Street, in 1903 by local businessman John Scates. Over the years, it housed the Scates Company, a post office, city hall, municipal court, Temple Lodge No. 86, Ancient Free & Accepted Masons, Cumberland County Power and Light, LaChance Drug Store, Phil's Pizza, Hub Furniture Co., and the Urban Renewal Authority, the last tenant before it was demolished. The CVS Pharmacy and parking lot currently occupy the space. (Mike Sanphy collection.)

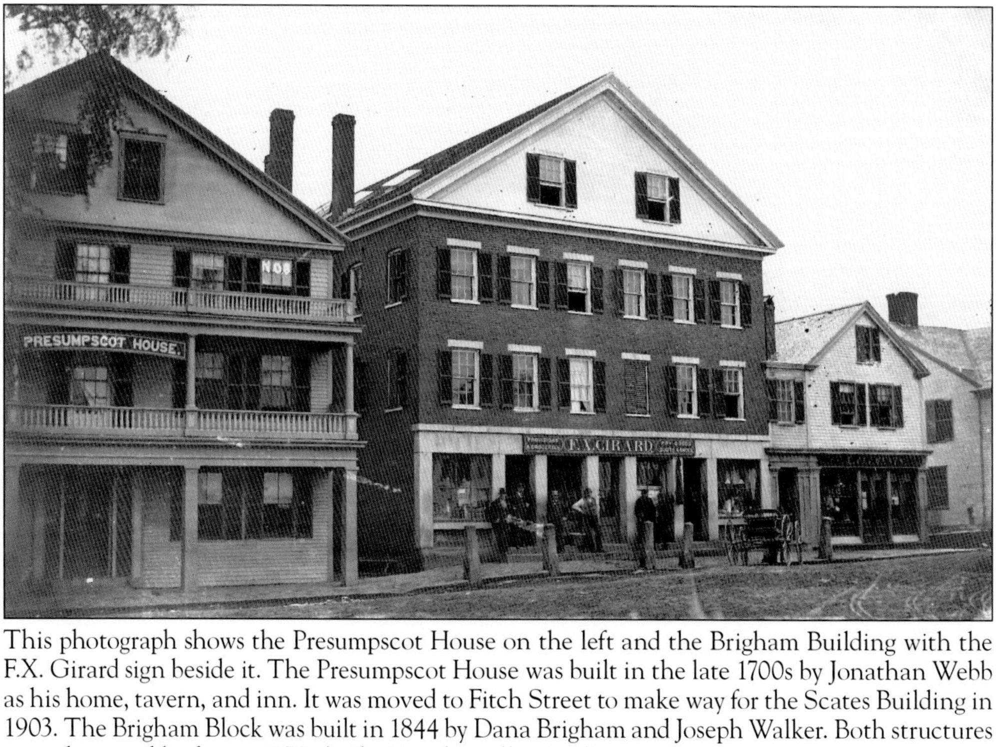

This photograph shows the Presumpscot House on the left and the Brigham Building with the F.X. Girard sign beside it. The Presumpscot House was built in the late 1700s by Jonathan Webb as his home, tavern, and inn. It was moved to Fitch Street to make way for the Scates Building in 1903. The Brigham Block was built in 1844 by Dana Brigham and Joseph Walker. Both structures were destroyed by fire in 1978. (Mike Sanphy collection.)

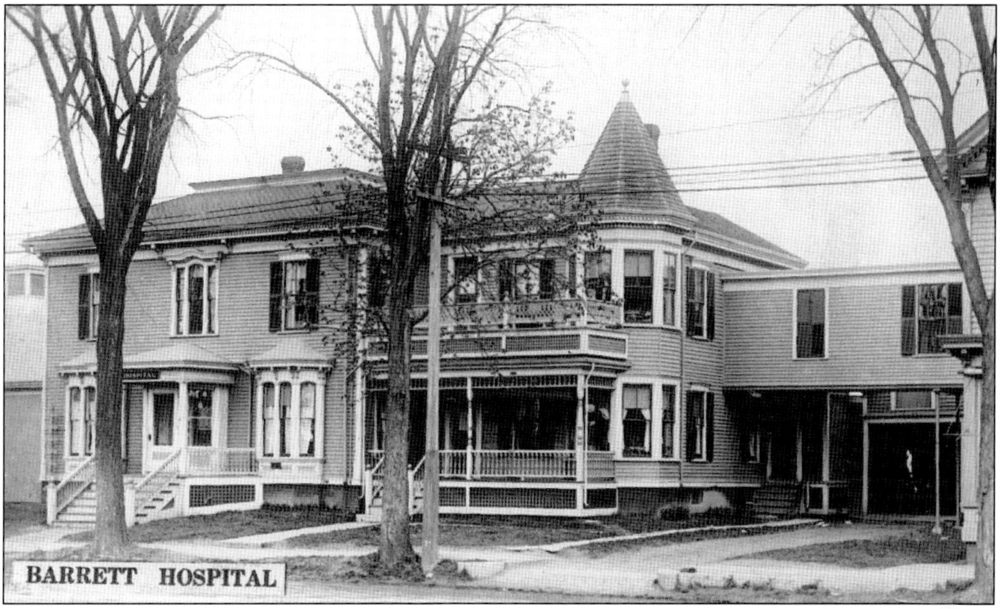

The Ansel Stevens house was on Main Street, opposite where Rochester Street meets Main Street. In 1909, Dr. Felix Barrett opened the Barrett Hospital in this building. This hospital served Westbrook and its surrounding communities for many years, closing in 1962 when the Westbrook Community Hospital opened on Park Road. The old hospital still stands as an apartment building. (Mike Sanphy collection.)

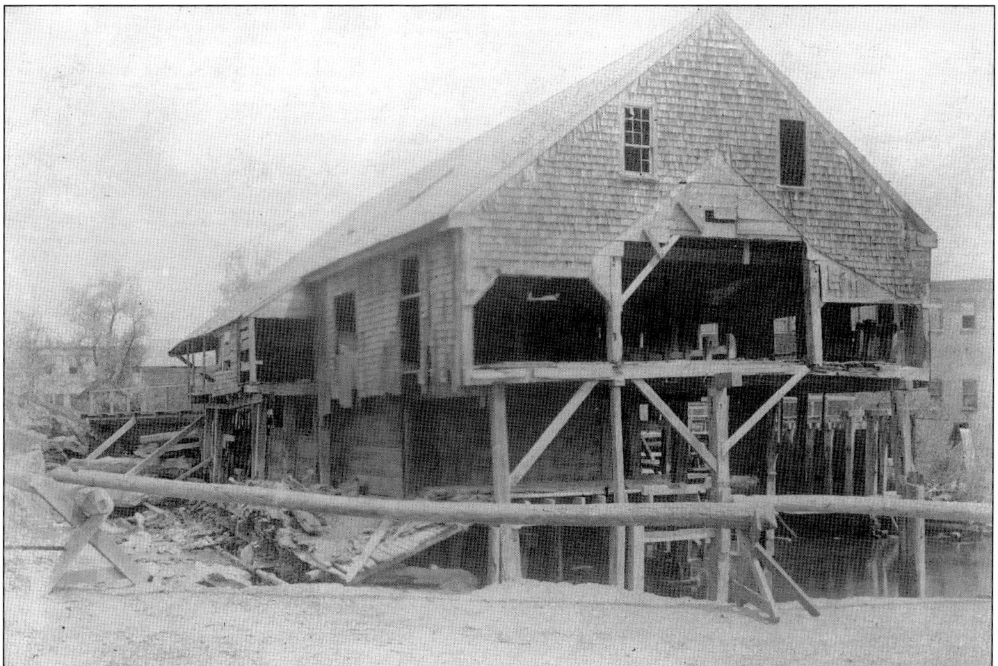

This is one of the many sawmills that stood on the banks of the Presumpscot River. Early settlers built dams and sawmills on the Presumpscot River, and this resulted in hostilities with the local Indians for many years. (Mike Sanphy collection.)

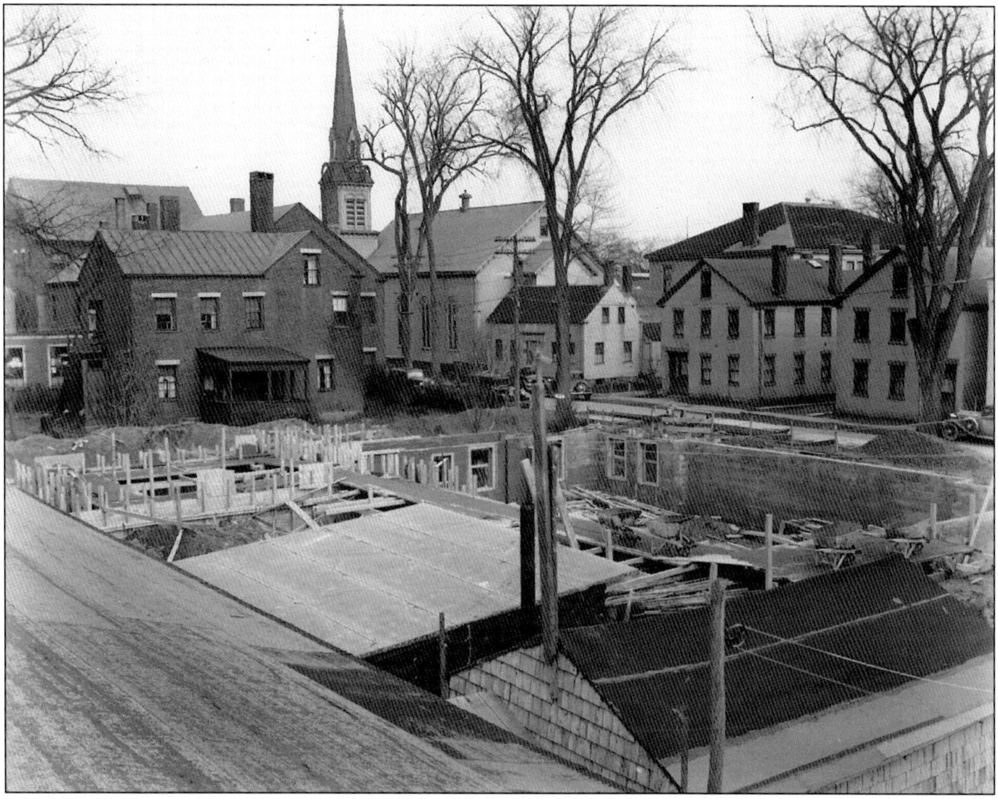

This photograph shows the foundation of the Brackett Street Post Office, built in 1935. In the background, the old Brackett-LaFond Block can be seen on the left, and the Westbrook Congregational Church is next to it. The church and the Brackett-LaFond Block were demolished, and the lower end of Brackett Street was closed off during urban renewal. Ocean Communities Federal Credit Union presently occupies the old post office building. (Mike Sanphy collection.)

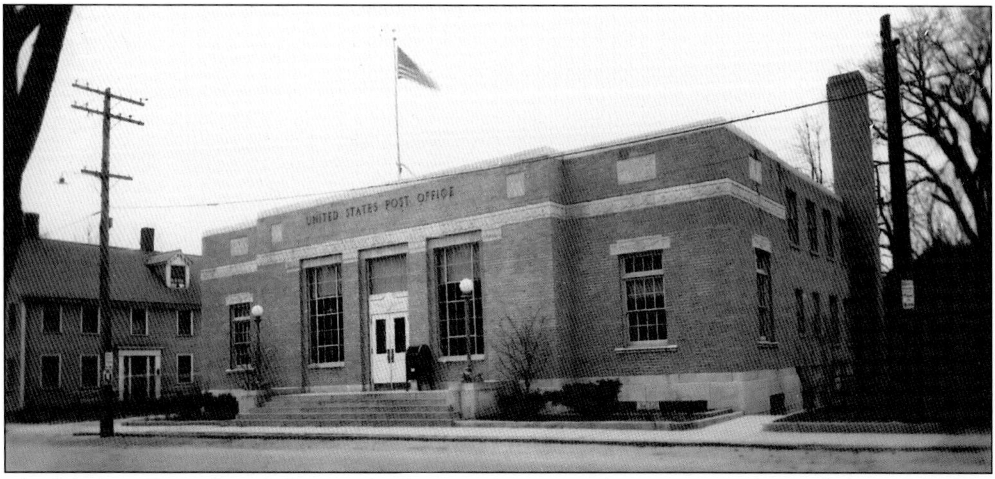

The Brackett Street Post Office was built in 1935 at 19 Brackett Street and served the community along with a branch office space in Cumberland Mills. Both of these facilities were closed when the new post office at 775 Main Street opened in 1978. The structure is presently occupied by Oceans Community Federal Credit Union. (Mike Sanphy collection.)

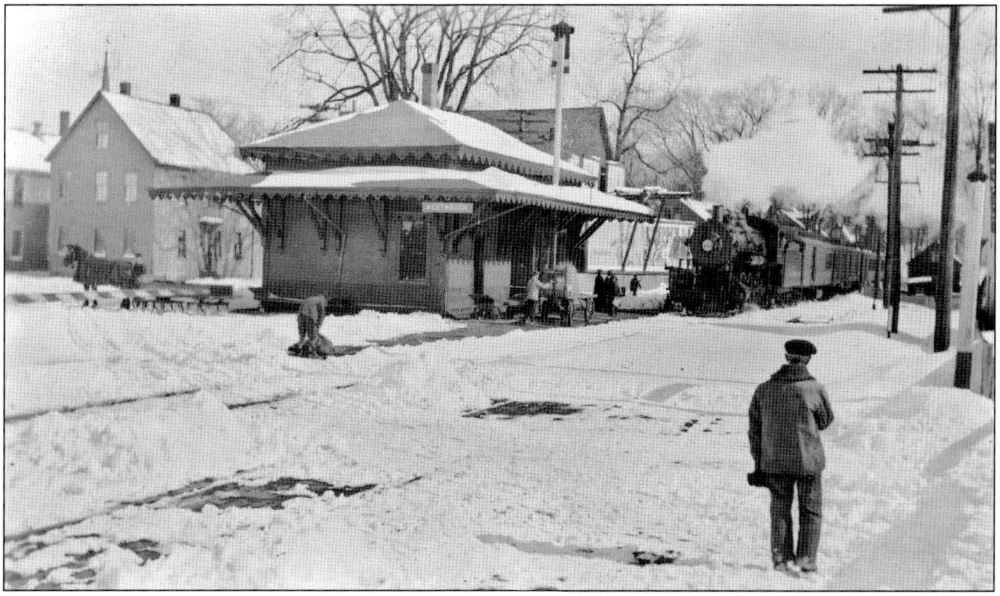

The old Boston & Maine Railroad Station was located in the present-day municipal parking lot facing William Clarke Drive, which was built over the railroad tracks that once branched off the tracks in Cumberland Mills and ran from Westbrook to Rochester, New Hampshire. This building was situated between present-day Fitch Street and Central Street. The old station closed in 1916 and was later demolished. (Mike Sanphy collection.)

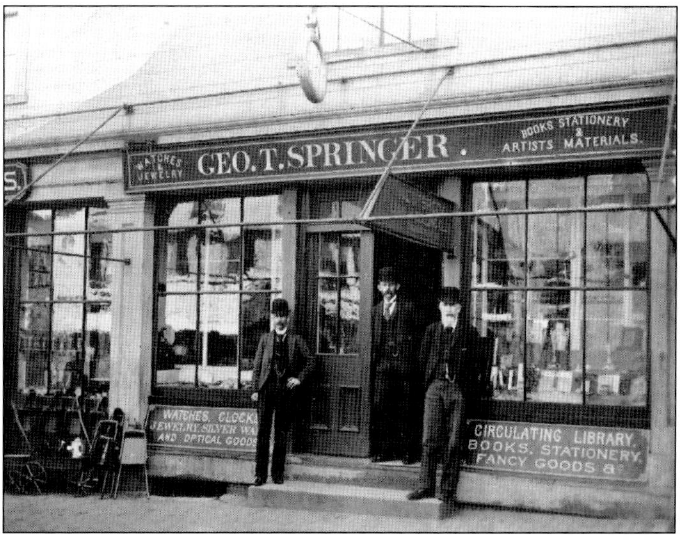

George T. Springer's store, located on Bridge Street around the corner from Main Street, sold jewelry, watches, books, stationary, artists' materials, and other goods. The store eventually moved to Portland. This building was adjacent the Vallee Block and was destroyed in the Vallee Block fire of February 1942. The structure was rebuilt as a one-story building, and the Frog & Turtle Restaurant currently occupies the space. (Mike Sanphy collection.)

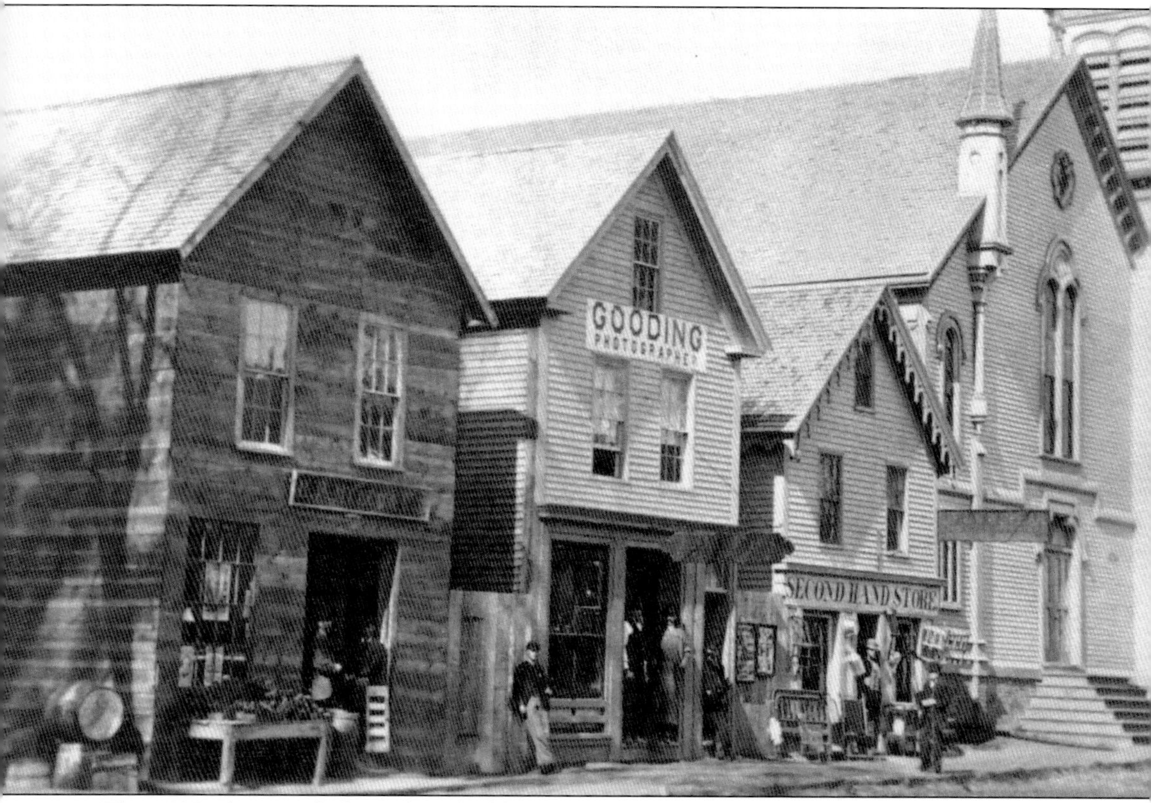

This 1800s photograph shows three buildings on Main Street, east of the Westbrook Congregational Church. In later years, these buildings were renovated. Parker's Dress Shop occupied the building on the left, Lane's Shoe Store was next, and the third building was a doctor's office. Parker's and Lane's were demolished to make way for a new medical building connecting to the structure next to the church. (Mike Sanphy collection.)

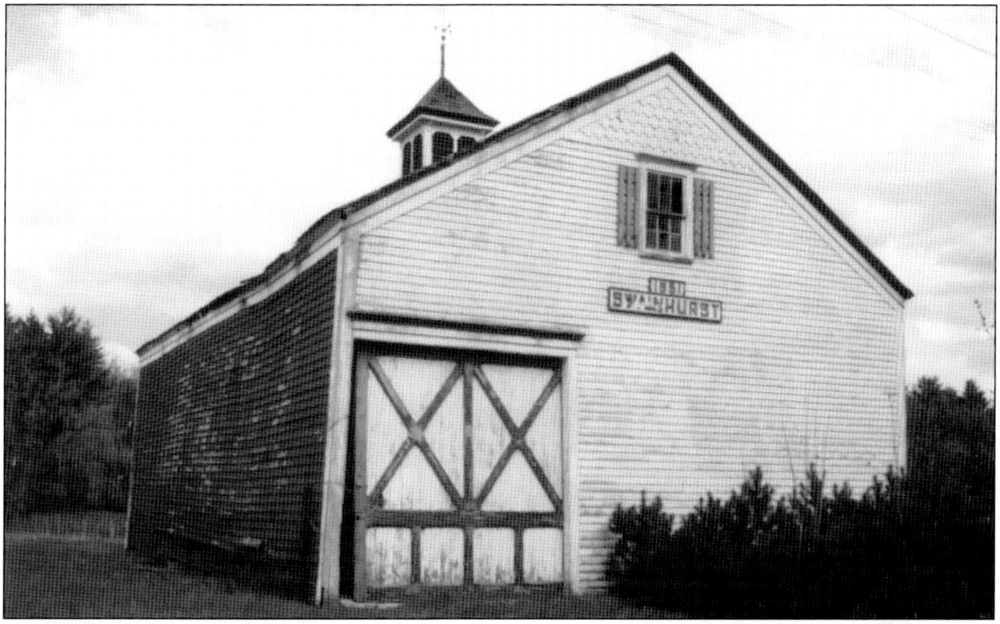

This barn on Duck Pond Road was for many years a landmark. It bore the name Swainhurst and the date 1851 and was originally part of the Knight farm. The barn fell into neglect, and it was demolished in 2000. (Mike Sanphy collection.)

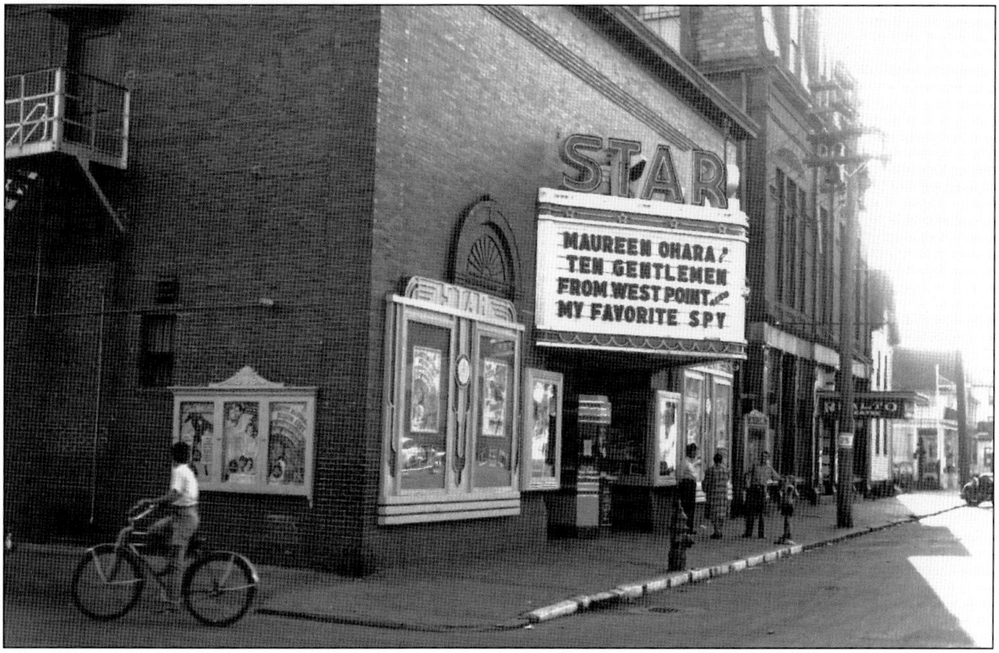

The Star Theatre was built in 1912 on Main Street at Central Street as a performing arts theater. Later, it changed from stage shows to motion pictures. In the 1960s, Cinema City, a multiscreen theater, opened in Westbrook, and this, coupled with several other multiscreen theaters in surrounding communities, spelled an end to the small theaters. Star Theatre closed and was demolished in 1974. Martini Lane occupies the space where the theater once stood. (Mike Sanphy collection.)

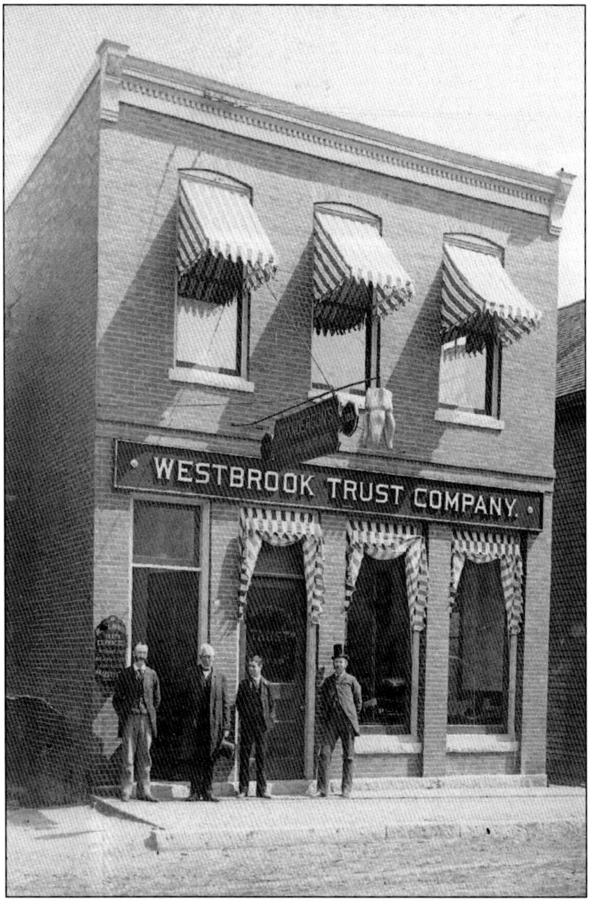

This is the original Westbrook Trust Company on Main Street in 1890. Dr. Anderson's Dental Parlors occupied the second floor. Leander Valentine, pictured second from left, was the first president of Westbrook Trust Company and the first mayor of Westbrook when it became a city in 1891. A new, larger bank was built to the left of this structure. This building became a millinery shop and was later demolished. (Mike Sanphy collection.)

The Westbrook Trust Company was built in the 1920s, replacing a smaller building that once stood to the right it. At one time, Westbrook Trust Company had branch banks in the Cumberland Mills and Prides Corner areas of the city. Westbrook Trust Company was bought out, and after several owners, Bank of America presently occupies this building. The branch offices were closed over the years. (Mike Sanphy collection.)

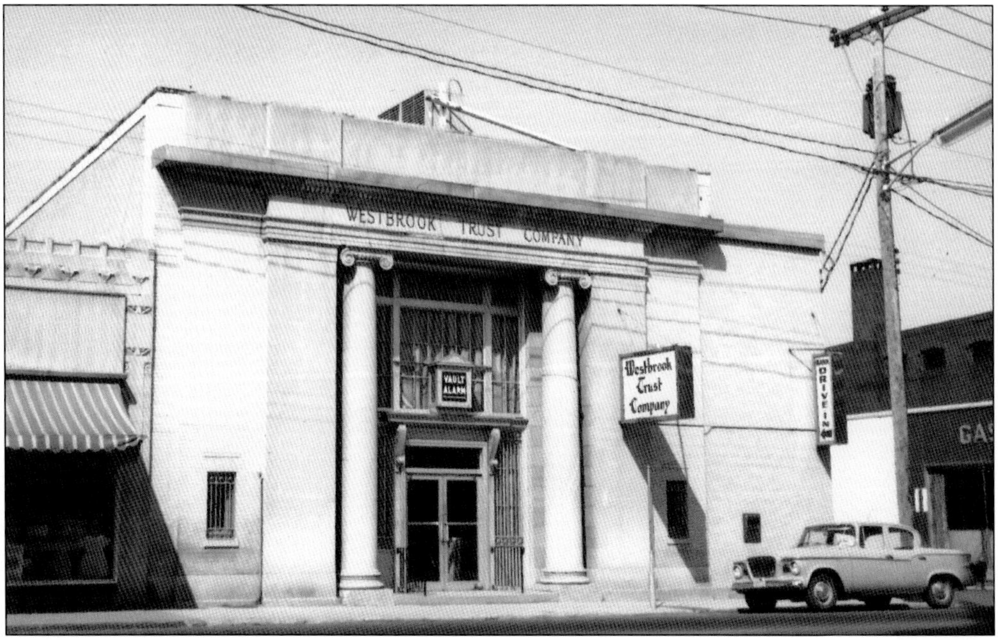

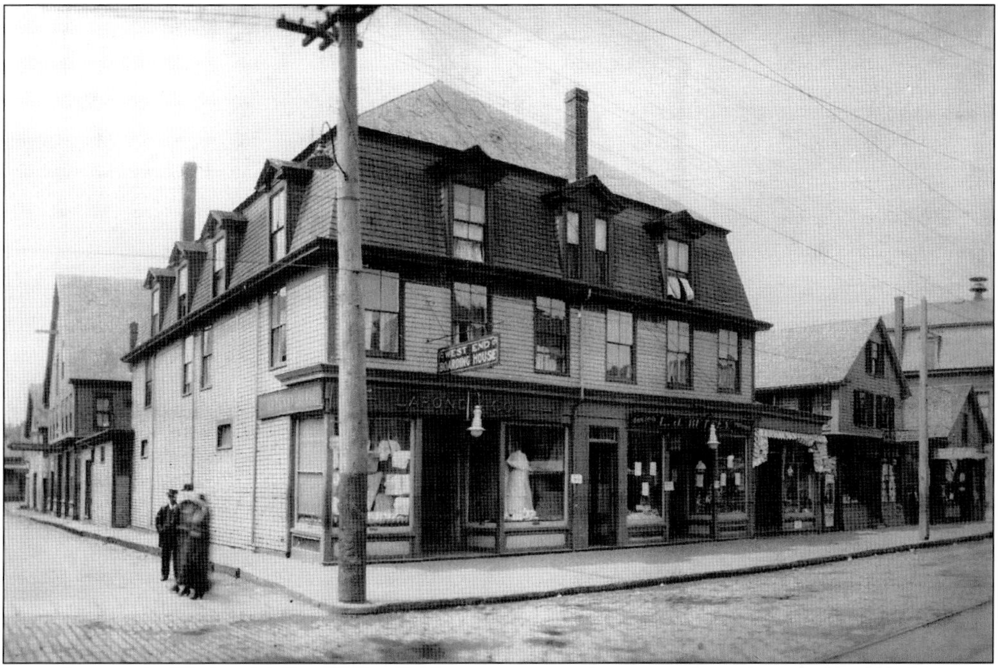

The Pride Block was located on Main Street at Fitch Street. The first floor had LaFond & Co. dry goods and L.J. Bettey groceries and provisions. West End Boarding House occupied the upper floors. LaFond & Co. later moved into the Brackett Block, and the Atlantic & Pacific Tea Company (A&P) moved here. This building was demolished to make way for a larger A&P store. A Family Dollar store now occupies this space. (Mike Sanphy collection.)

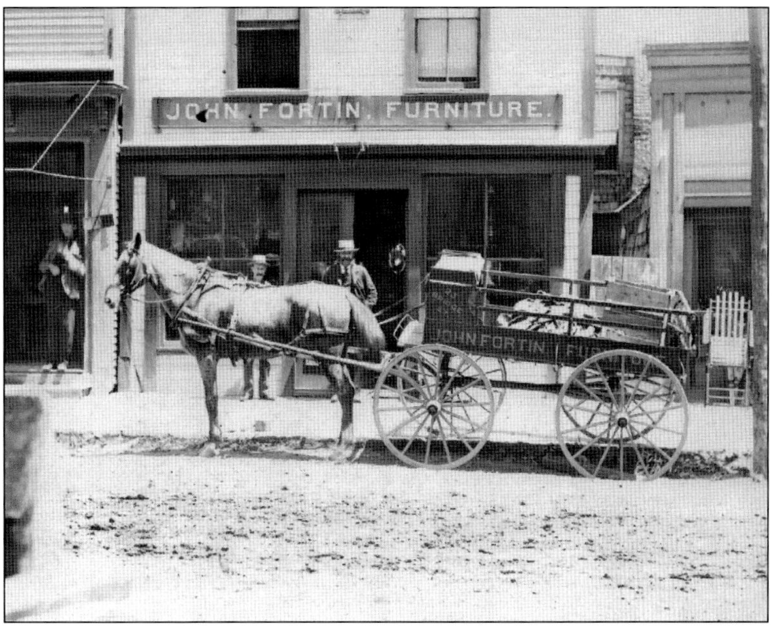

John Fortin's horse and wagon wait outside his business at 25 Bridge Street. Wires over his doorway show that electricity has arrived to downtown Westbrook, and the sign next to the unidentified gentleman in the doorway on the left shows that Moxie has arrived. (EG/BFC.)

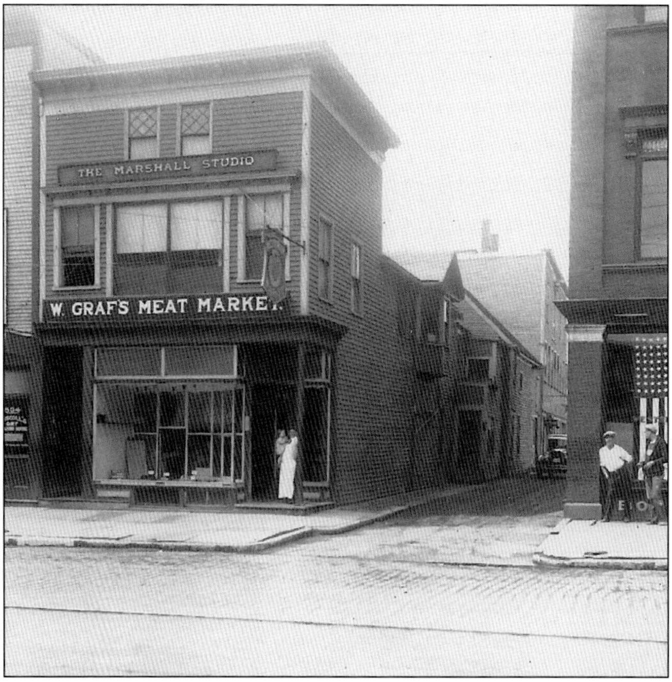

Walter Graf was an immigrant from Switzerland who had learned his trade as a butcher there. In this 1928 photograph, he holds his daughter Emily as he stands in front of his market on Main Street at Carpenter Street, opposite where Bridge Street meets Main Street. (EG/BFC.)

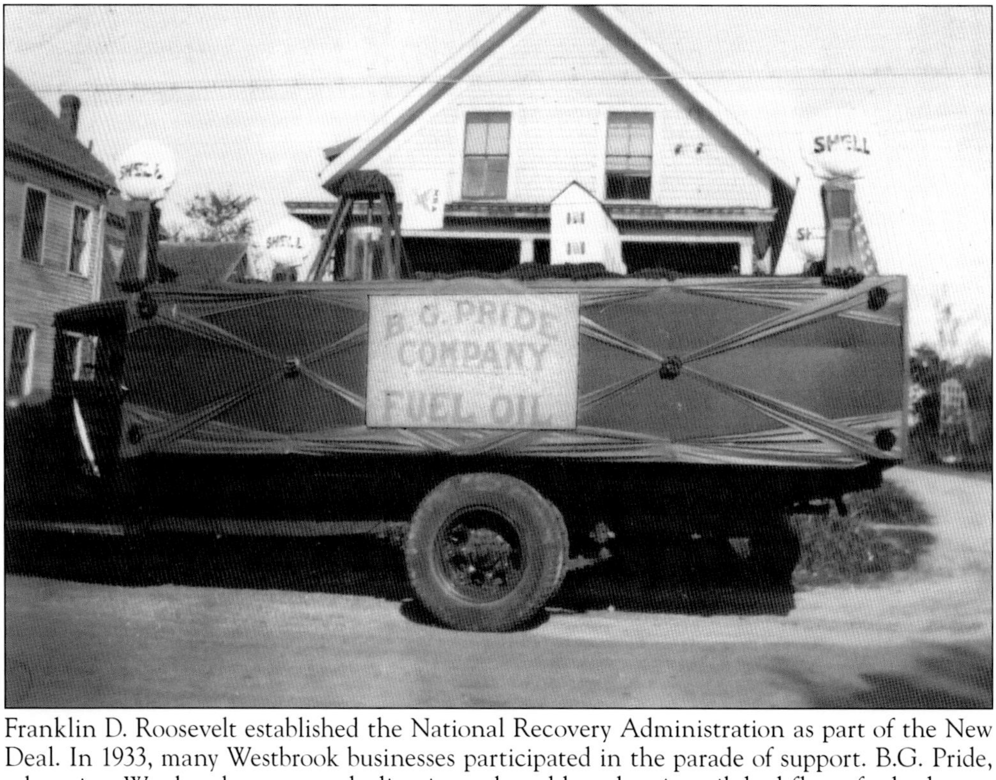

Franklin D. Roosevelt established the National Recovery Administration as part of the New Deal. In 1933, many Westbrook businesses participated in the parade of support. B.G. Pride, a longtime Westbrook company dealing in coal, and later heating oil, had floats for both: one with a full cart exiting a coal mine, and this one, which features an oil rig and Shell gasoline pump. (EG/BFC.)

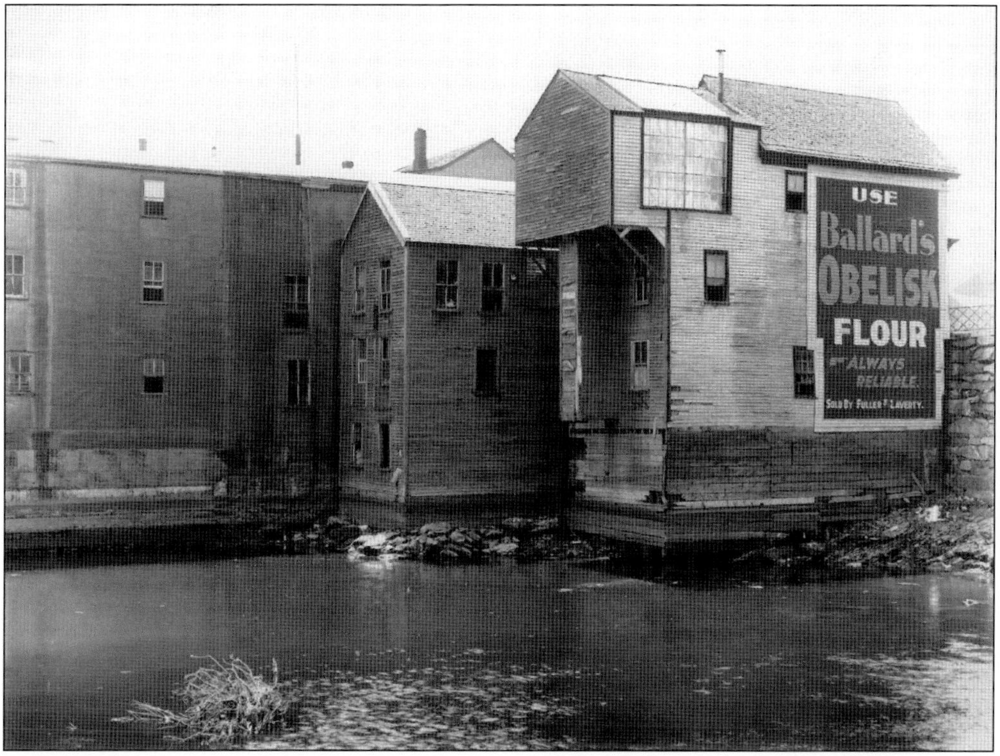

This was the view across the river from the north side, a bit downstream from Bridge Street's iron bridge. Part of the bridge's stone abutment can be seen on the far right. The three buildings all face Bridge Street, and this view is of the structures' backs and sides. The largest of the three, extending out to the left, once housed the Federal Furniture Company. (EG/BFC.)

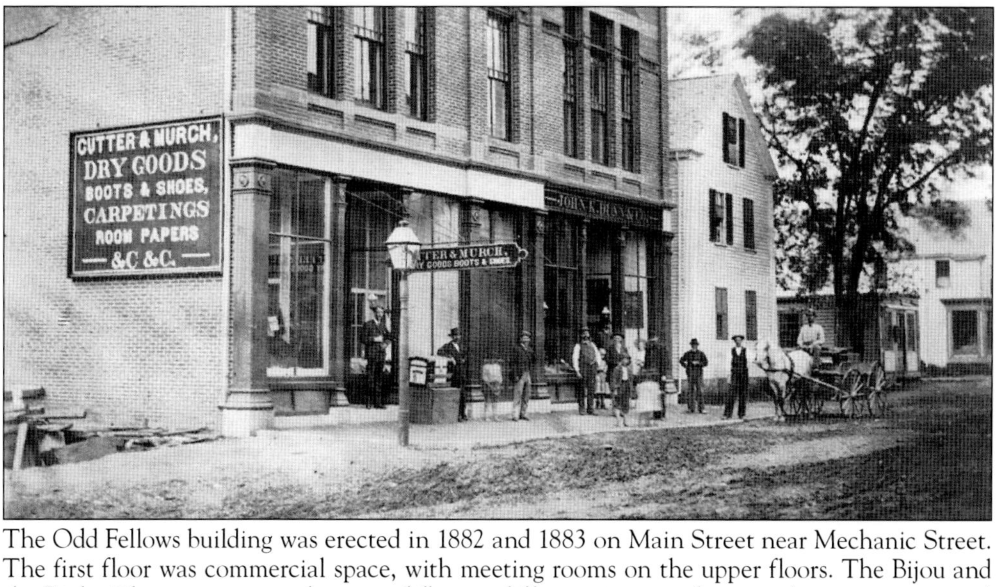

The Odd Fellows building was erected in 1882 and 1883 on Main Street near Mechanic Street. The first floor was commercial space, with meeting rooms on the upper floors. The Bijou and the Rialto Theatres were on the second floor at different times, and various businesses occupied the first floor over the years. American Legion Post No. 197 was the last owner of the building before it was demolished by urban renewal. (Westbrook Historical Society collection.)

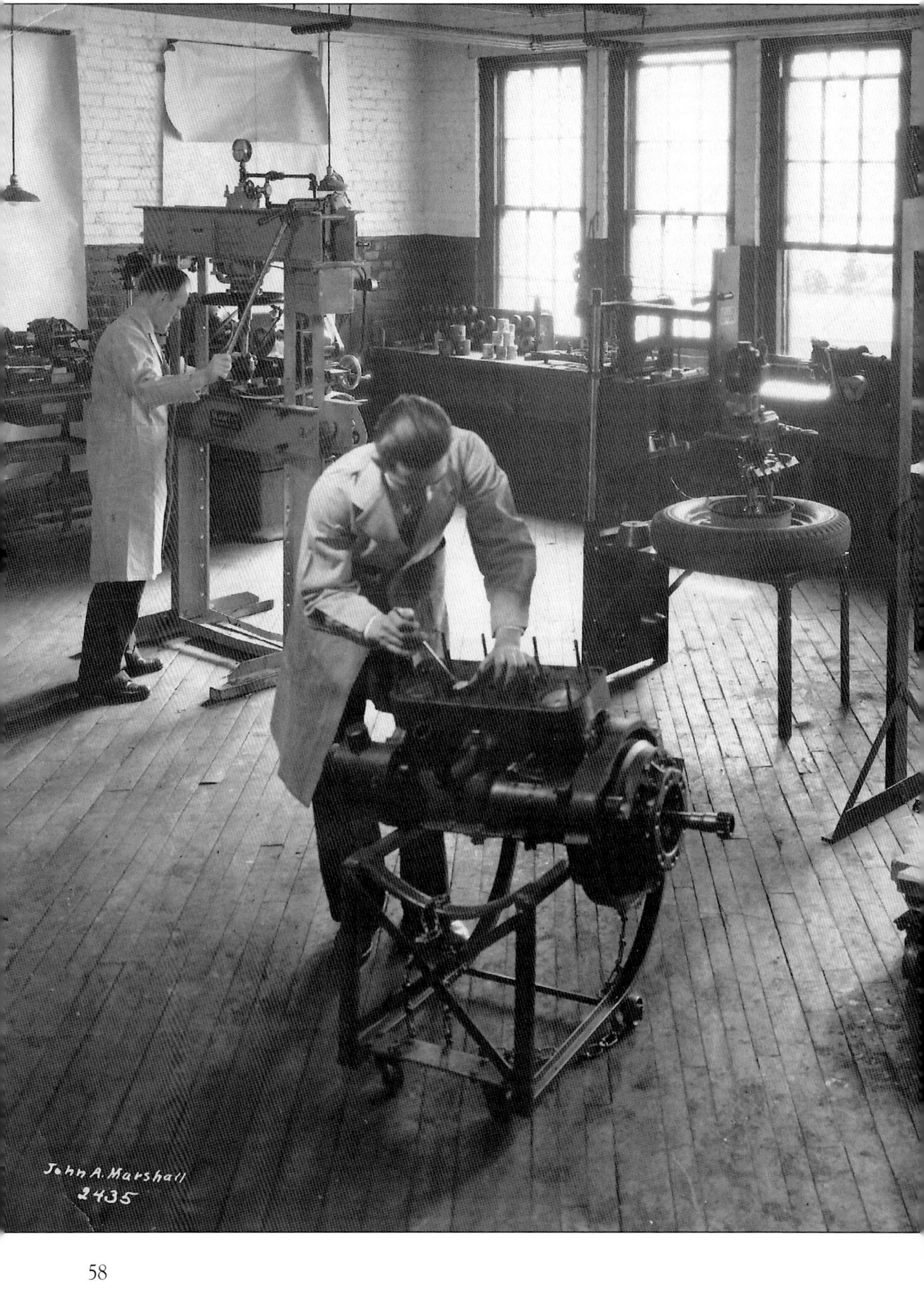
John A. Marshall
2435

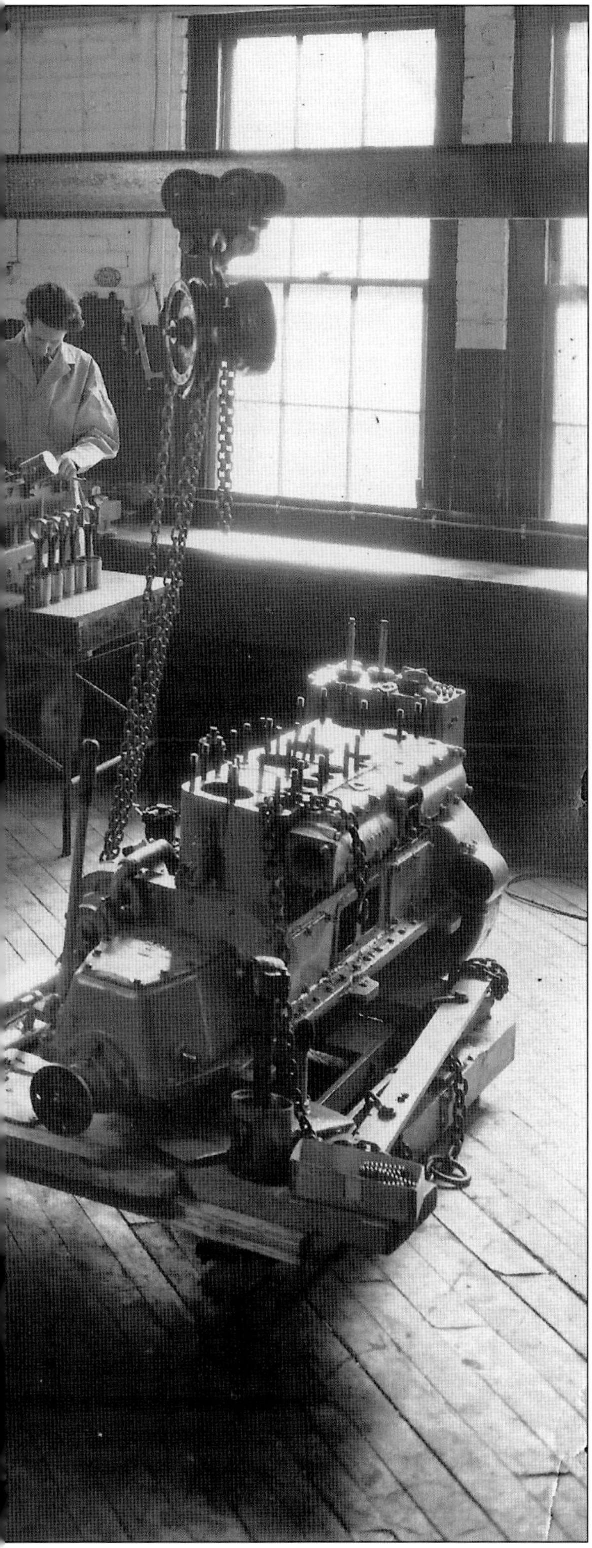

Roland Turgeon (in the foreground) works on an engine at the Bailey Auto Shops. This is a professional photograph taken by Marshall Studios of Westbrook. It may have been used for promotional purposes. (Westbrook Historical Society collection.)

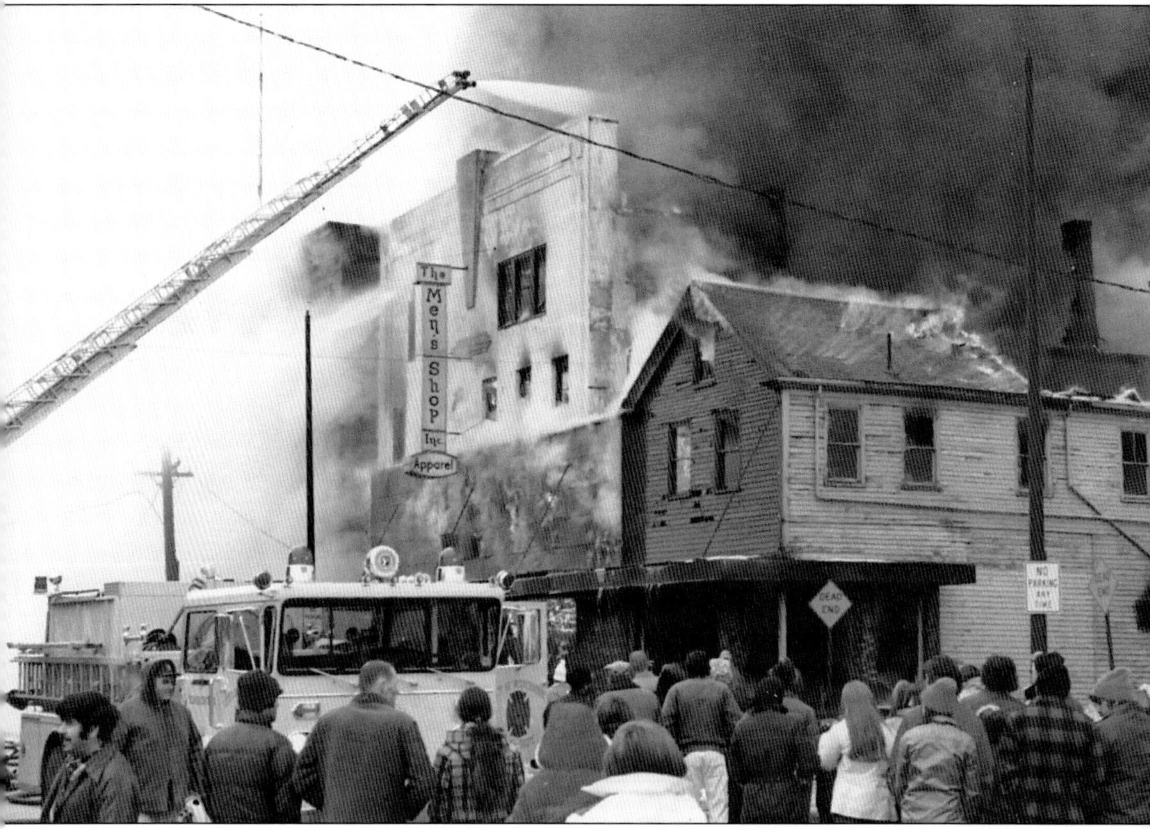

On Sunday morning, January 8, 1978, a fire of undetermined origin swept through the vacant Men's Shop, Inc., building that had been slated for demolition by the Urban Renewal Authority on the following day. The large Men's Shop structure was built in 1844 by Dana Brigham and Joseph Walker. The smaller building, once the West End Drug Company, was an annex to the Men's Shop. A third vacant building behind this one, Bevo's Rooming House, was also destroyed. This structure was the old Presumpscot House, built in the late 1700s and later moved from Main Street to make way for the construction of the Scates Building in 1903. CVS Pharmacy presently occupies this site. (Mike Sanphy collection.)

Four

CHURCHES

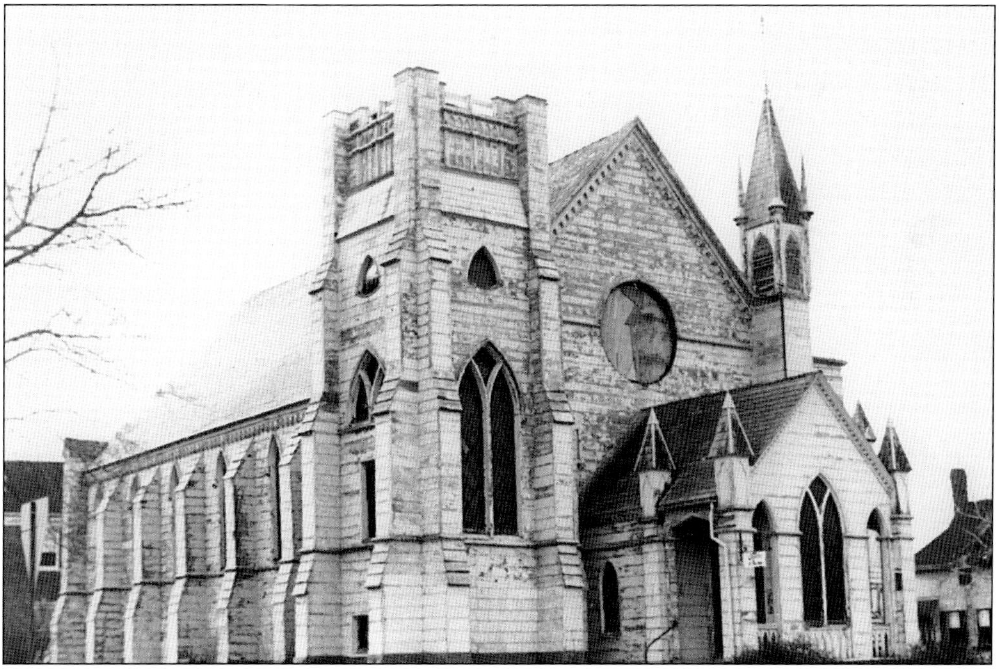

The Warren Congregational Church was built in 1869 by members of the Westbrook Congregational Church who had been given permission to separate and build a church in the Cumberland Mills area of Westbrook. This photograph shows it vacant prior to demolition in 1978. The original Westbrook Congregational Church, built in 1834, was demolished by urban renewal in 1974. Members of these two churches reunited to build the Westbrook Warren Congregational Church at 810 Main Street. (Photograph by Neil Cobisi.)

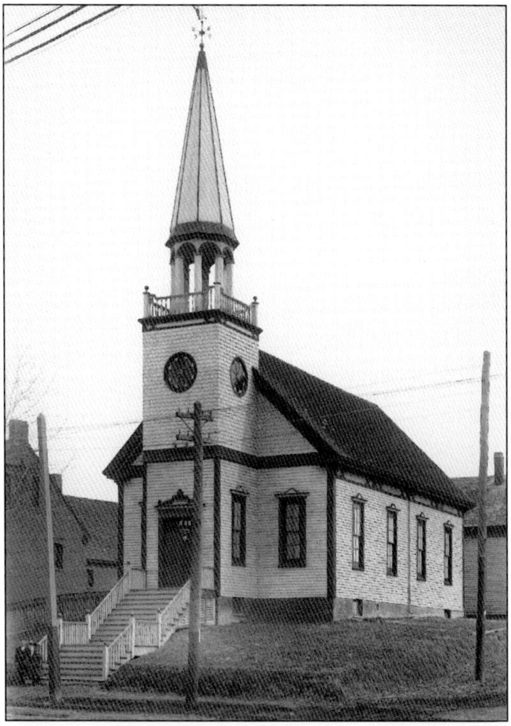

On November 2, 1882, the First Danish Evangelical Lutheran Church was organized in a home on Reservoir Street. As the congregation grew, the need for a church became evident, and fundraisers were started. This church was dedicated on January 1, 1893. The parsonage was purchased in 1908 and remodeled. In 1928, a church bell was installed. This church has been expanded and remodeled over the years. (Mike Sanphy collection.)

The First Baptist Church on Main Street was dedicated on October 28, 1888. A house at 65 Stroudwater Street was purchased in 1923 for a parsonage. On December 14, 1947, the church was badly damaged by fire. At that time, the damage was repaired, but the church has been renovated and enlarged several times. The bell in the tower is said to be from the old Westbrook Manufacturing Company bell tower. (Mike Sanphy collection.)

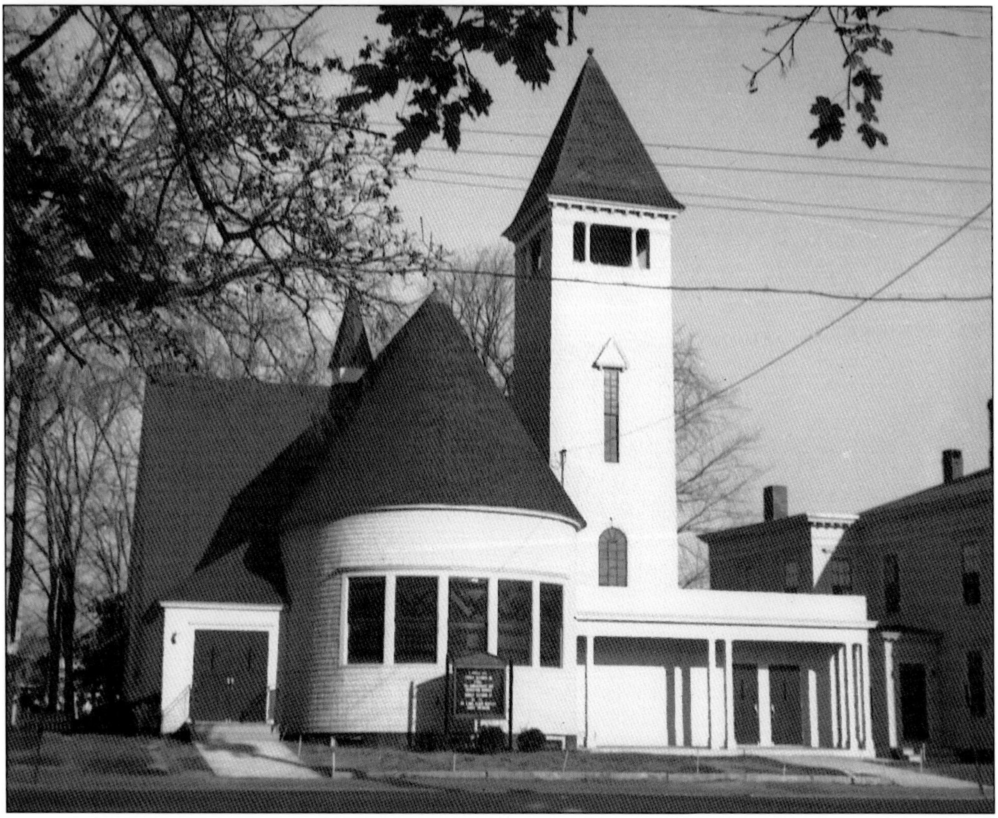

The Universalist church at 709 Main Street was built in 1887 and 1888, replacing an older church constructed in 1840 at 907 Main Street. This building was renovated several times over the years, with structural changes inside and out. In later years, the congregation dwindled, and this church was closed and sold. The church now serves as a Hindu church. (Mike Sanphy collection.)

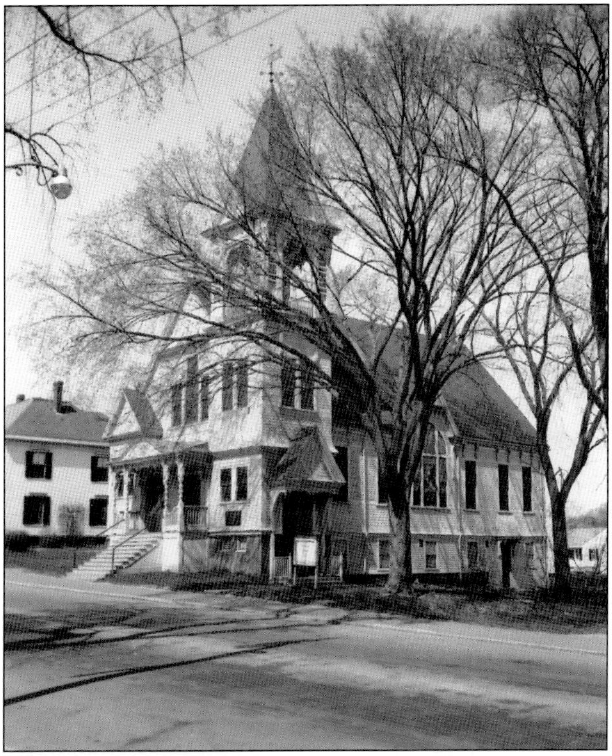

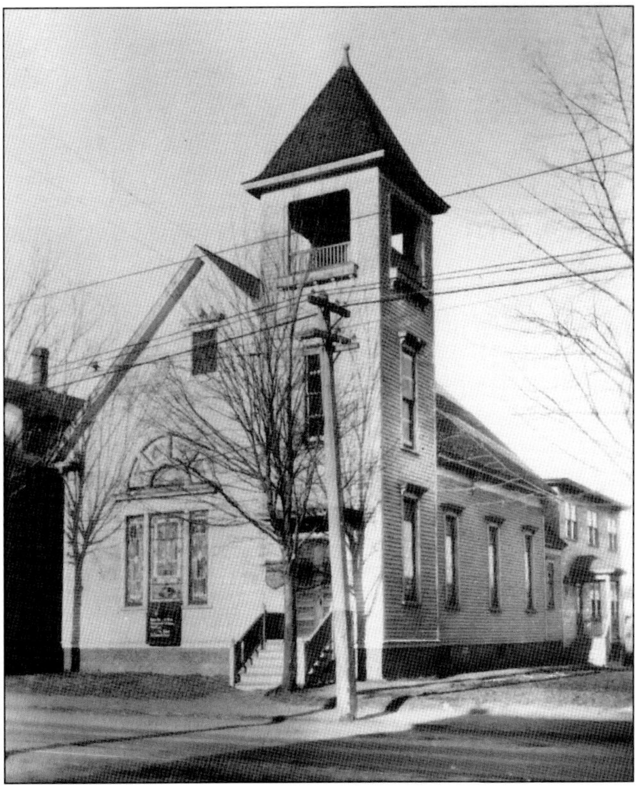

The Advent Christian Church building on Main Street was dedicated in December 1886. The original structure has undergone several renovations, including additions. (Mike Sanphy collection.)

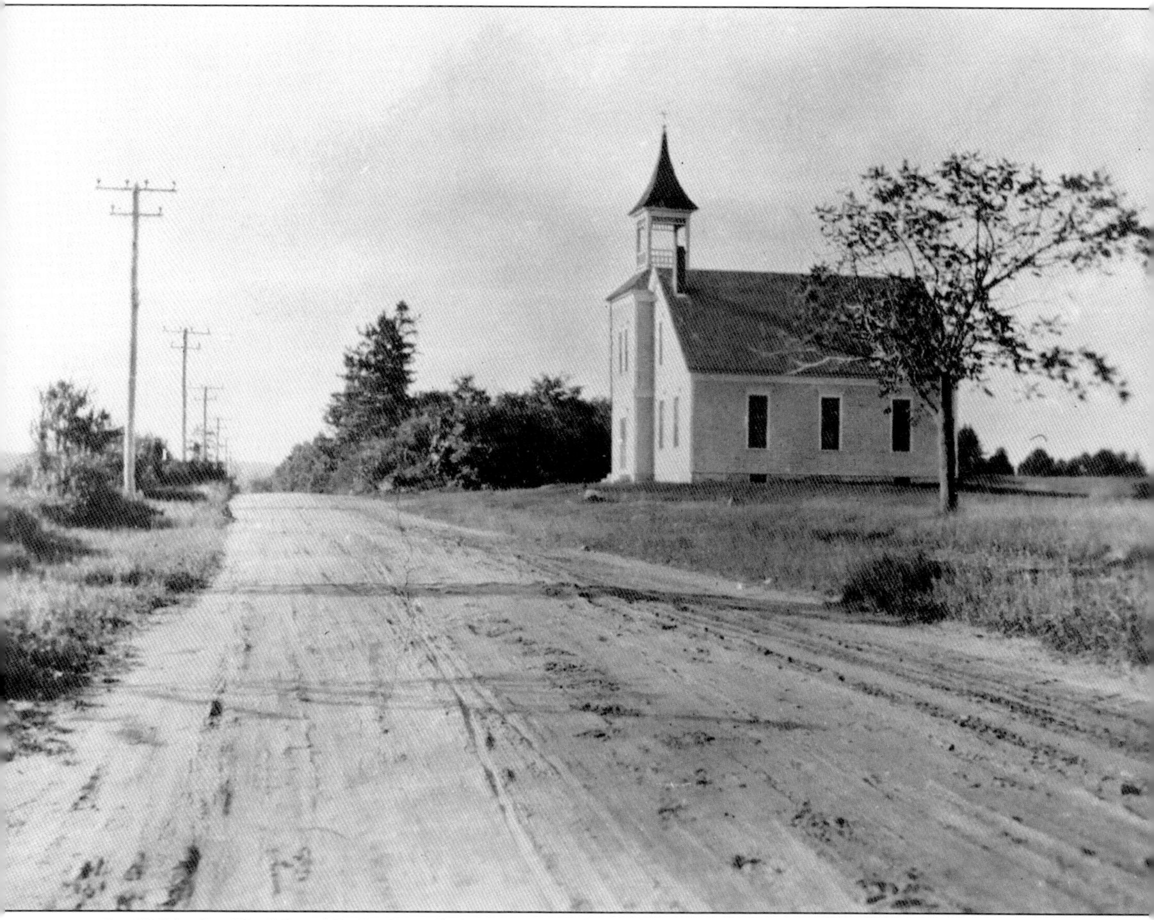

In 1904, the Highland Lake Parish Society purchased land on Bridgton Road with plans for a new church. The new church was completed in 1907. Over the years, the church has been renovated and expanded several times. A bell was added in 1938. In 1949, the basement was renovated into Sunday school classrooms; a kitchen and furnaces were also added. Highland Lake Congregational Church is at 1303 Bridgton Road. (Mike Sanphy collection.)

Five

MANUFACTURING

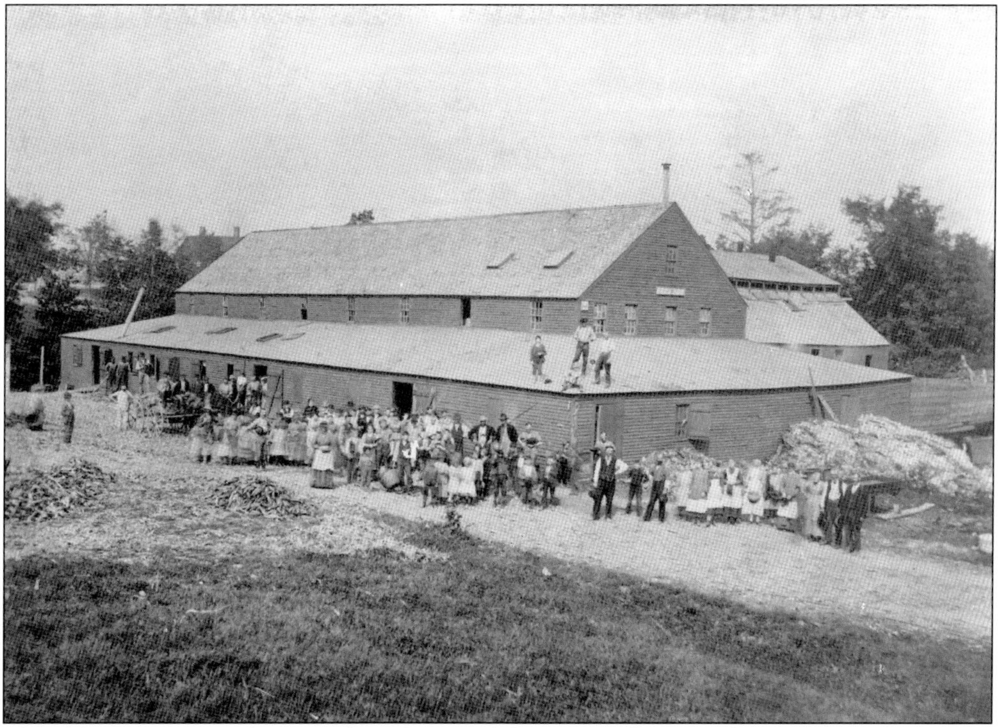

The old corn canning plant stood on the site of the present-day Cornelia Warren Pool. The first canned corn in the nation was canned here. (Mike Sanphy collection.)

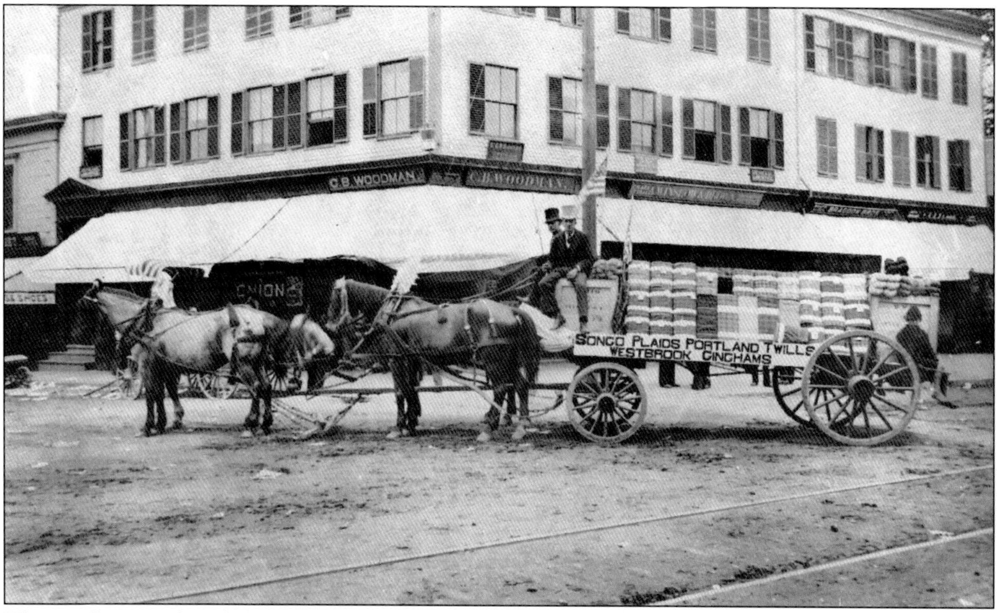

This is the Westbrook Manufacturing Company wagon turning from Main Street onto Bridge Street. The company was located on Bridge Street on the banks of the Presumpscot River. Damages caused by the flood of 1896 forced the company out of business. (Mike Sanphy collection.)

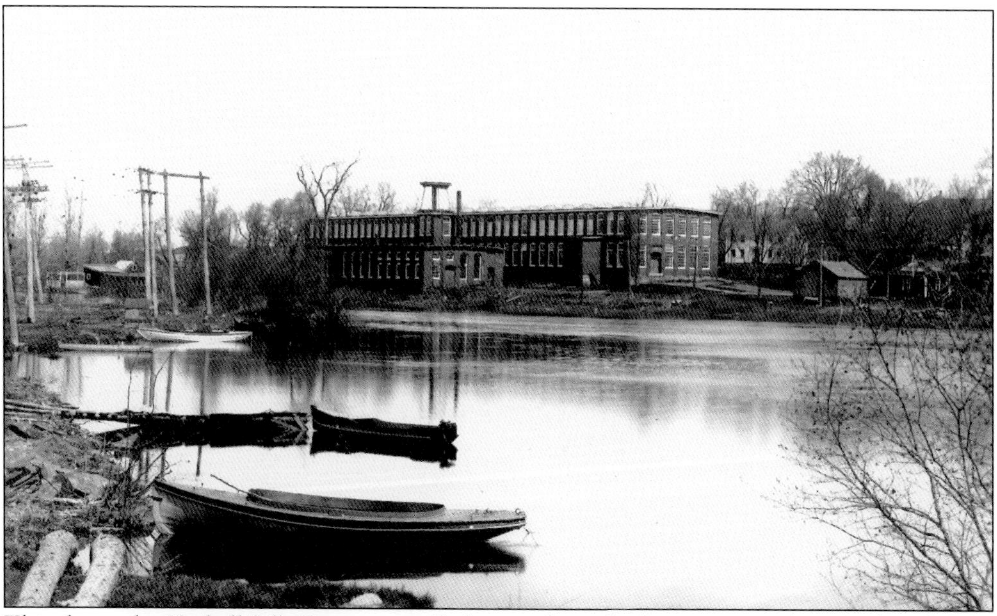

This shows the Haskell Silk Company mill plant on Lincoln Street as seen from Park Hill. The company built this plant in 1900 to replace their original mill that was located on Bridge Street alongside the river. The company went out of business in 1933. This structure later served as a plant for the Sebago Moc Company. The building was later sold and renovated into a condominium complex. (Mike Sanphy collection.)

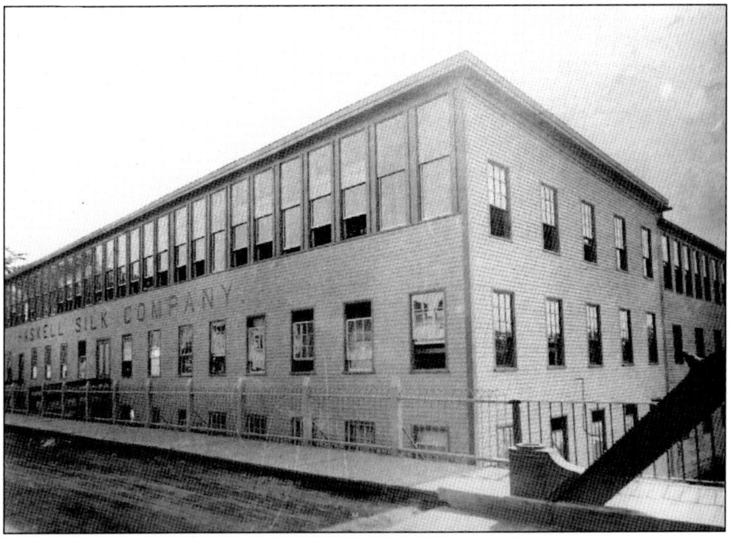

The original Haskell Silk Company mill plant was located on Bridge Street. The company was organized in 1874 and started in this building. As the company grew, the need for more space became evident, and a new mill was constructed on Lincoln Street in 1900. This building was later demolished. (Mike Sanphy collection.)

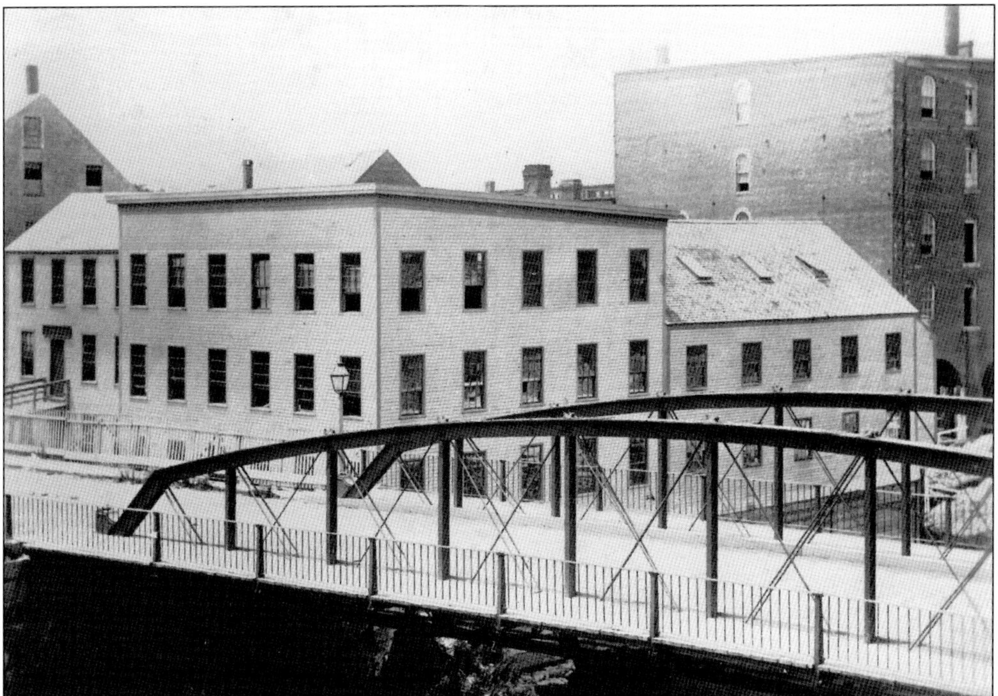

This view shows the building prior to being occupied by the Haskell Silk Company. The bridge in the foreground is the old iron bridge that crosses the Presumpscot River on Bridge Street. This bridge was replaced once in 1957 and is scheduled to be replaced again in the near future. (Mike Sanphy collection.)

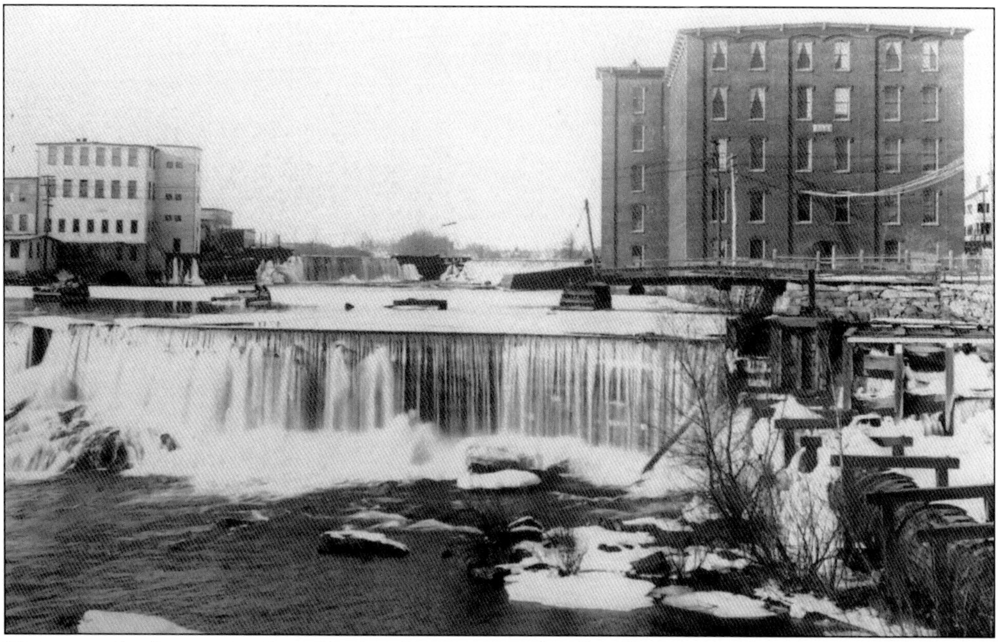

This view looks upriver from Bridge Street after the flood of 1896. The building on the left is Woodbury Dana's Island Mill. The building on the right is Mill No. 3 of the Westbrook Manufacturing Company. The S.D. Warren Company purchased this building in 1896 and sold it to Woodbury Dana in 1900. This building became Dana's primary mill, and the island building was used as a warehouse. (Mike Sanphy collection.)

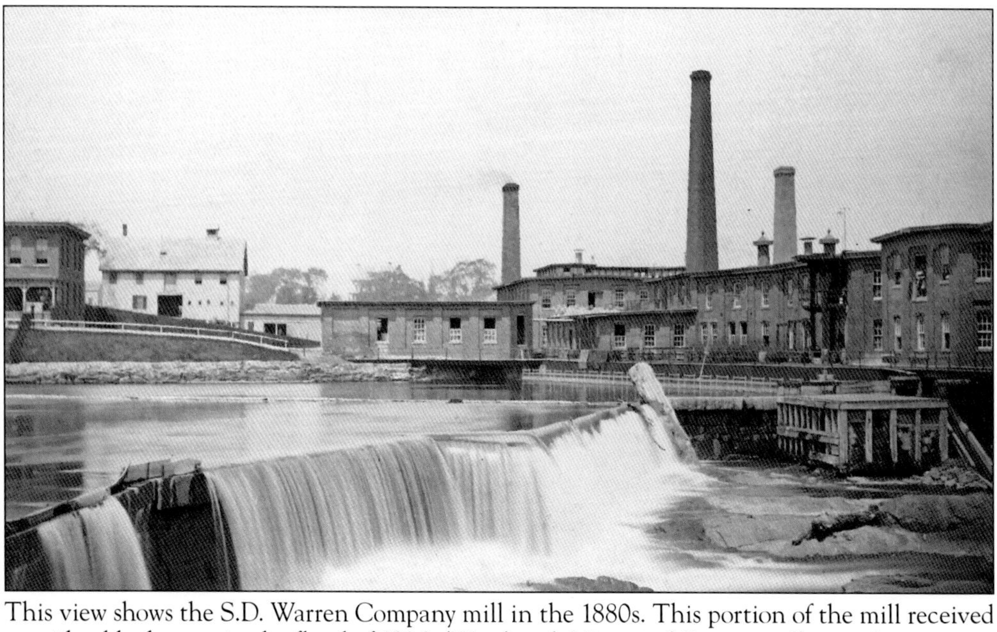

This view shows the S.D. Warren Company mill in the 1880s. This portion of the mill received considerable damage in the flood of 1896. (Westbrook Historical Society collection.)

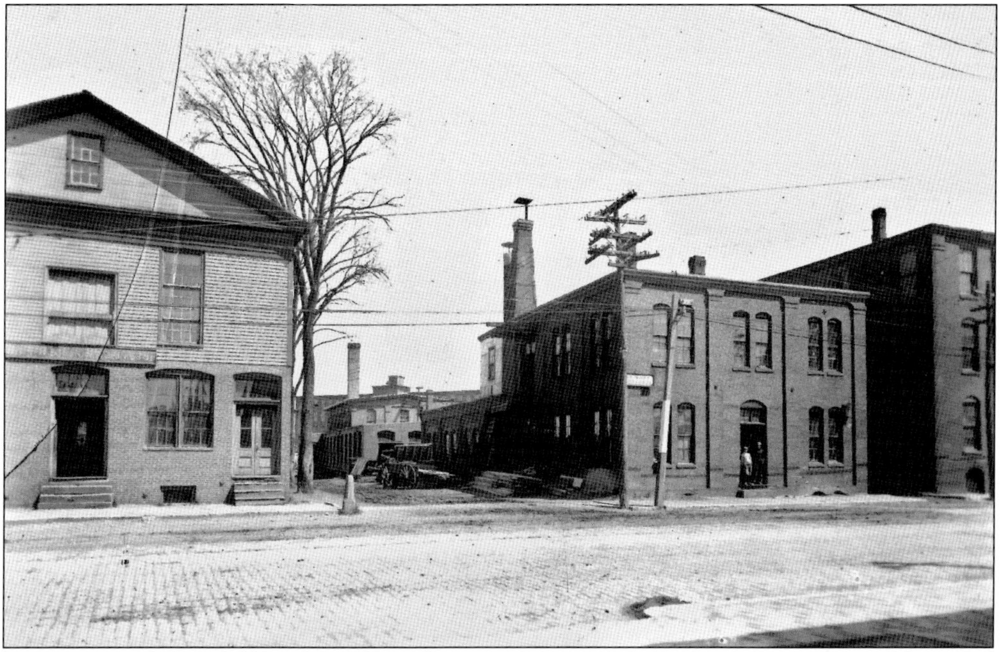

This photograph shows Dana Street from Main Street. The street was named after Woodbury Dana as it led to a bridge that crossed over the river to his island mill. The building on the left at 917 Main Street was demolished several years ago. The building on the right at 907 Main Street still stands today. The building at the end of the street was the Rufus Jordan Foundry, later Knowlton Machine. This building was destroyed by fire on December 31, 1981. (Mike Sanphy collection.)

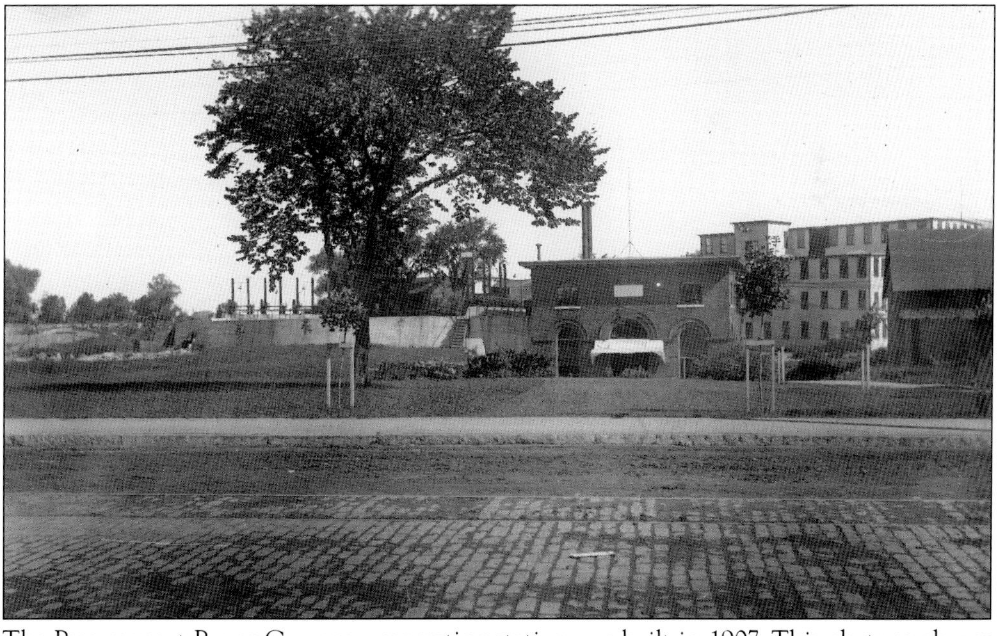

The Presumpscot Power Company generating station was built in 1907. This photograph was taken looking across Main Street near Mechanic Street. The power station is now owned and operated by SAPPI. The large building in the background was Woodbury Dana's island mill. (Mike Sanphy collection.)

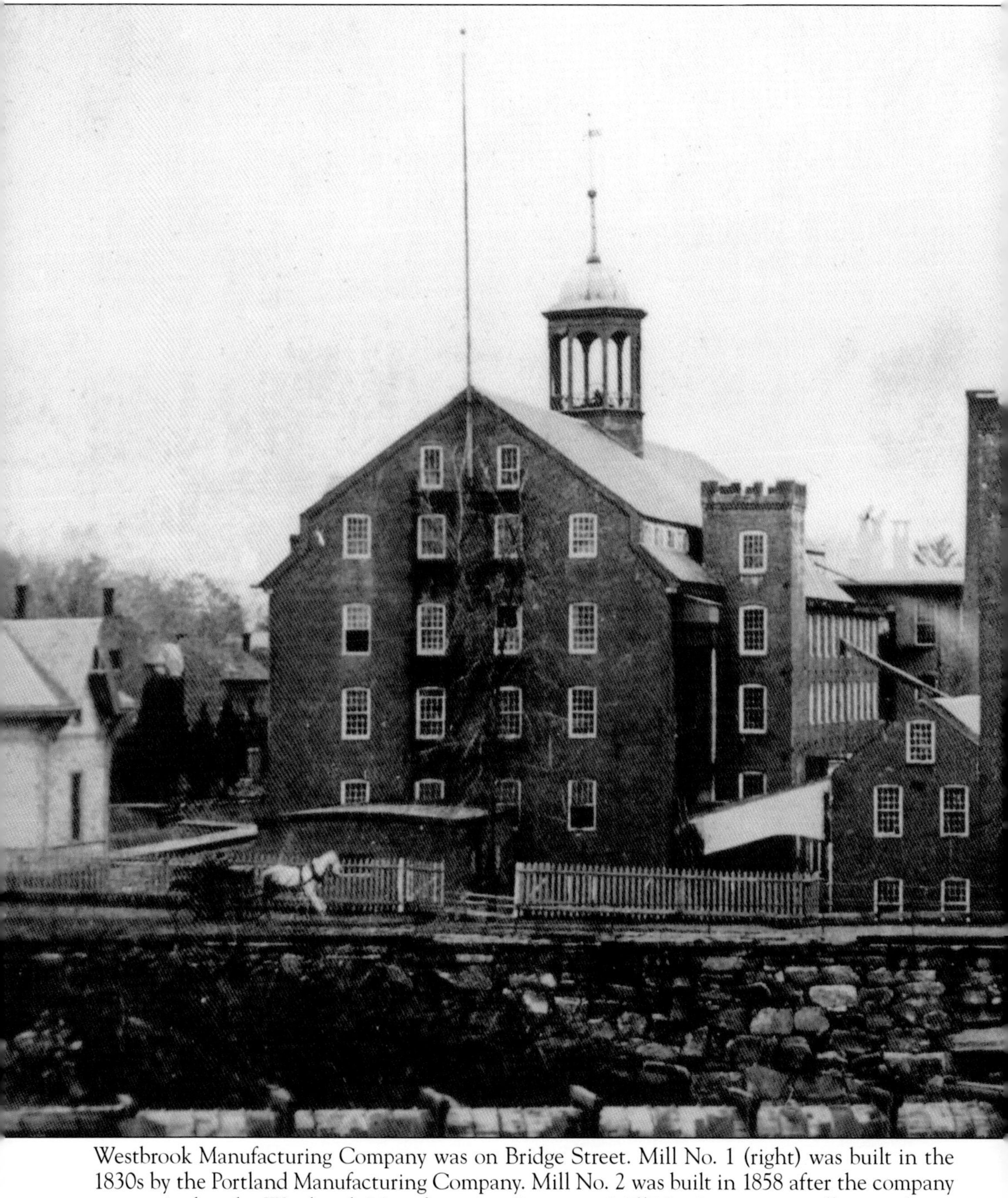

Westbrook Manufacturing Company was on Bridge Street. Mill No. 1 (right) was built in the 1830s by the Portland Manufacturing Company. Mill No. 2 was built in 1858 after the company reorganized as the Westbrook Manufacturing Company. Mill No. 1 was eventually torn down, as it became structurally unstable. The foundation is still visible on the riverbank. The company prospered greatly during the Civil War, and in 1881, a third mill was built alongside the river on

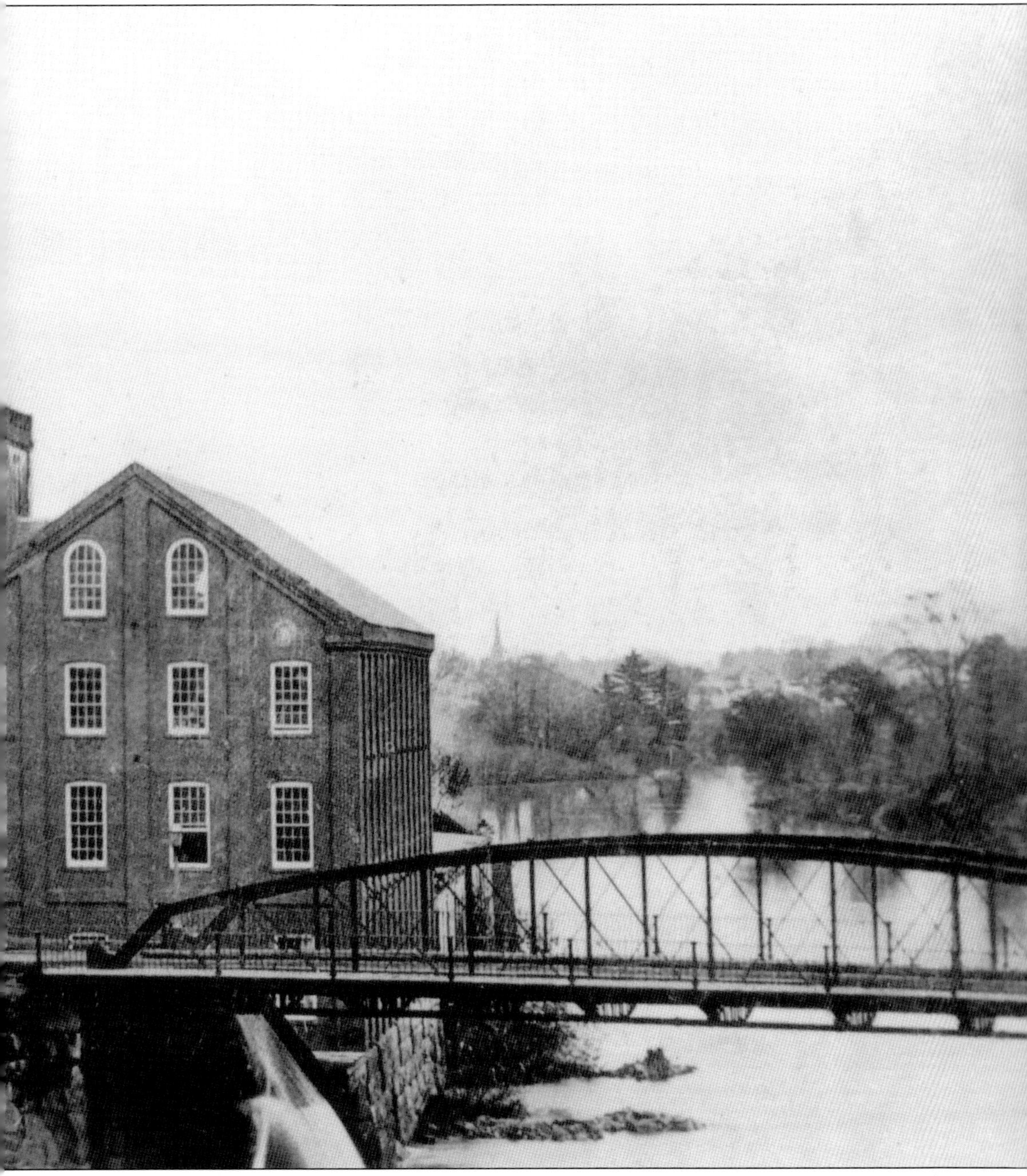

the opposite side of Bridge Street. The flood of 1896 did considerable damage to the buildings and products and forced the company out of business. The upper floors of Mill No. 2 were later taken down because of structural problems, and the bell was given to the Westbrook Baptist Church. Stultz Electric Company was the last occupant. The building was eventually sold and demolished, and today, the Riverfront Office complex occupies the site. (Mike Sanphy collection.)

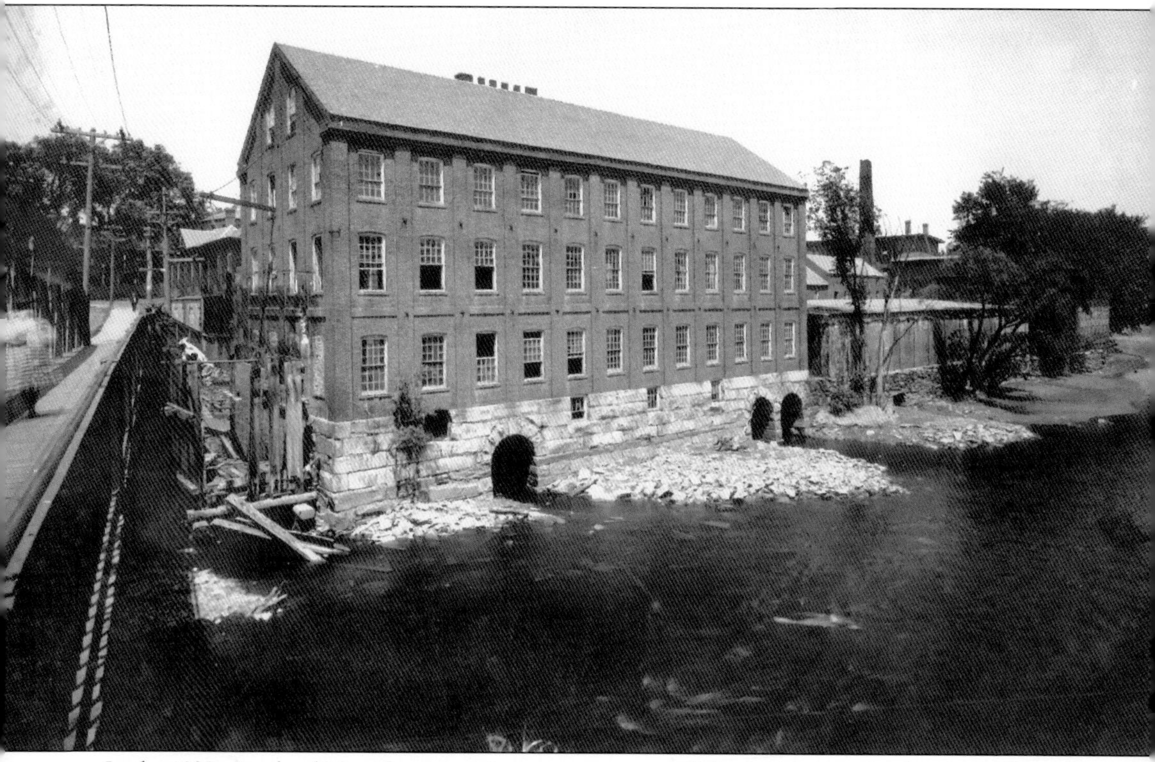

In the 1830s, Portland Manufacturing Company constructed this building on Bridge Street alongside the Presumpscot River. In 1858, the company reorganized as the Westbrook Manufacturing Company. They built Mill No. 2 next to this building and in 1881 constructed another mill on the opposite side of Bridge Street. This building was later torn down when it was found to be unsafe. The foundation is still visible on the riverbank. (Mike Sanphy collection.)

Six

SCHOOLS

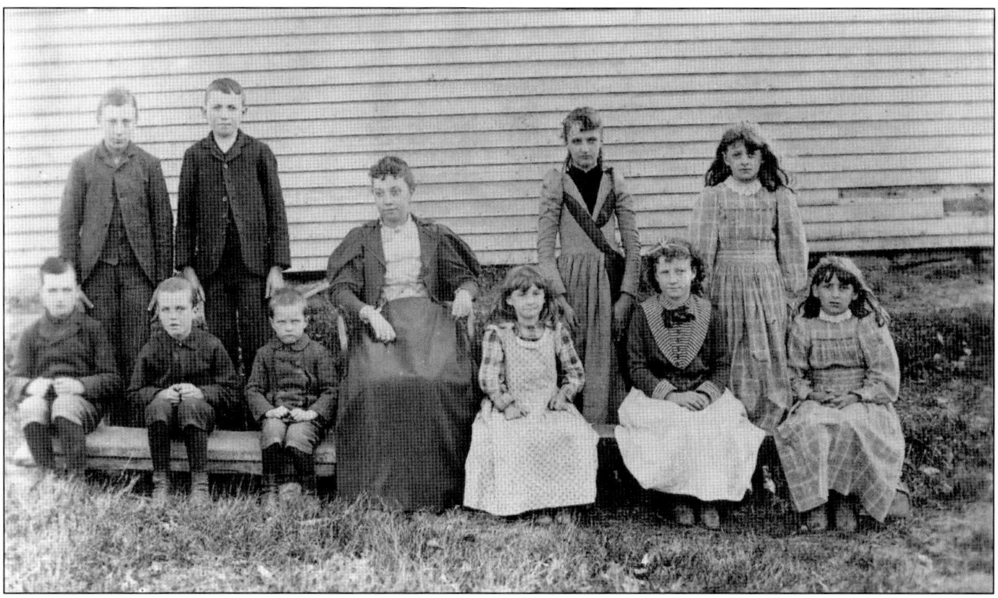

This photograph shows unidentified schoolchildren with their teacher. Upon close inspection, it appears that some of these children were siblings. It is possible these children were students at the Rocky Hill School. (Warren Library collection.)

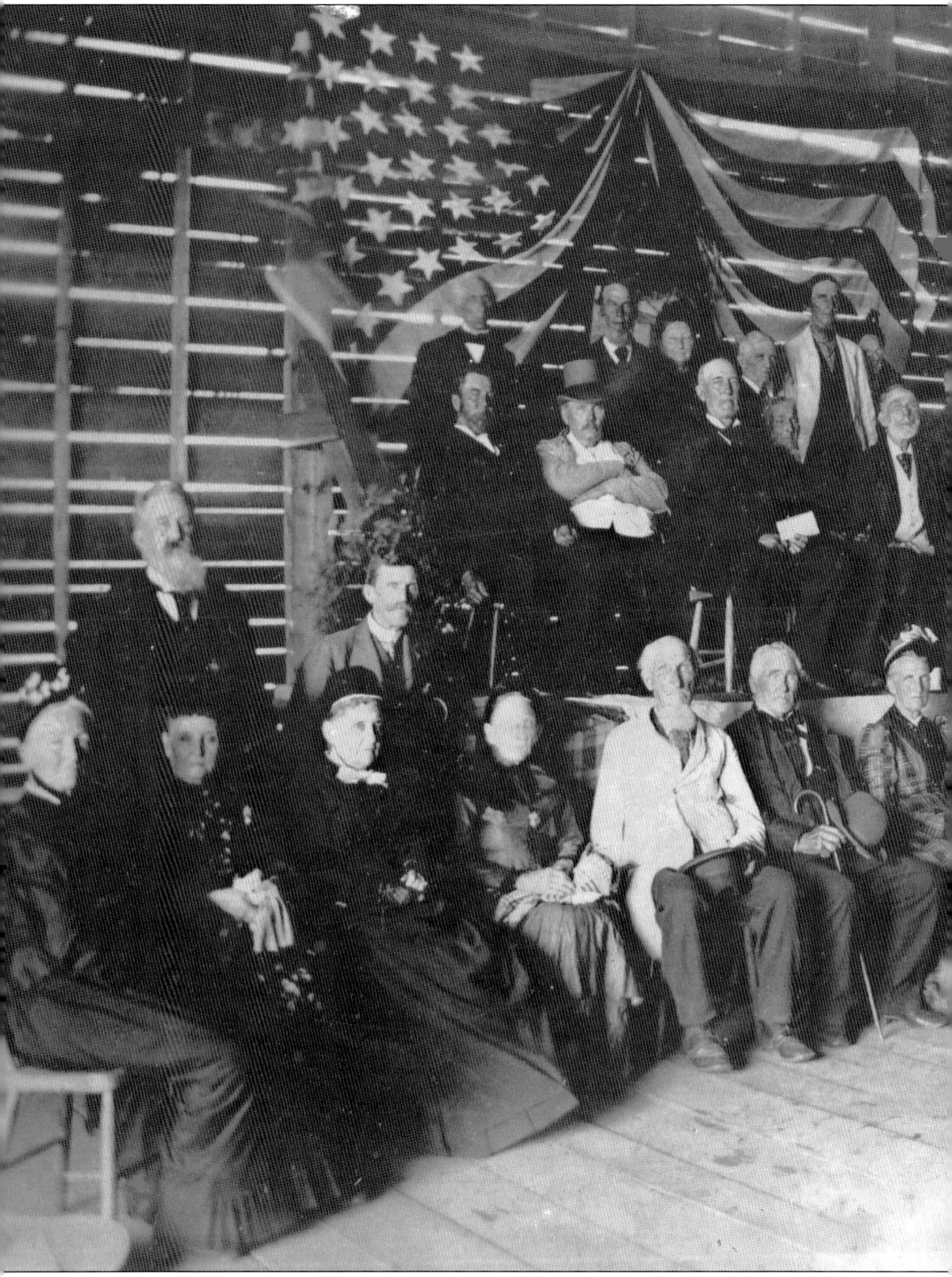

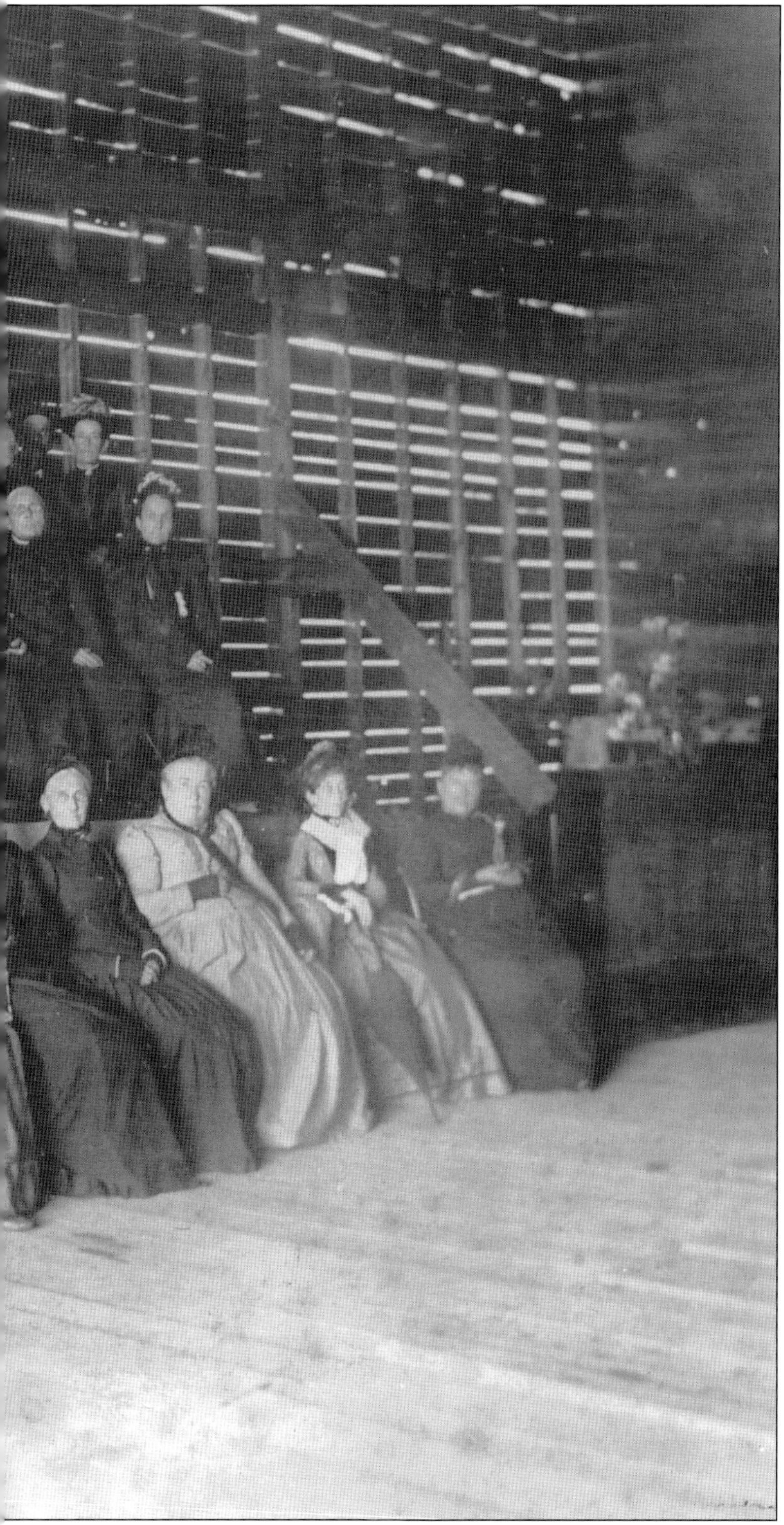

The Old North School was built in 1811 at what was known as the four corners, where Bridge and Cumberland Streets cross today. In the early 1890s, a reunion of teachers and students of the Old North School was held in the barn of Captain Chase. The barn was built on the site of the old school. (Westbrook Historical Society collection.)

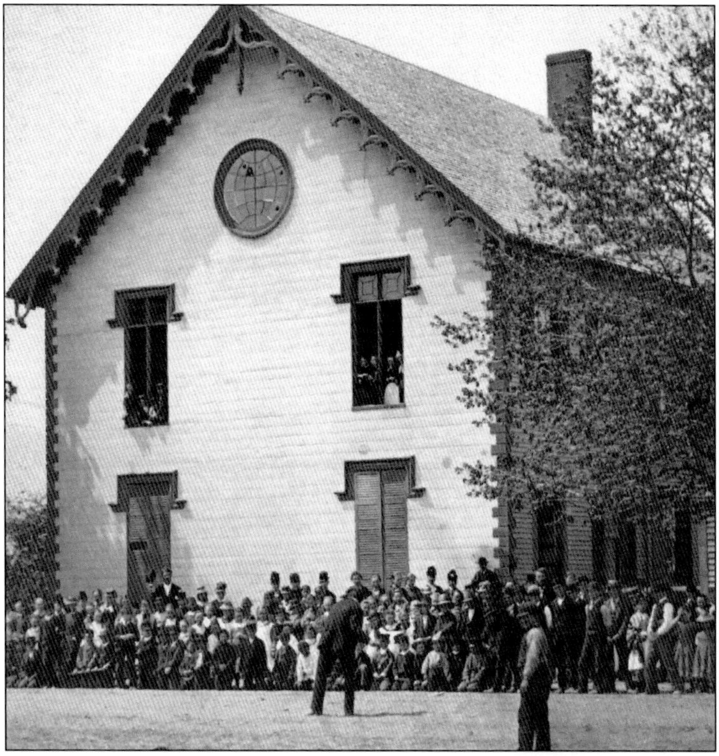

The old Westbrook High School was located on Main Street in the area of the post office. The building was moved to East Valentine Street in 1885 to make way for a new high school structure. The old building served as a high school until the new one was constructed later, serving many years as the Valentine Street School. The building is now a privately owned apartment building. (Mike Sanphy collection.)

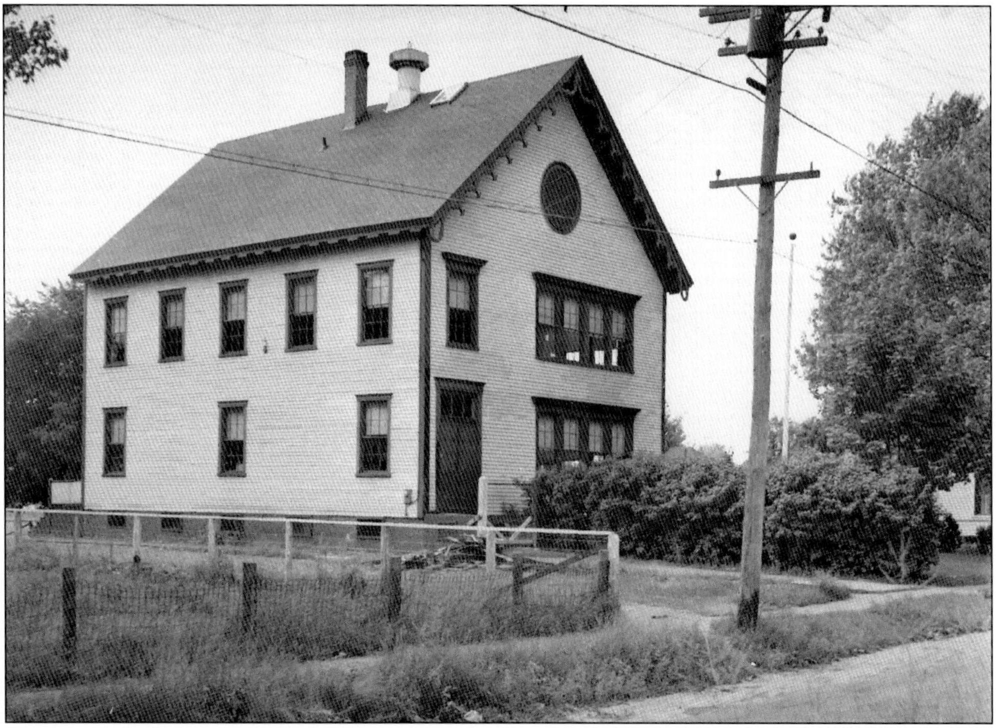

This photograph shows the old Westbrook High School building as the Valentine Street School. Today, the building consists of apartment units. (Mike Sanphy collection.)

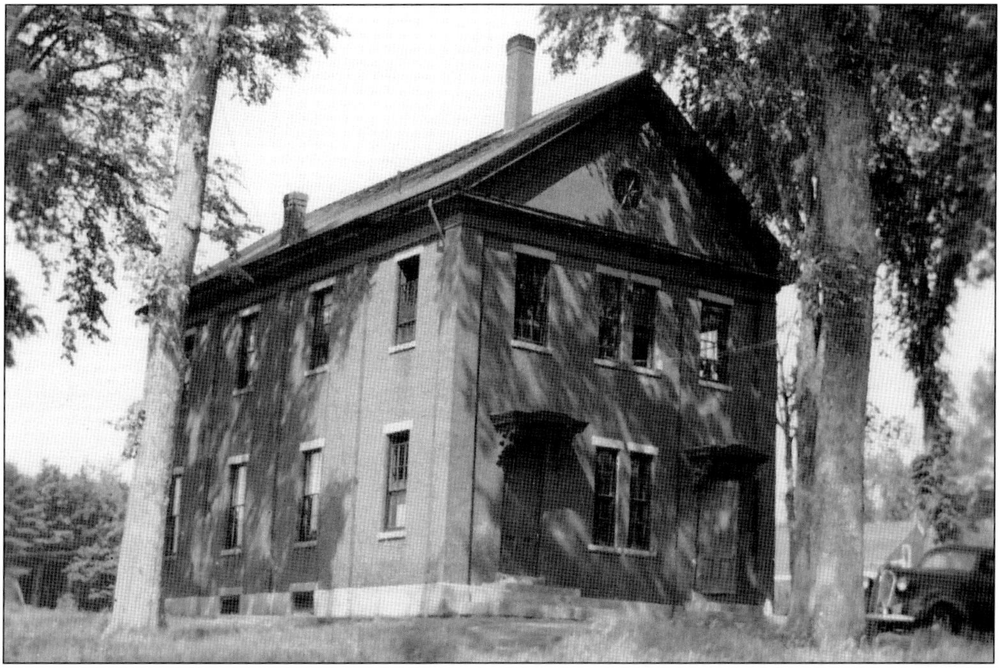

The Old Prides Corner School, built in 1869, served the Prides Corner area from 1870 to 1951 when a new school was erected on Pride Street. This building was eventually purchased by the Westbrook Trust Company and torn down to make way for a new branch office. The bank building was eventually sold, and a new structure was constructed alongside it and connected. The buildings are now real estate offices. (Mike Sanphy collection.)

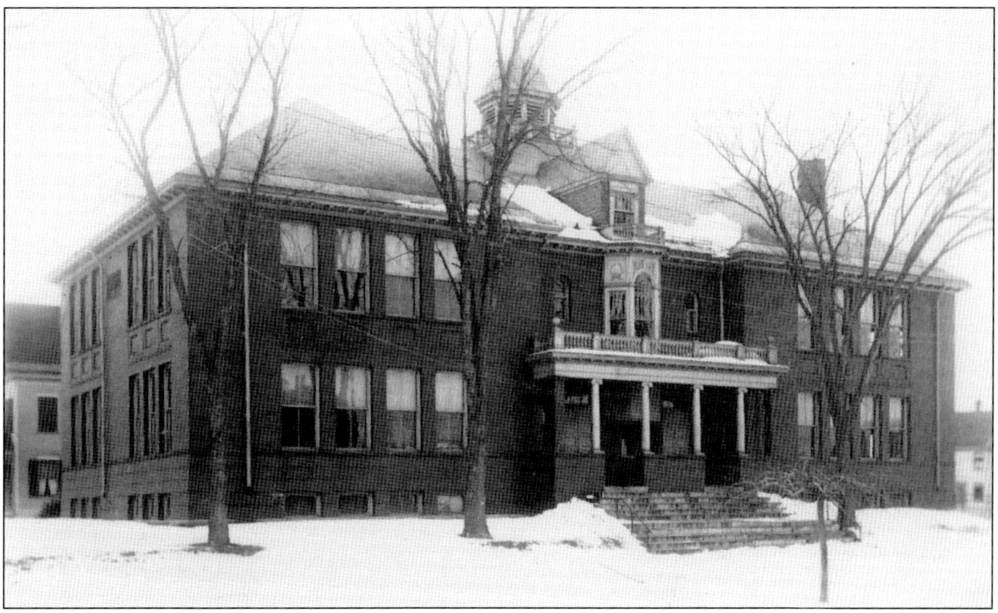

The Forest Street School was built in 1894 on Forest Street at Main Street. The school closed when the new Congin School opened on Bridge Street. The building was leased by a performing arts group and then eventually sold. The structure has been converted in condominiums. (Mike Sanphy collection.)

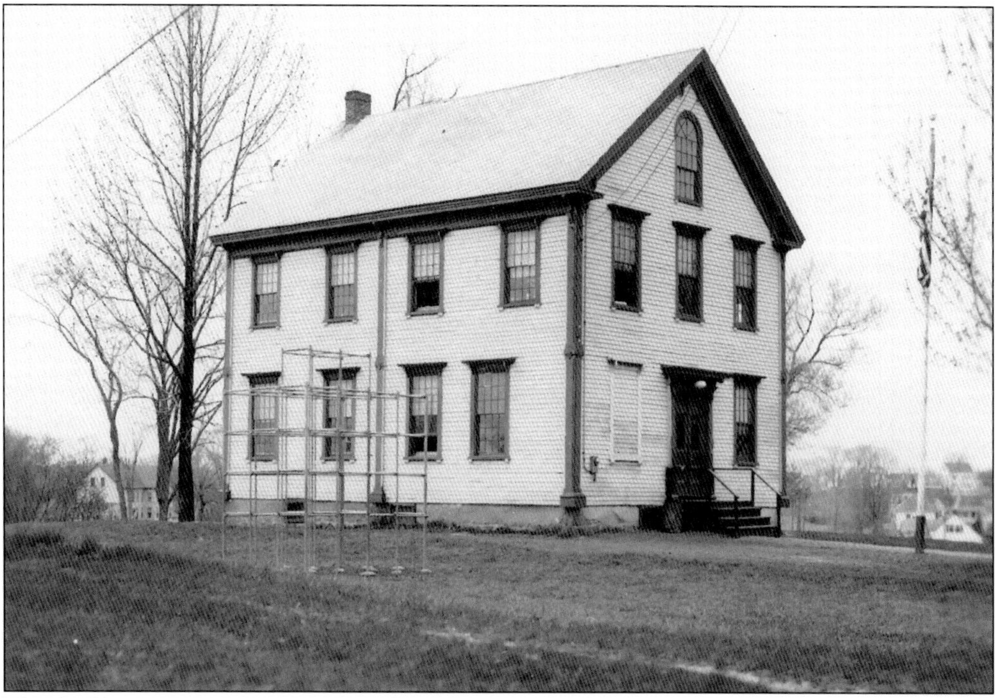

This building at 89 Saco Street served as Saco Street School for many years. It closed when the new Saccarappa School was built. Westbrook Eagles Club now occupies this building.

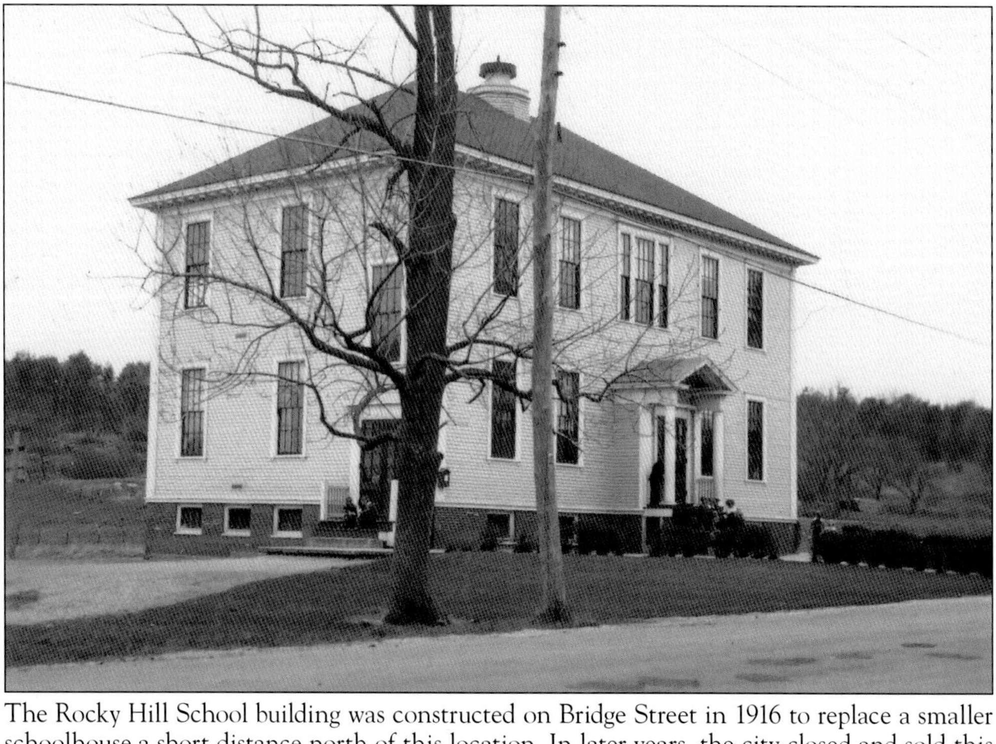

The Rocky Hill School building was constructed on Bridge Street in 1916 to replace a smaller schoolhouse a short distance north of this location. In later years, the city closed and sold this structure, which now serves as an apartment building. (Mike Sanphy collection.)

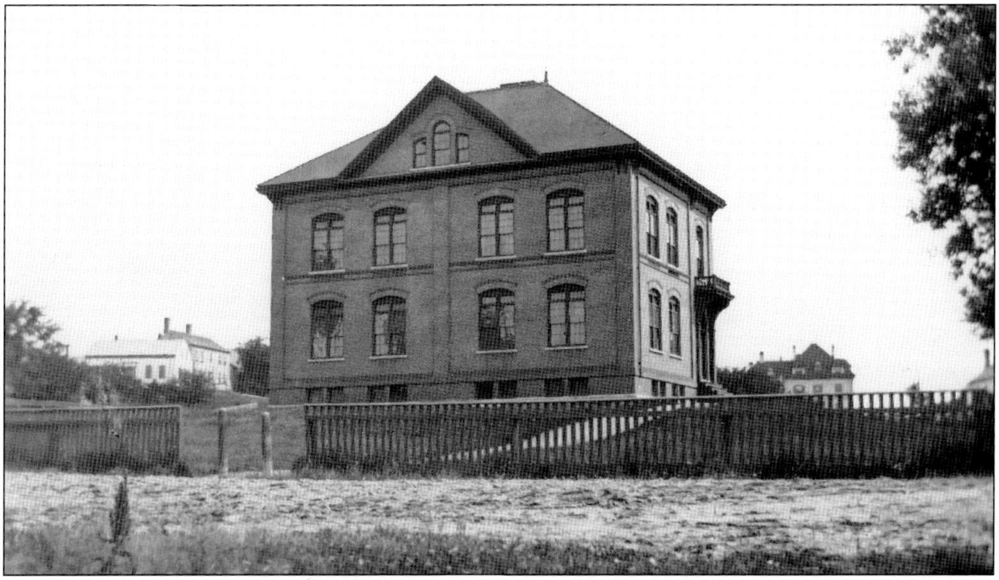

The Bridge Street School was built in 1882 as a brick four-room schoolhouse. This building was later enlarged and served as a school until the new Congin School was opened. The structure is now rental apartments. (Mike Sanphy collection.)

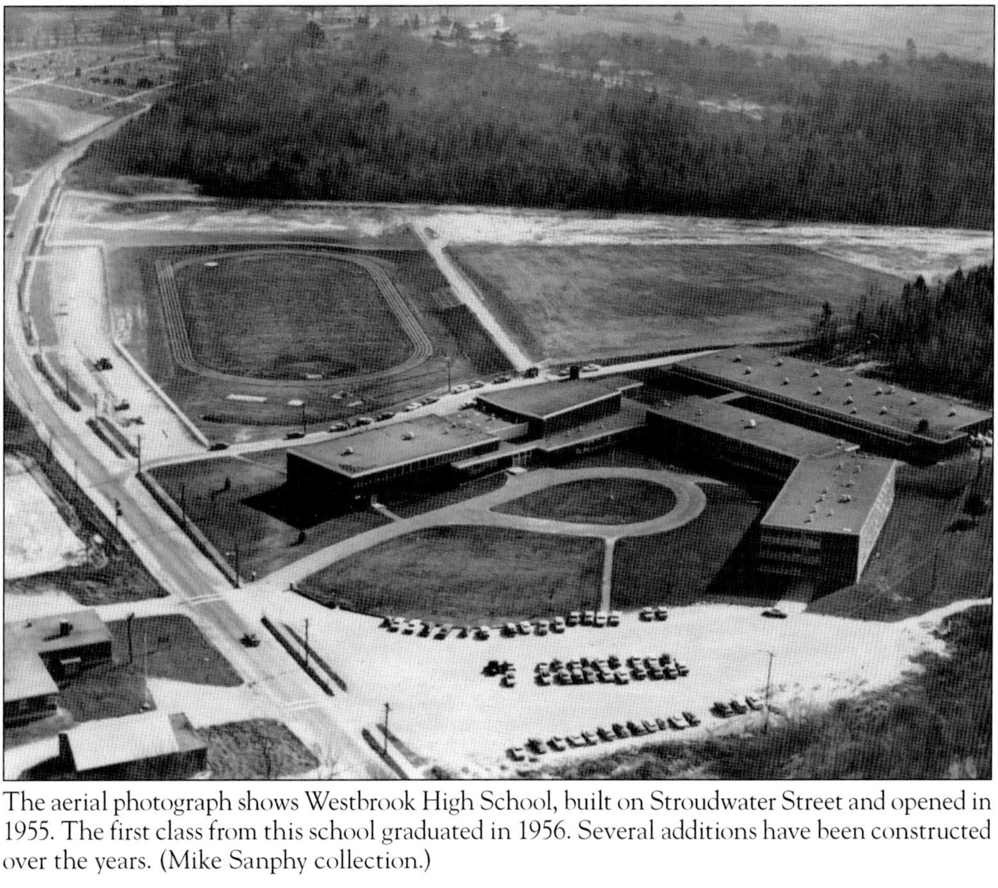

The aerial photograph shows Westbrook High School, built on Stroudwater Street and opened in 1955. The first class from this school graduated in 1956. Several additions have been constructed over the years. (Mike Sanphy collection.)

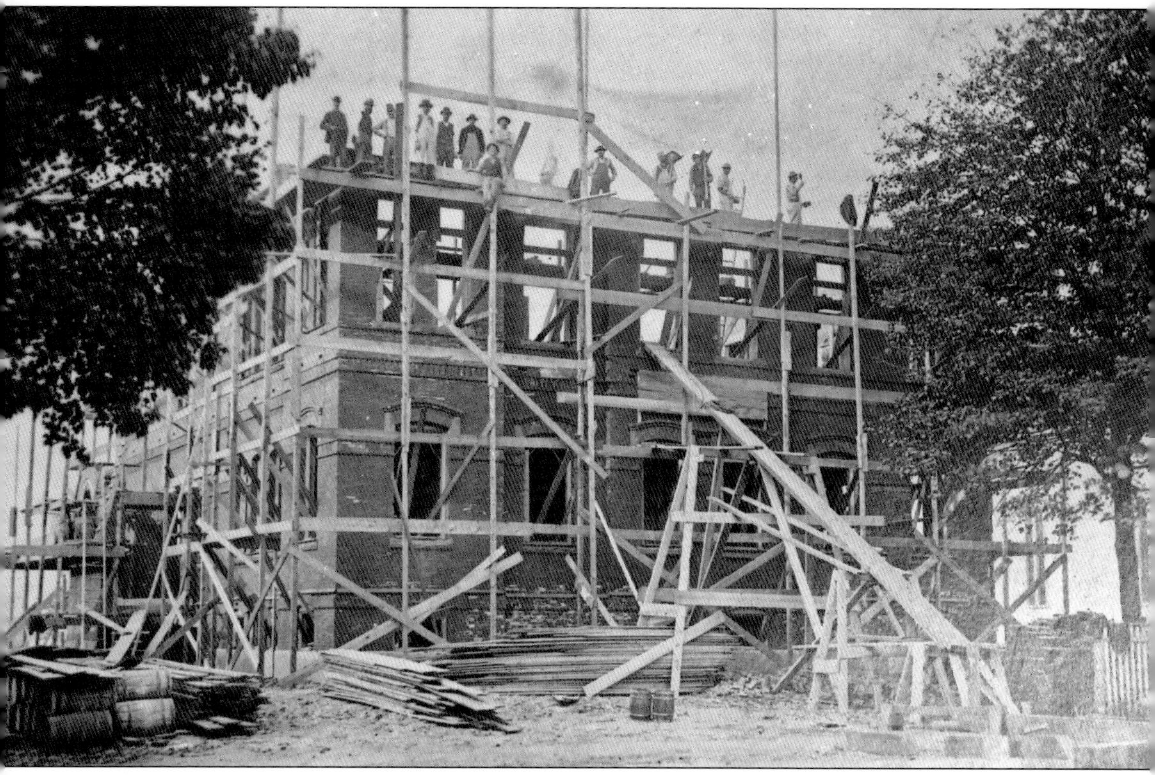

This is construction of the new high school on Main Street. This building replaced a much smaller high school that was moved from this site to East Valentine Street to serve as a temporary high school while this one was being constructed. This high school opened in 1886 and was converted to a junior high school when a newer high school opened on Stroudwater Street in 1955. The junior high school program later moved to the Wescott Junior High School. (Mike Sanphy collection.)

Seven

PEOPLE

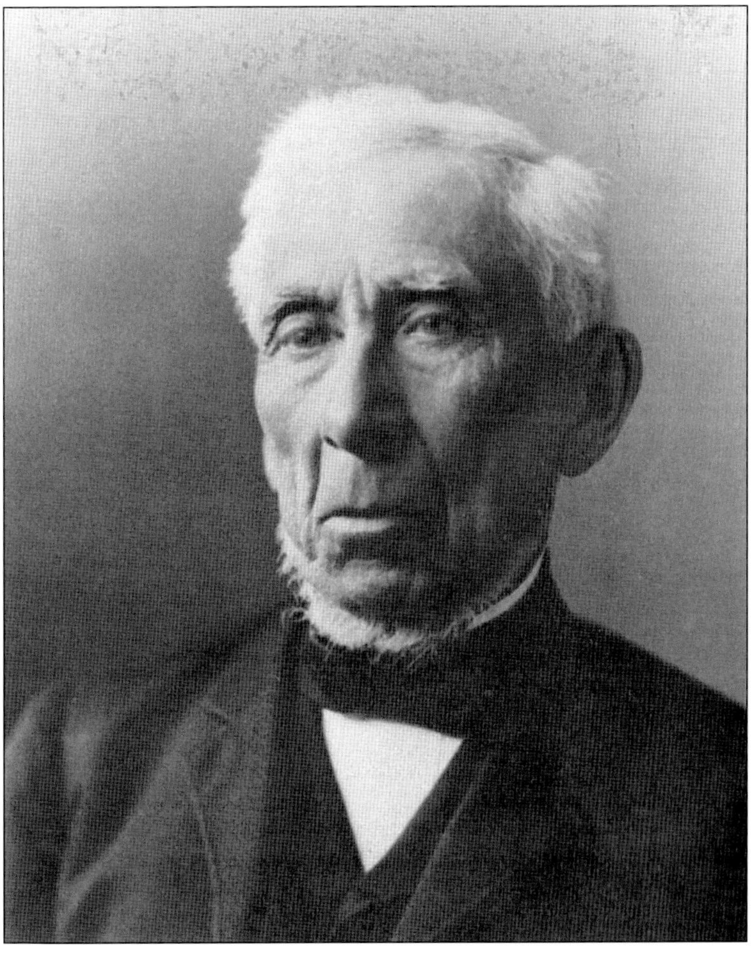

Leander Valentine was born in 1814 to William and Abigail Spring Valentine. Leander had a long active life and the distinction of being the first president of Westbrook Trust Company, serving from 1890 to 1895. Leander was also the first mayor of Westbrook in 1891. Leander was married to Margaret Coolbroth of Gorham. He passed away in 1895. (Mike Sanphy collection.)

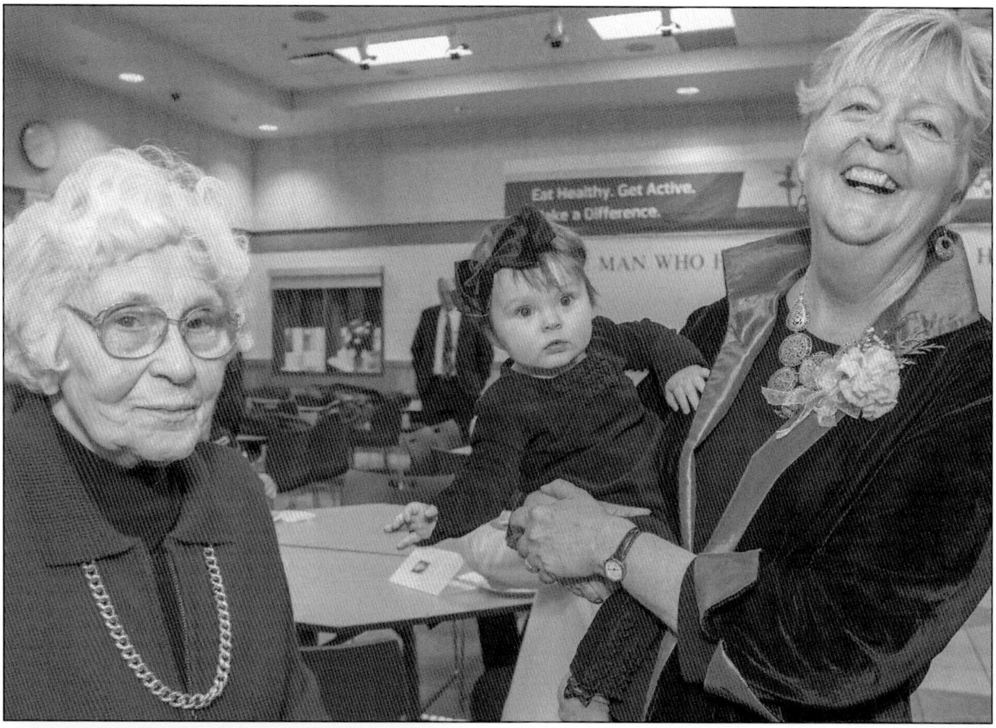

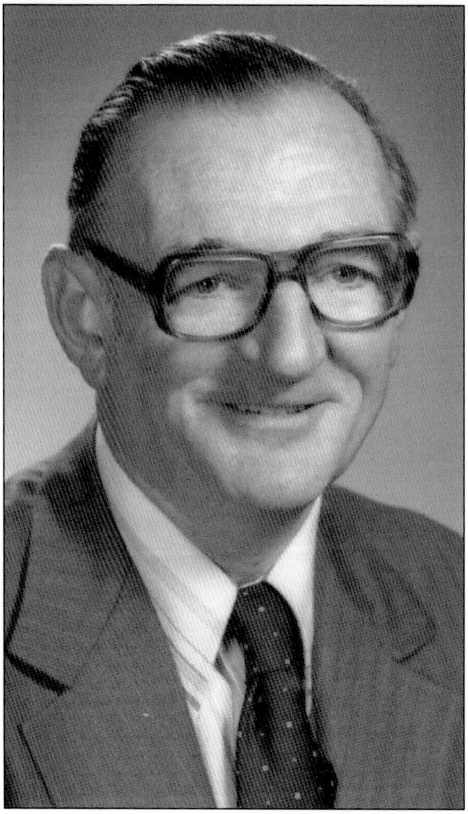

Westbrook mayor Coleen Hilton holds her granddaughter, eight-month-old Colleen Mary Conner, as she chats with Eleanor Conant Saunders after the city's inauguration ceremony at the Westbrook Performing Arts Center in January 2014. Hilton took the oath of office to begin her third term, and Saunders was the guest of honor, recognized for her many years of service to the city. Hilton is Westbrook's first woman mayor and is serving as the bicentennial mayor. Saunders is a descendant of Joseph Conant, who is recognized as the first permanent settler of Westbrook. (Photograph by Rich Obrey; courtesy of American Journal.)

William Clarke was born in Westbrook on September 30, 1919. His parents, Lee and Millie Clarke, bought a house at 333 Spring Street the next year. William lived there all his life. He started Blue Spruce farm and delivered milk door to door until 1960. He then started selling milk to Oakhurst Dairy. Bill was active in politics, serving on the Westbrook Council from 1943 to 1949 and as city clerk for 38 years, from 1956 to 1994. He was married to Jacqueline Rocheleau, and they had four children. (Westbrook Historical Society collection.)

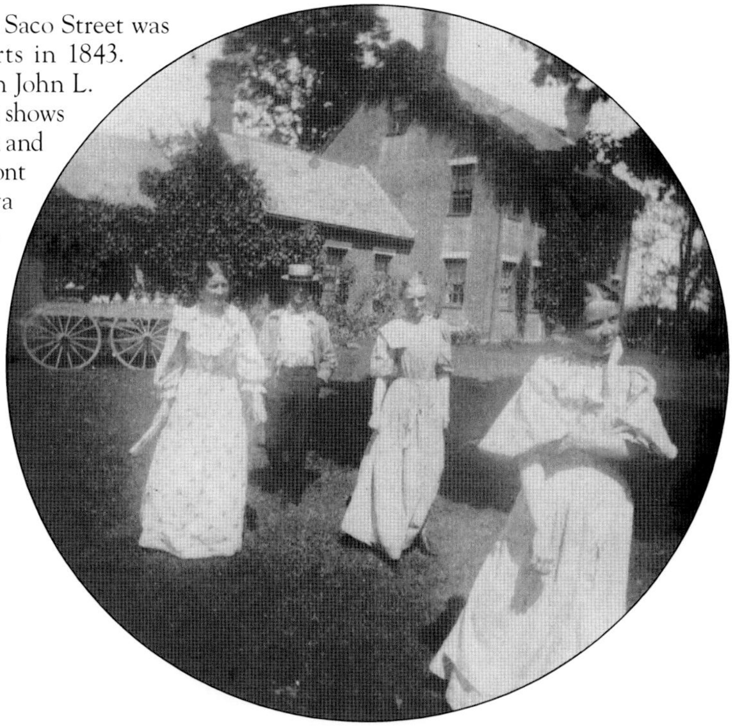

This brick farmhouse on Saco Street was built by William Roberts in 1843. He left it to his grandson John L. Roberts. This photograph shows the adult children of John and Martha Roberts. In the front is Westbrook teacher Eva Roberts (born in 1868), and Marietta Roberts (1872) holds a newspaper. Florence Roberts (1860) is on right, and in the back is Perley Chenery Roberts (1878). None of the sisters married and spent their lives in this house.

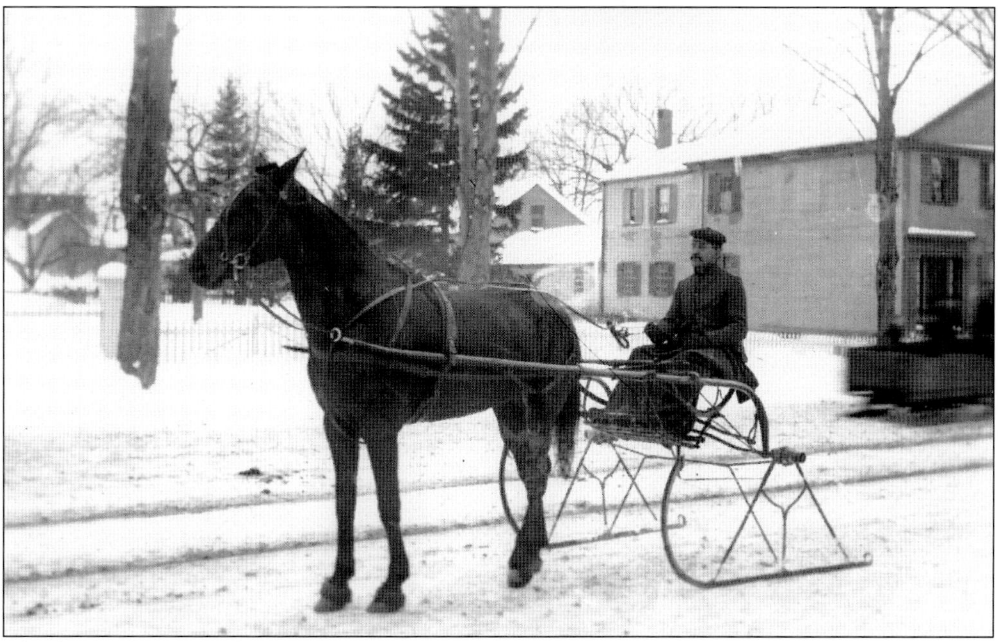

This horse-drawn sleigh is seen on Main Street around 1892. The house in the background still stands on Main Street today, at the corner with Church Street. Dr. George Woodman lived there when this photograph was taken. The vacant lot is now occupied by a brick structure once known as the telephone building. Westbrook's telephone operators were located on the second floor. Oxford Bank and the *American Journal* newspaper offices were also once located here. (Warren Library collection.)

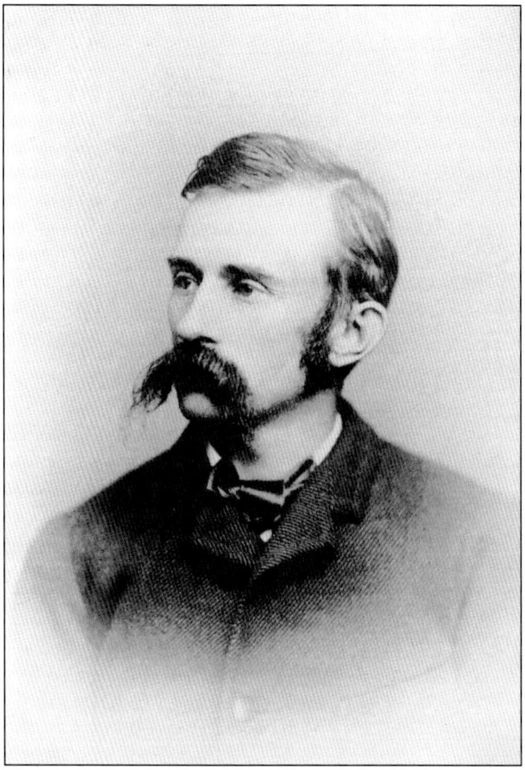

In 1874, the Haskell Silk Company was established by James Haskell, who resigned as agent of the Westbrook Manufacturing Company. His son Frank was appointed treasurer. Frank also took over his father's position as agent for the Westbrook Manufacturing Company, holding both jobs until 1889 when he was forced to resign from Haskell Silk Company to devote his time to Westbrook Manufacturing Company. He died suddenly in 1896. (Mike Sanphy collection.)

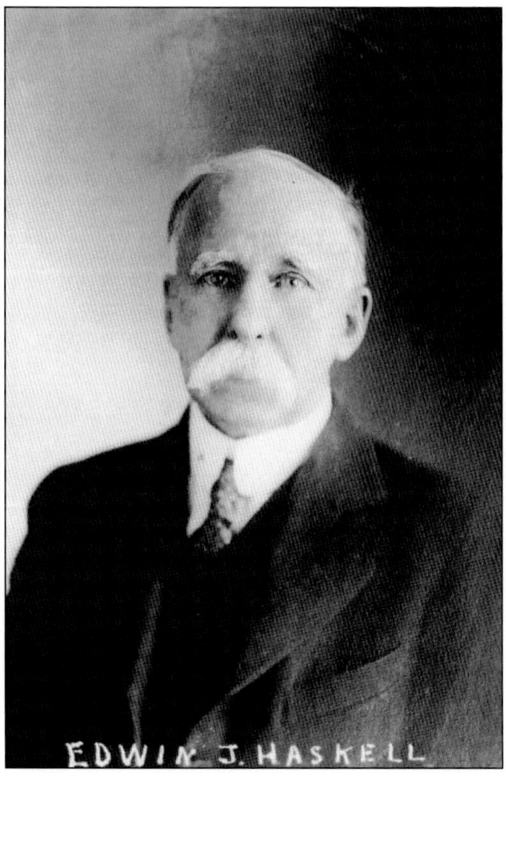

Edwin J. Haskell came to Westbrook from Rockport, Massachusetts, with his mother; his father, James Haskell; brother Frank; and three sisters in 1858 when his father became agent of the Westbrook Manufacturing Company. In 1874, James established the Haskell Silk Company, and Edwin was appointed general manager. Edwin also served for many years on the Westbrook School Committee and was a trustee of the University of Maine. (Mike Sanphy collection.)

John E. Warren, nephew of Samuel Dennis Warren, was born in Grafton, Massachusetts. Shortly after his birth, his family resettled along the frontier in Wisconsin. Warren had originally intended to pursue a college education, but he left after just one year to enlist in the military, joining the Union army in the Civil War. While Warren did see combat, a considerable portion of his service was spent as a prisoner in the Andersonville prison of the South. After the war, Warren came to Maine, where he worked his way up through the Warren Paper Company to later become one of the plant's most admired and beloved mill agents. (Mike Sanphy collection.)

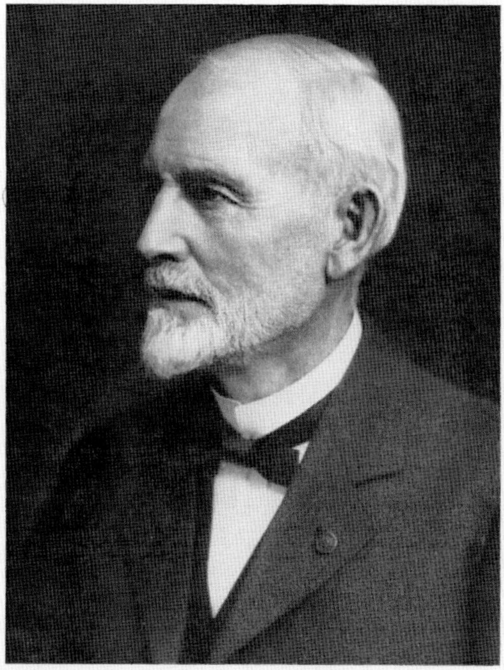

JOHN E. WARREN

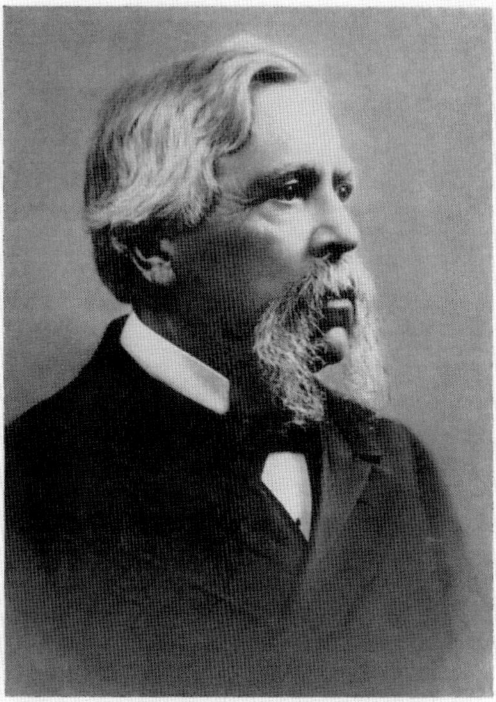

SAMUEL DENNIS WARREN

Samuel Dennis Warren grew up in a religious family that placed a high value on knowledge, service, and education. Although he lost his father when he was just a youth, his mother ensured that he completed his education. After some time employed with a Boston paper supplier, he decided to purchase a small Westbrook paper mill in 1854. Eventually, Warren became the sole proprietor of the business. Warren Standard Paper would go on to become one of the most successful paper manufacturing companies in the nation. (Mike Sanphy collection.)

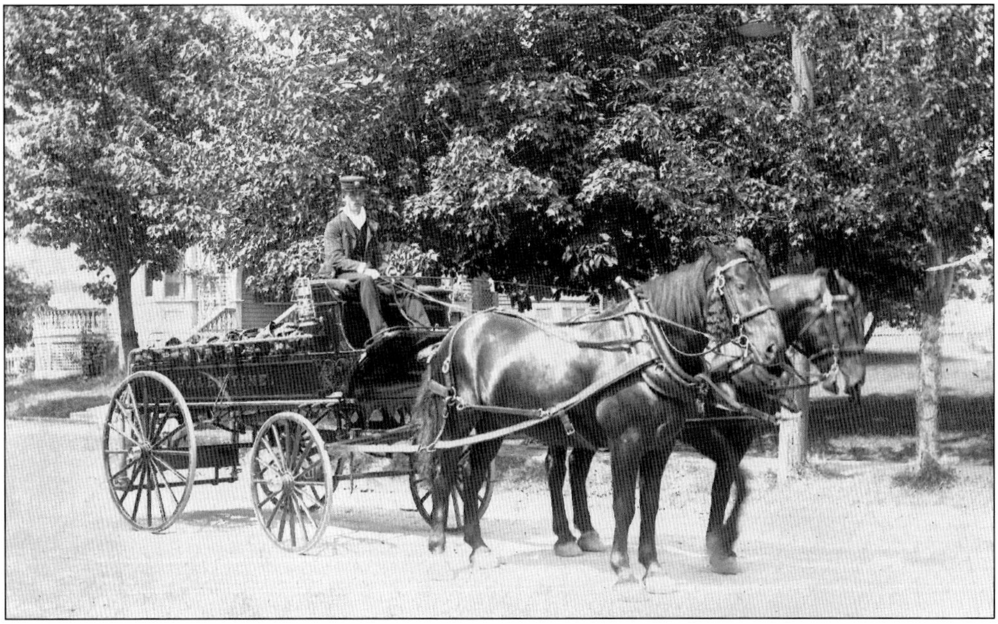

Pictured here is the Westbrook Fire Department Valentine Hose 2 Wagon. This wagon was located at the Mechanic Street Fire Station. Valentine Hose Company was named after Leander Valentine, the first mayor of Westbrook. (Mike Sanphy collection.)

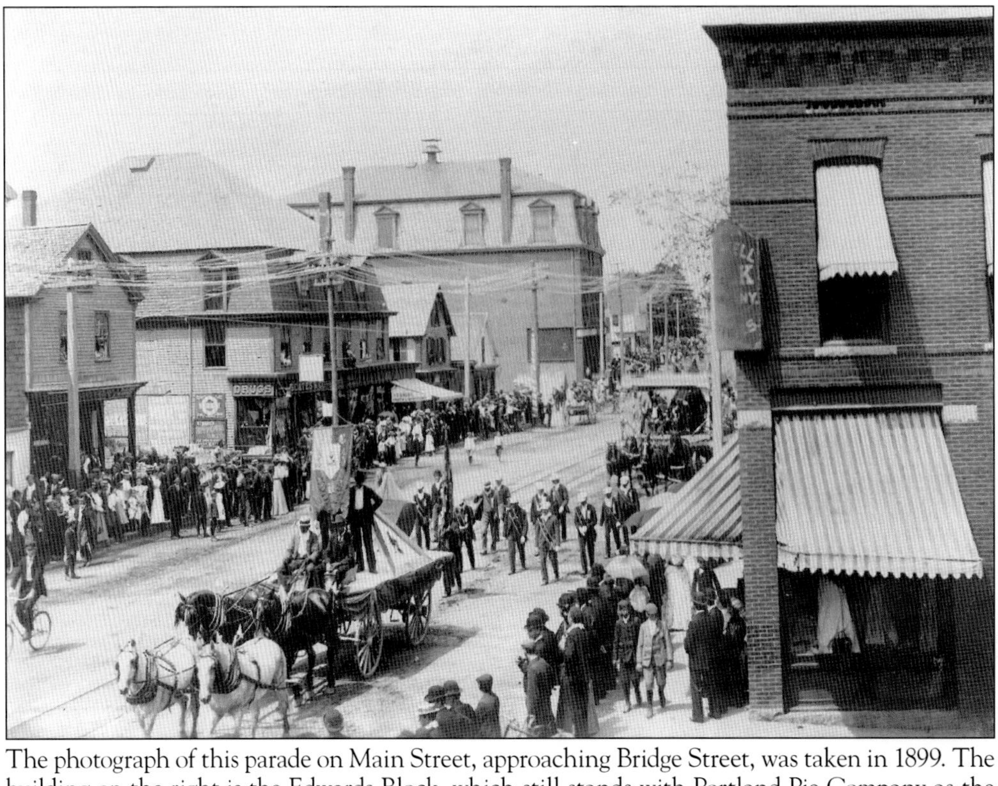

The photograph of this parade on Main Street, approaching Bridge Street, was taken in 1899. The building on the right is the Edwards Block, which still stands with Portland Pie Company as the primary tenant. All the other structures in the photograph are gone. (Mike Sanphy collection.)

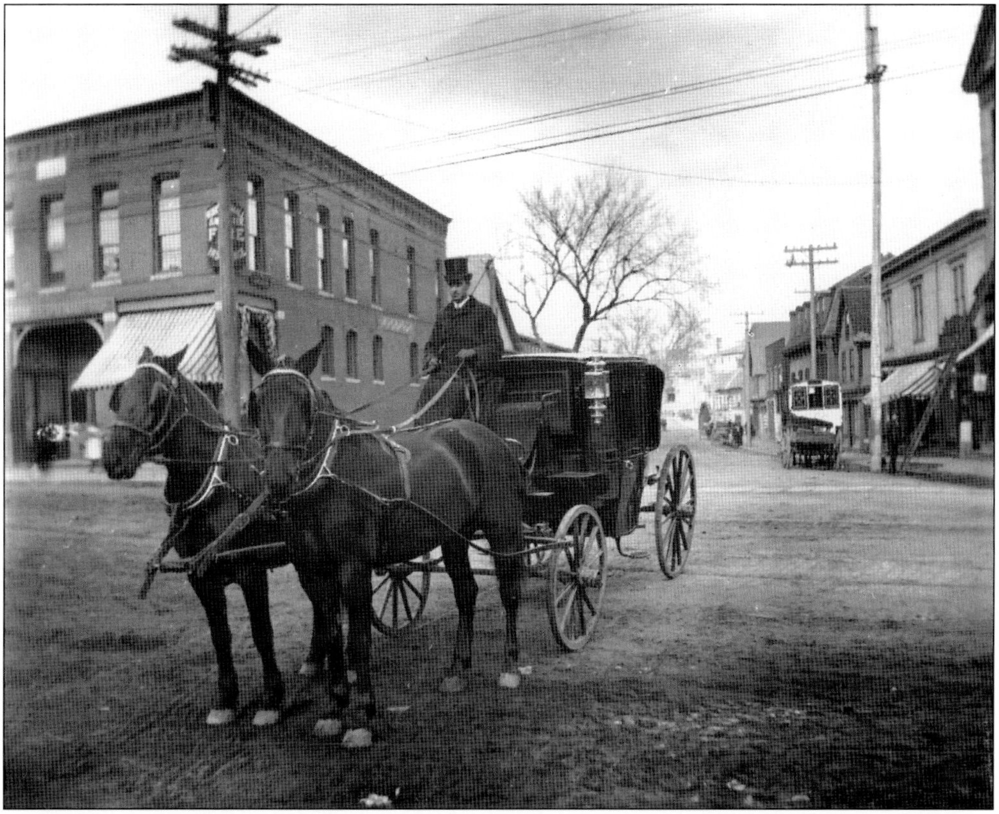

The hack on Main Street at Vallee Square is heading into Arthur Robert's Stable, located behind 866 Main Street. The entrance road to the stable later became Carpenter Street, and the old stable building was later occupied by the Westbrook Star Laundry. The Westbrook Police Station later occupied a building on Carpenter Street, across from the laundry. Urban renewal demolished both buildings, and Carpenter Street no longer exists today. (Mike Sanphy collection.)

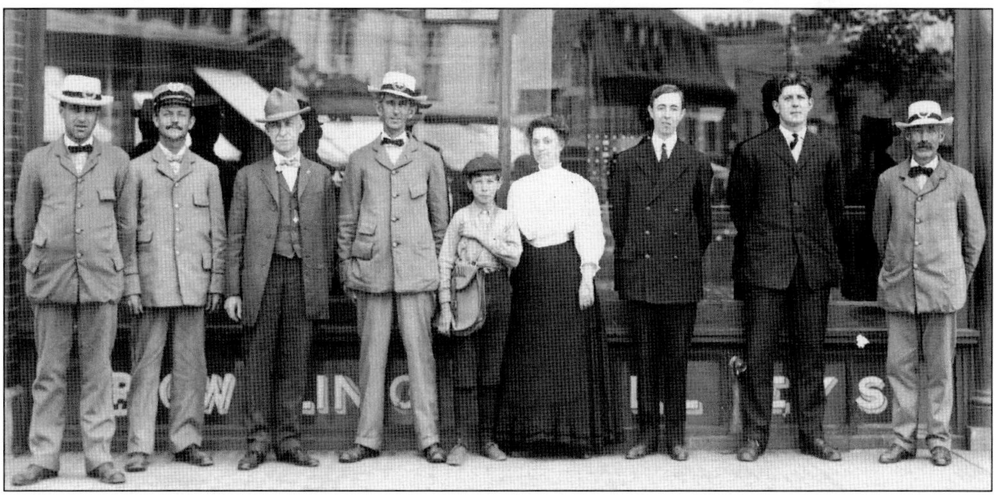

This photograph of the post office crew was taken on Main Street in front of the Scates Building where the downtown branch of the post office was located from 1903 to 1935 when the Brackett Street Post Office opened. (Mike Sanphy collection.)

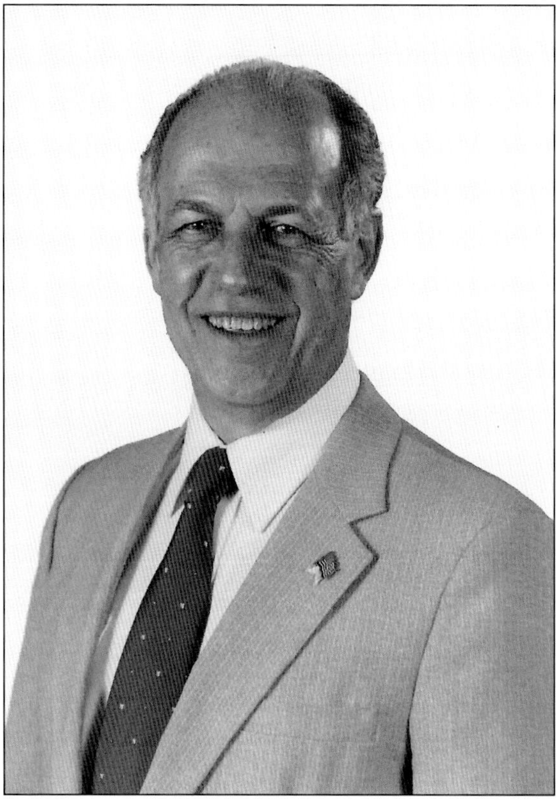

Al Hawkes was born on Christmas Day in Providence, Rhode Island, to Maine parents who moved back to the old farm homestead in Westbrook, Maine, when Al was 10 years old. He has been in Westbrook ever since, working his country music magic. He was inducted into the Maine Country Music Hall of Fame in 1980. He has also received numerous instrumentalist and recording awards for his bluegrass and country music. (*American Journal.*)

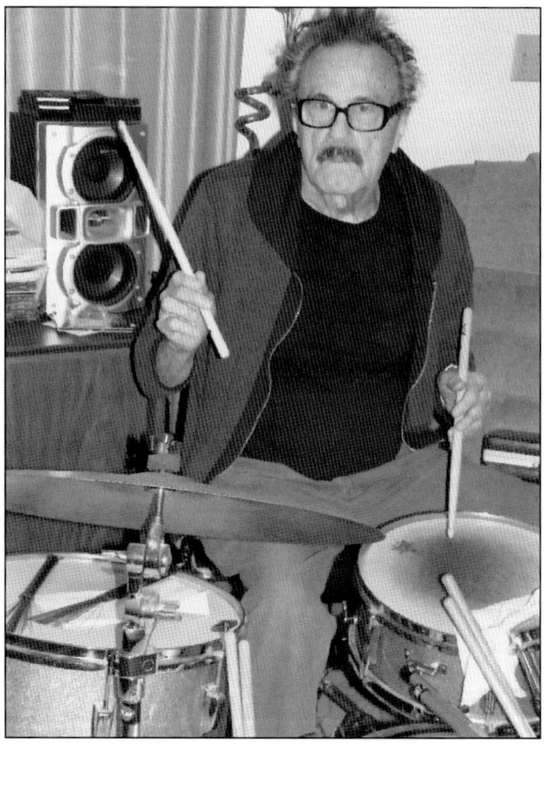

Artt Frank grew up in some of Westbrook's poorest neighborhoods. Although Frank had no formal musical training, he had natural talent and grew up playing in local musical bands. After service in the Navy, numerous jobs, and marriage, Frank left the East Coast for Los Angeles in the 1960s. There, his career flourished as he played with other jazz greats such as Chet Baker and Billie Holiday. In 2010, Frank was inducted into the Jazz Hall of Fame in Tulsa, Oklahoma. (Artt Frank.)

Eight

Centennial

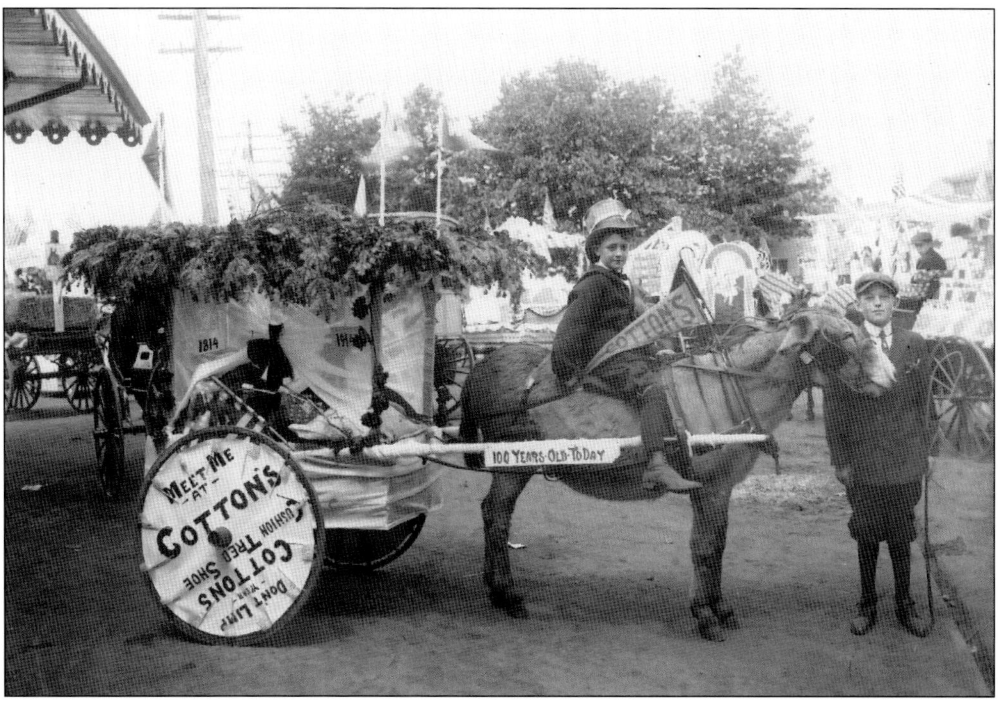

Cotton's Dry & Fancy Goods Store, located at 533 Main Street, had this entry in the 1914 centennial celebration. (Mike Sanphy collection.)

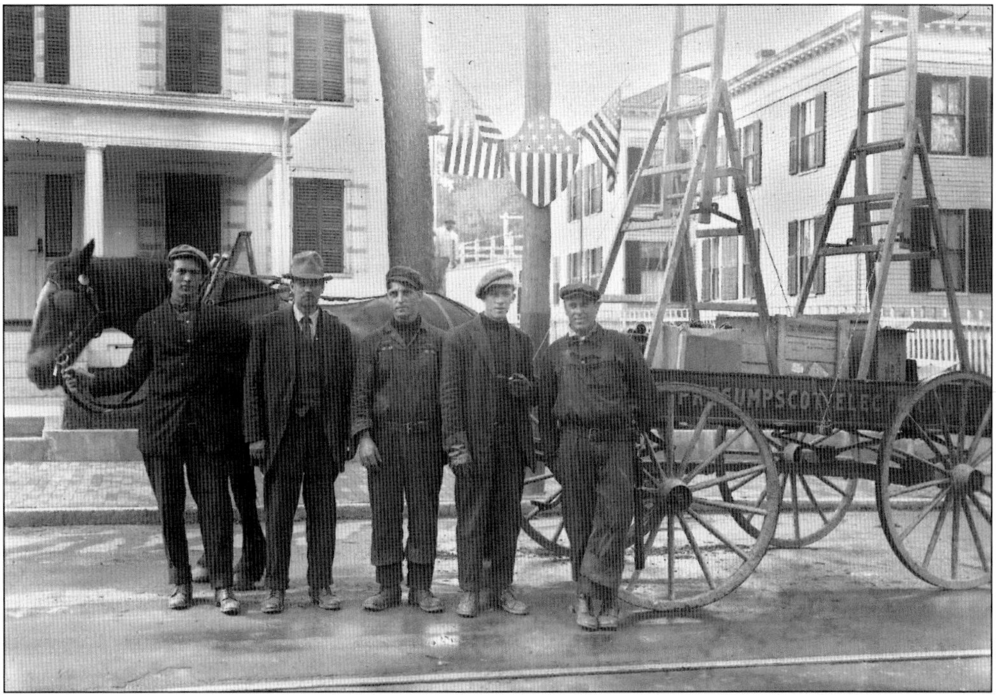

The Presumpscot Electric Company crew poses on Main Street with its wagon during the 1914 centennial celebration. The company had an office at 895 Main Street. General manager William B. Bragdon was appointed chairman of the centennial celebration by the chamber of commerce. Bragdon went on to become mayor of Westbrook in 1919. (Mike Sanphy collection.)

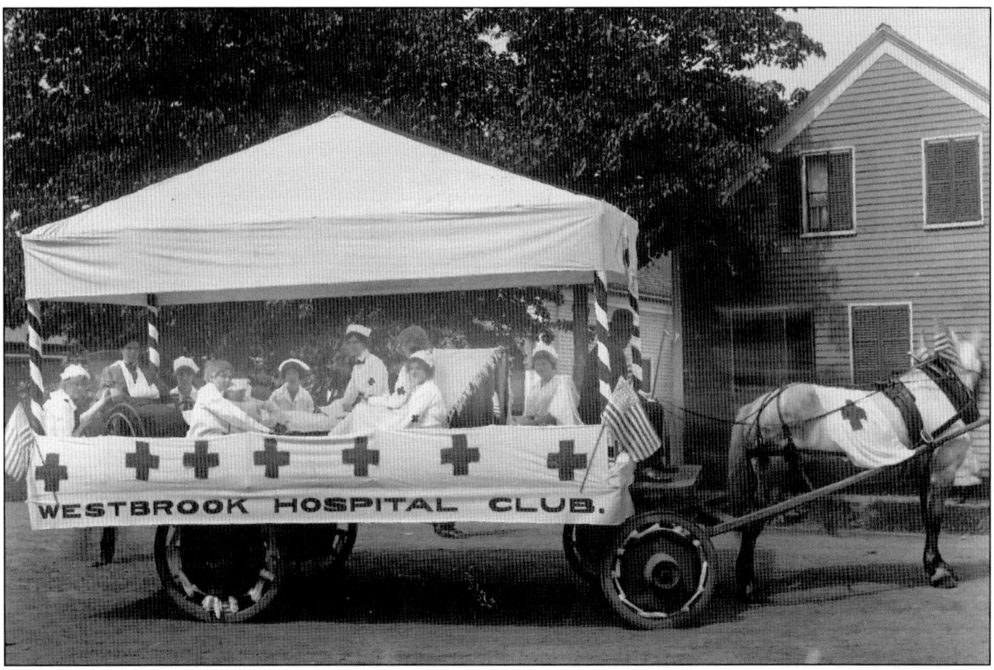

The Westbrook Hospital Club had this horse-drawn wagon in the centennial parade. (Westbrook Historical Society collection.)

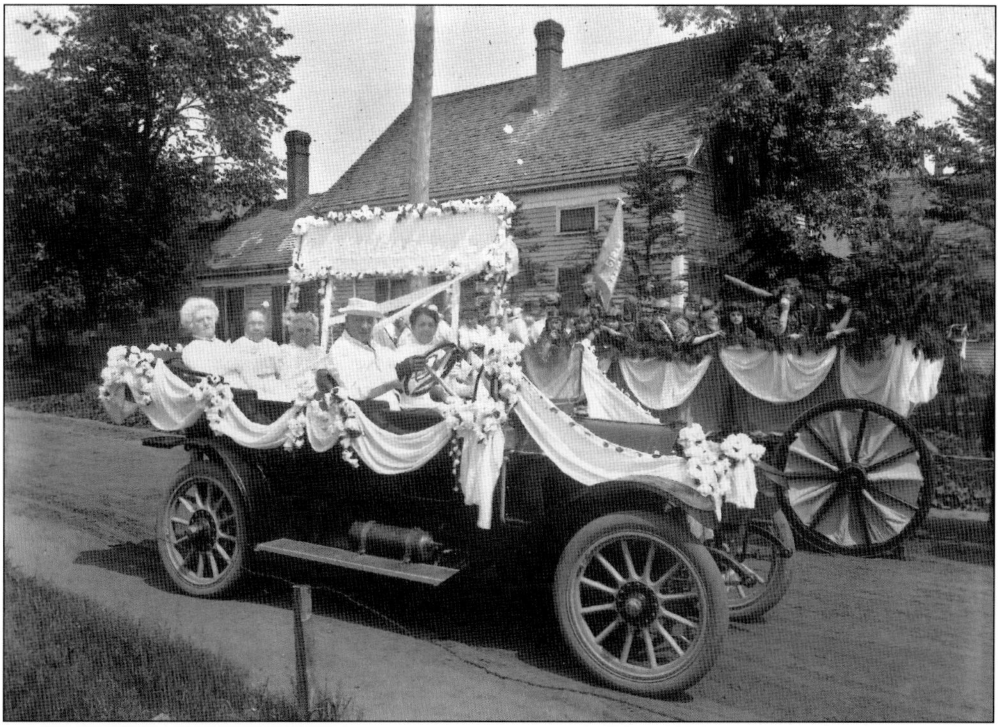

The S.D. Warren Company had this motorized entry in the centennial parade. The people in the car are unidentified. (Westbrook Historical Society collection.)

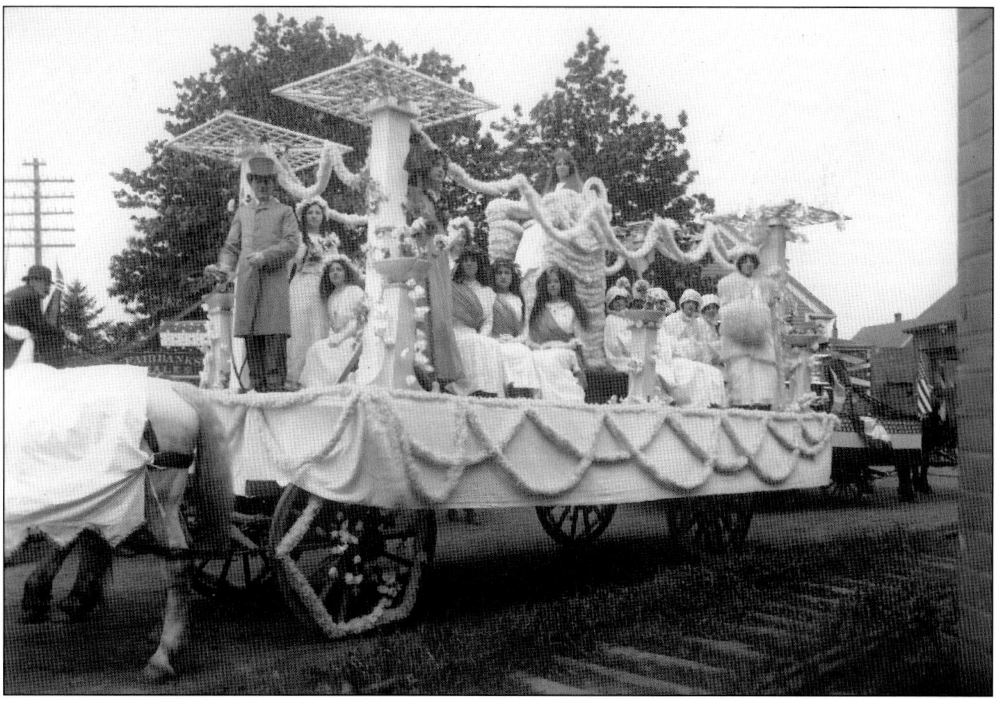

Pictured is an unidentified float in the centennial celebration parade. (Westbrook Historical Society collection.)

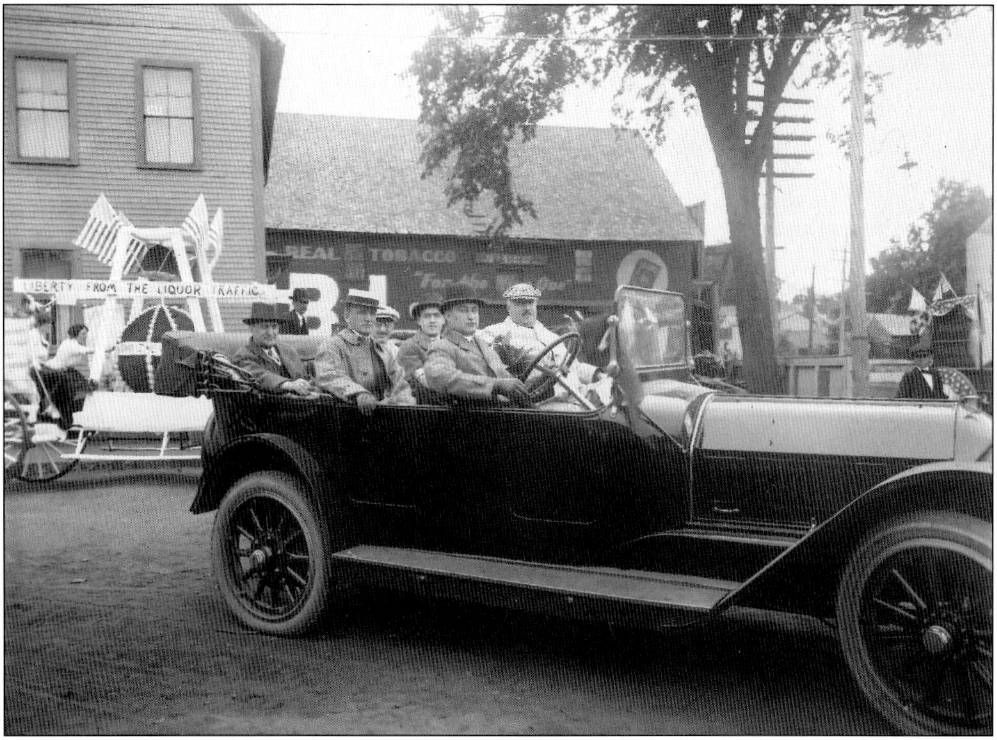

This is an unidentified group of local men, possibly chamber of commerce members, in the centennial parade. (Westbrook Historical Society collection.)

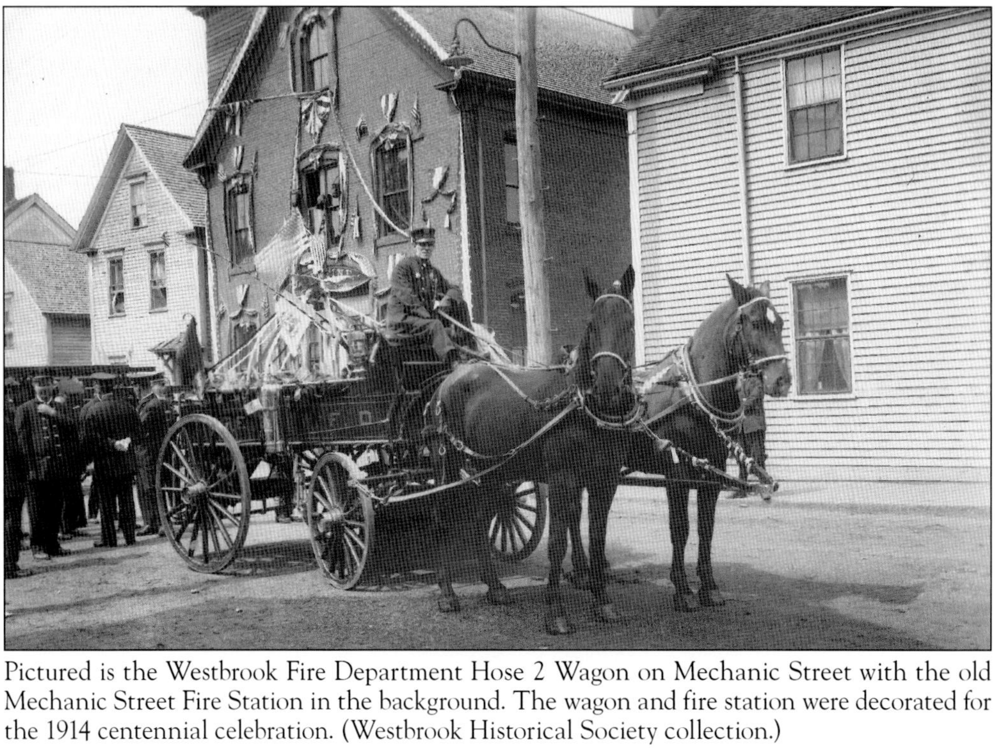

Pictured is the Westbrook Fire Department Hose 2 Wagon on Mechanic Street with the old Mechanic Street Fire Station in the background. The wagon and fire station were decorated for the 1914 centennial celebration. (Westbrook Historical Society collection.)

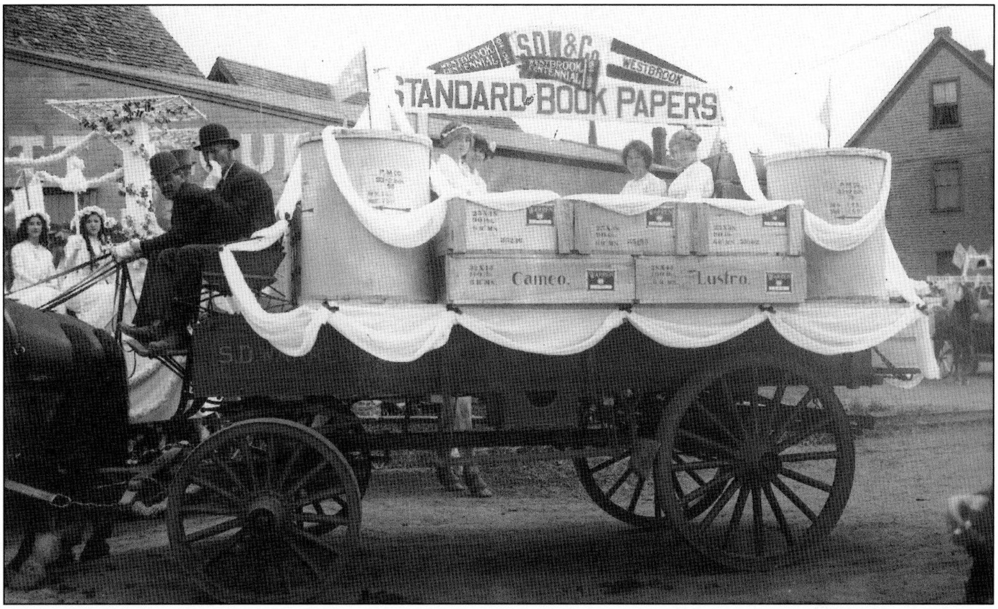

This shows the S.D. Warren Company float in the 1914 centennial parade. Ed Hulit was the driver (wearing white gloves), and a Mr. Tondreau was his assistant. Seated in back are, from left to right, Mina Mickelson, Dora Sullivan, Hattie Johnson, and Marion Shaw Goff. (Walker Memorial Library collection.)

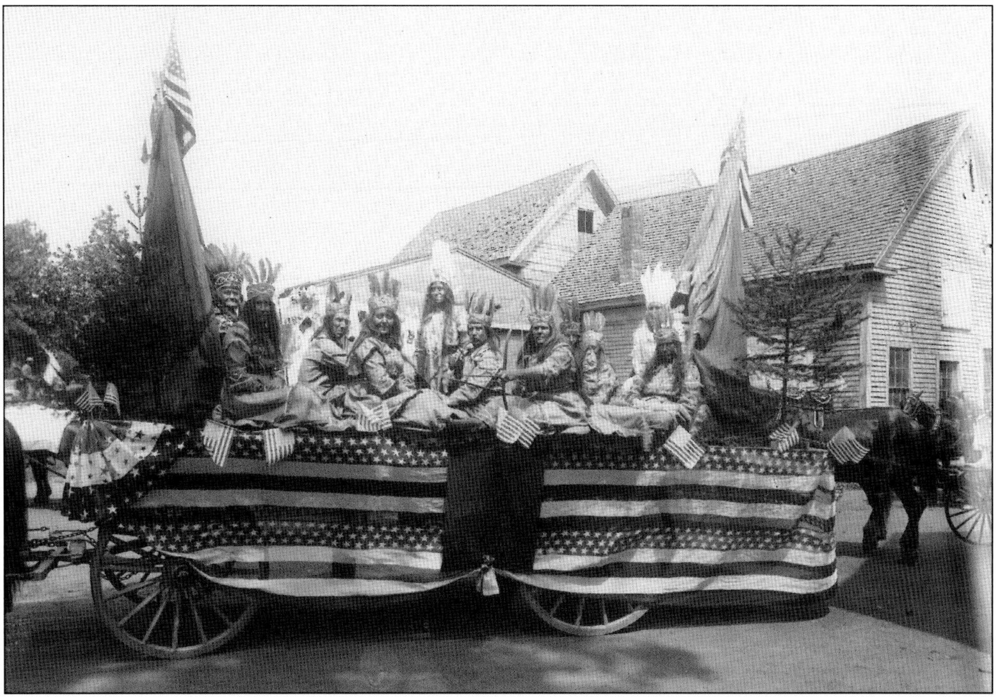

This photograph provided no information on this float, but it is believed to be that of the Improved Order of Red Men. Westbrook had Pequawket Tribe No. 17 and the Degree of Pocahontas, Minnehaha Council No. 6. Meetings were held in Red Men's Hall at 485 Main Street. (Westbrook Historical Society collection.)

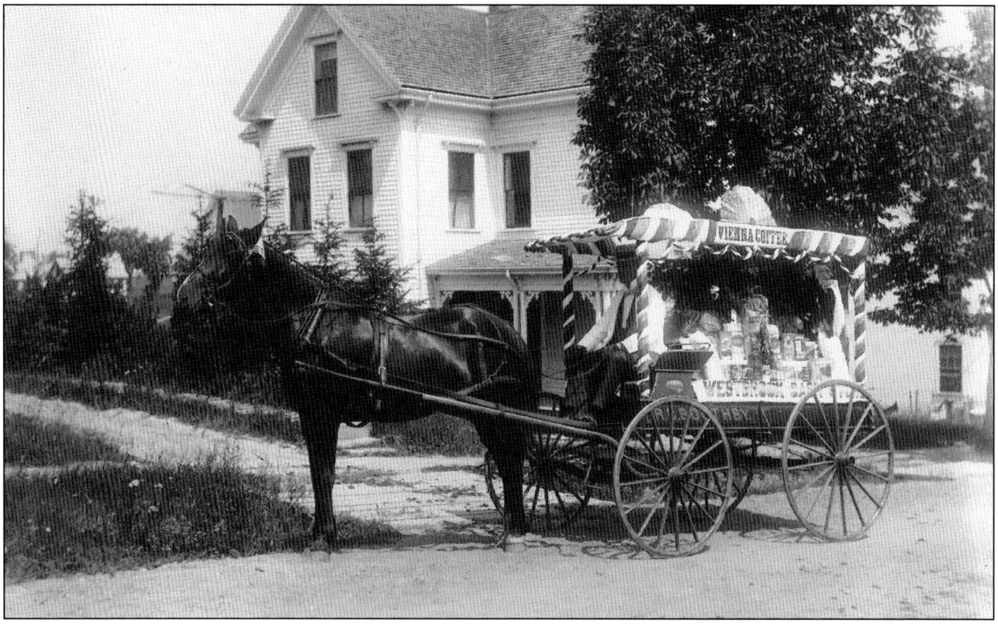

Richard C. Boothby, a grocer at 837 Main Street, entered this wagon in the centennial parade. The wagon had signs advertising Vienna Coffee and Westbrook Cash Store. Boothby's store was in the old Springer Block. Westbrook Hardware later occupied the space. Urban renewal demolished the building. (Mike Sanphy collection.)

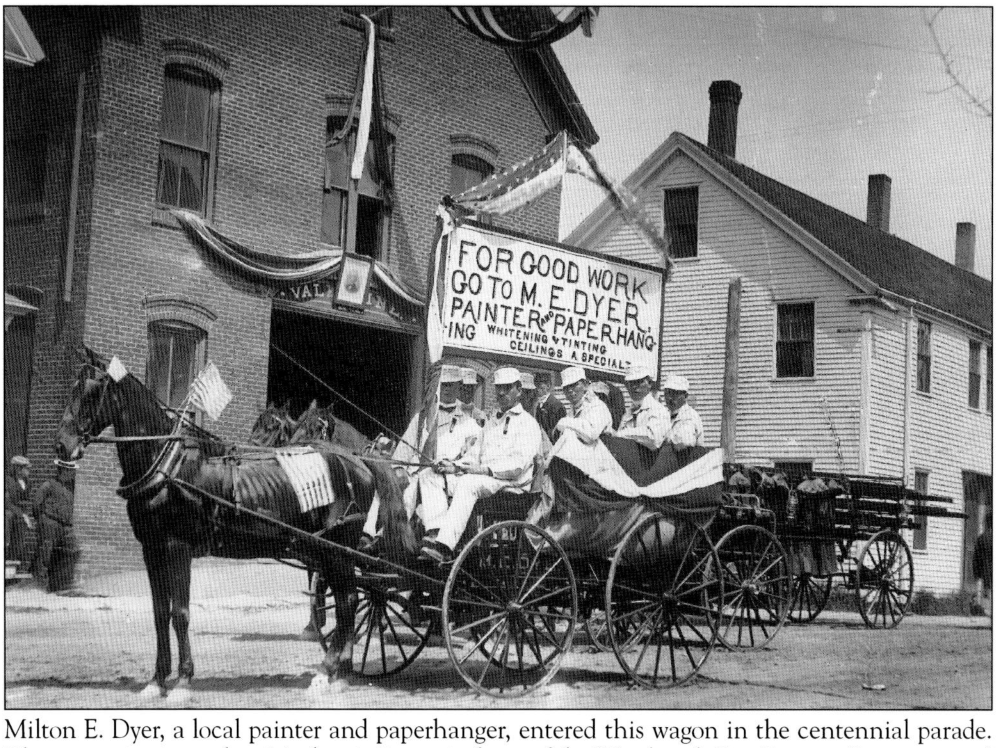

Milton E. Dyer, a local painter and paperhanger, entered this wagon in the centennial parade. The wagon is pictured on Mechanic Street in front of the Westbrook Fire Station. Dyer operated his business out of his home at 687 Main Street. (Mike Sanphy collection.)

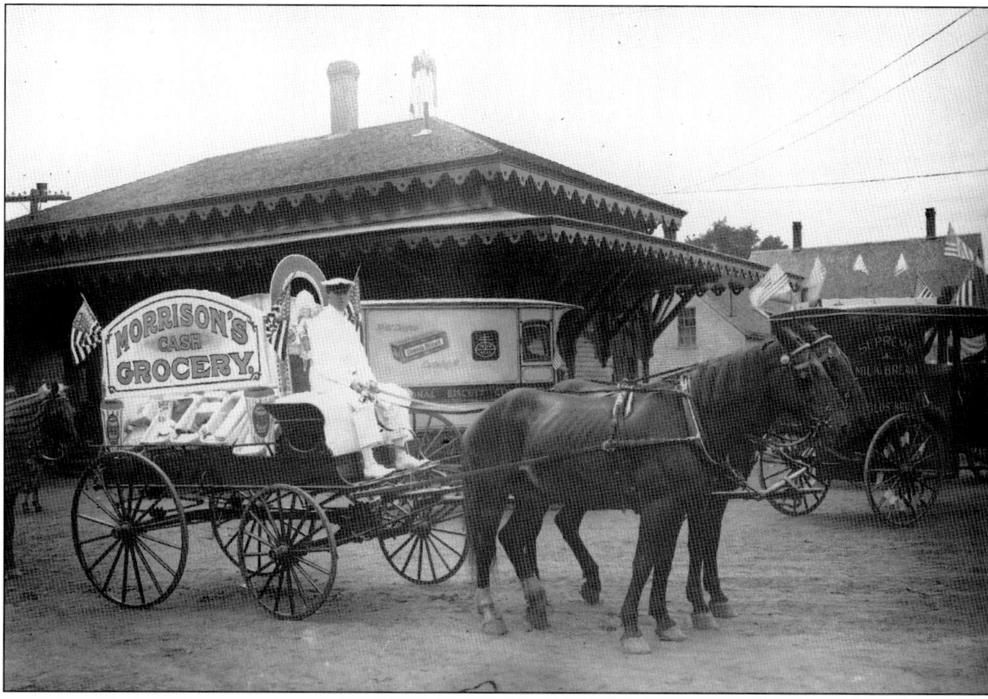

Morrison's Cash Grocery had this wagon in the centennial parade. Angus A. Morrison had a grocery and provision store at 694 Main Street. (Westbrook Historical Society collection.)

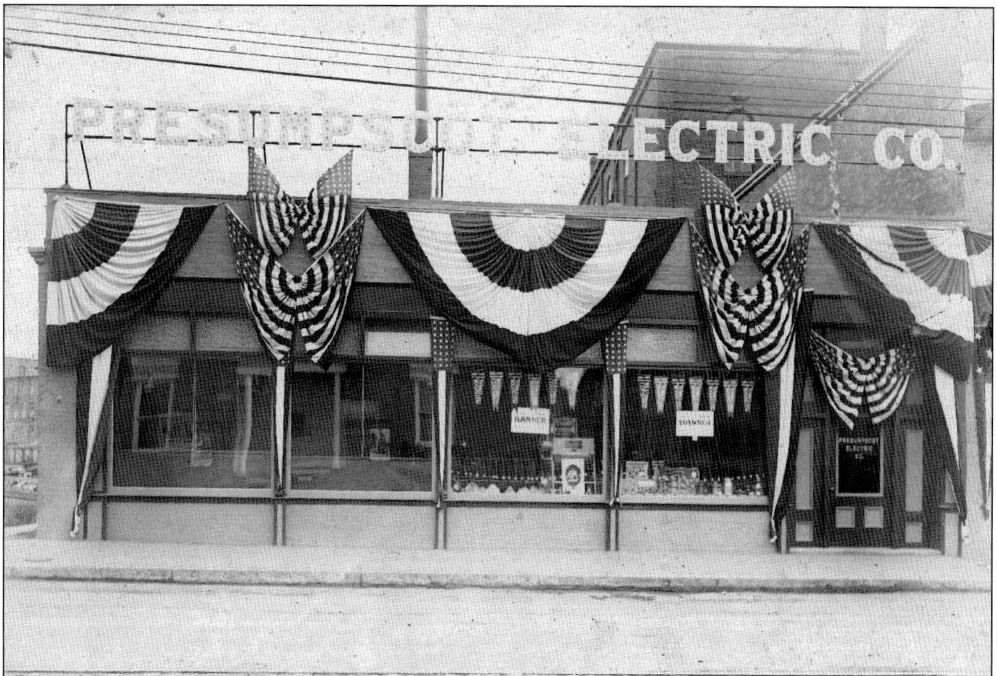

The Presumpscot Electric Company office, located at 895 Main Street, is decorated in celebration of Westbrook's 1914 centennial celebration. This building once stood on Main Street where the Bridge Street Spur enters Main Street. (Mike Sanphy collection.)

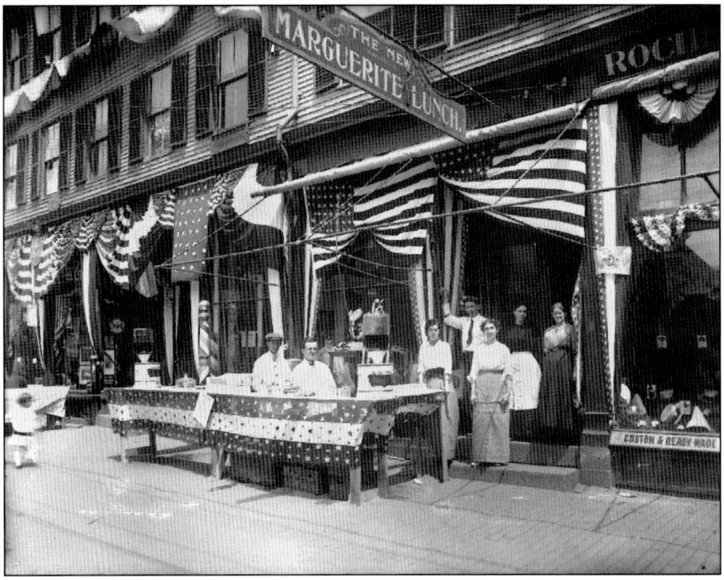

This is the New Marguerite Lunch, located on Main Street in the Vallee Block next to Rocheleau, Cash Clothier. This photograph shows the lunch spot and adjoining businesses displaying flags and bunting in celebration of the 1914 centennial. (Mike Sanphy collection.)

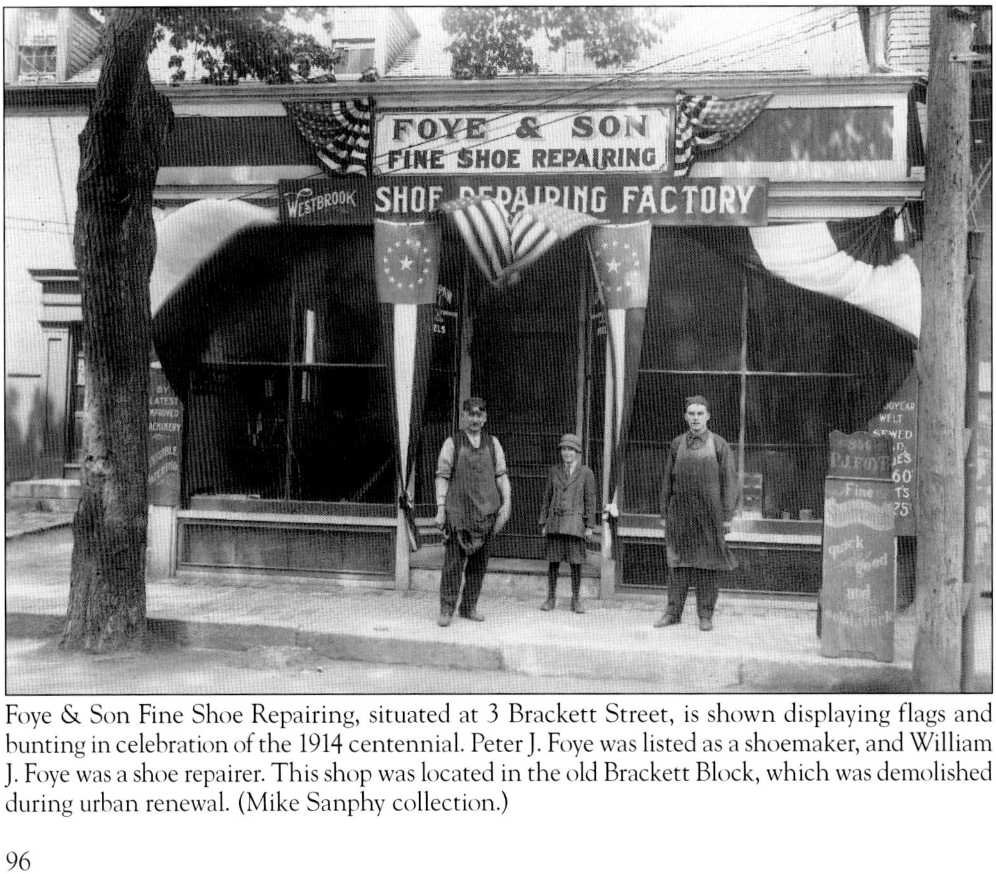

Foye & Son Fine Shoe Repairing, situated at 3 Brackett Street, is shown displaying flags and bunting in celebration of the 1914 centennial. Peter J. Foye was listed as a shoemaker, and William J. Foye was a shoe repairer. This shop was located in the old Brackett Block, which was demolished during urban renewal. (Mike Sanphy collection.)

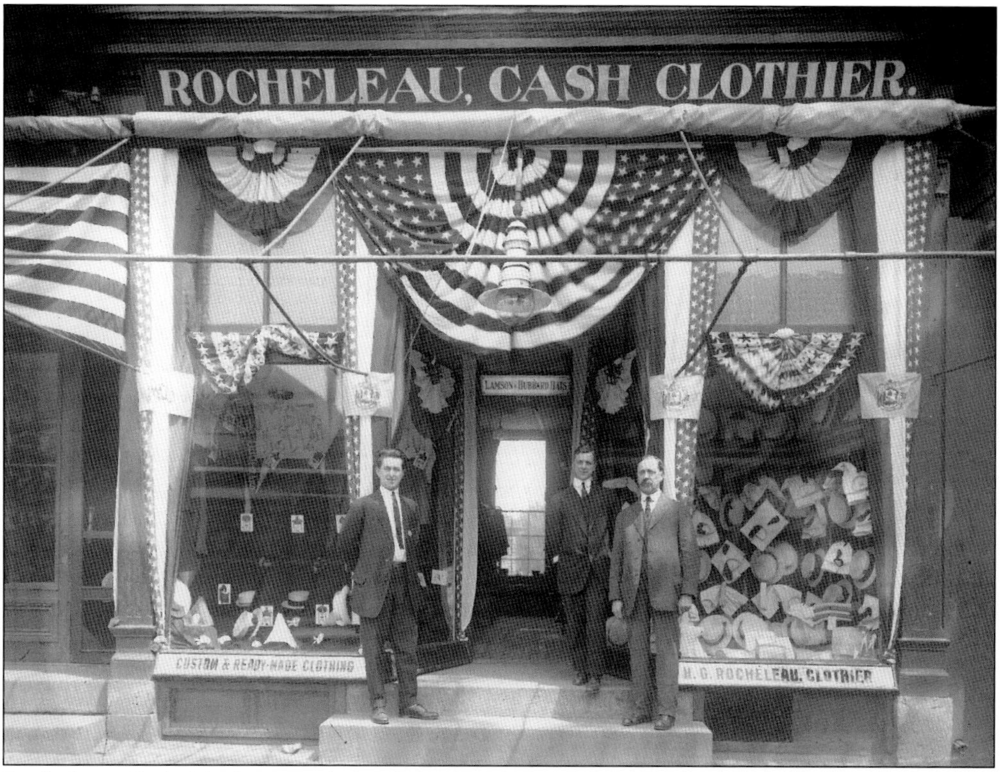

Rocheleau, Cash Clothier was located at 861 Main Street in the Vallee Block. The business is pictured during the 1914 centennial celebration. Henry G. Rocheleau owned and operated this business and also owned and operated the H.G. Rocheleau & Son Funeral Home at 71 Church Street. William Rocheleau closed the store in the 1980s, and the funeral business was moved to 35 Church Street and purchased by Robert Blais in 1953. (Mike Sanphy collection.)

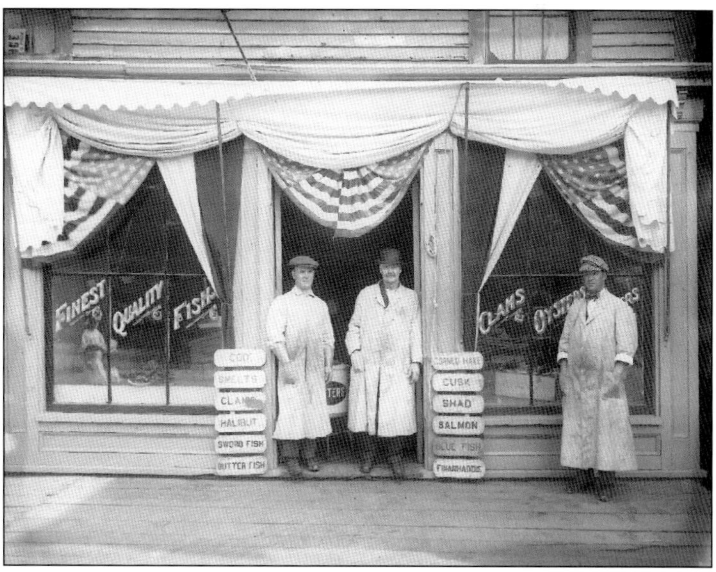

This photograph was taken for the centennial. In the window of this unidentified fish market, a pair of lobsters sits on a platter. The hand-lettered signs on the window, as well as the other signs advertising the types of fish carried, make for an interesting photograph. (Westbrook Historical Society collection.)

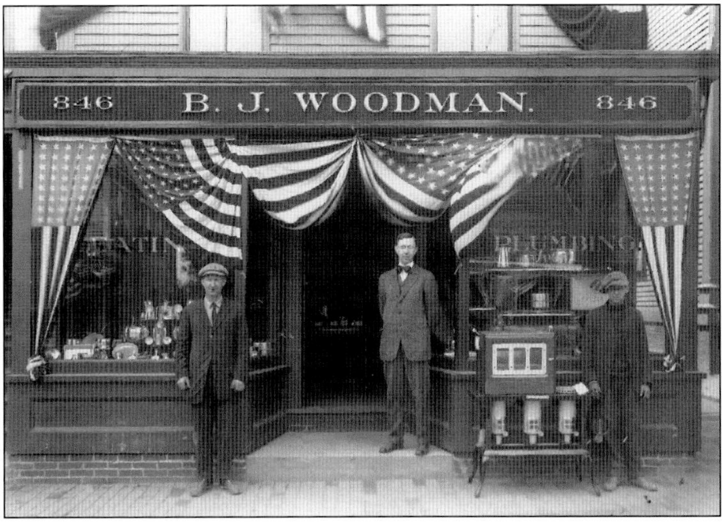

Benjamin J. Woodman's store at 846 Main Street is seen here during the 1914 centennial celebration. Woodman dealt in plumbing, heating, and sheet metal work. This building was next to the Westbrook Congregational Church and still stands today. (Mike Sanphy collection.)

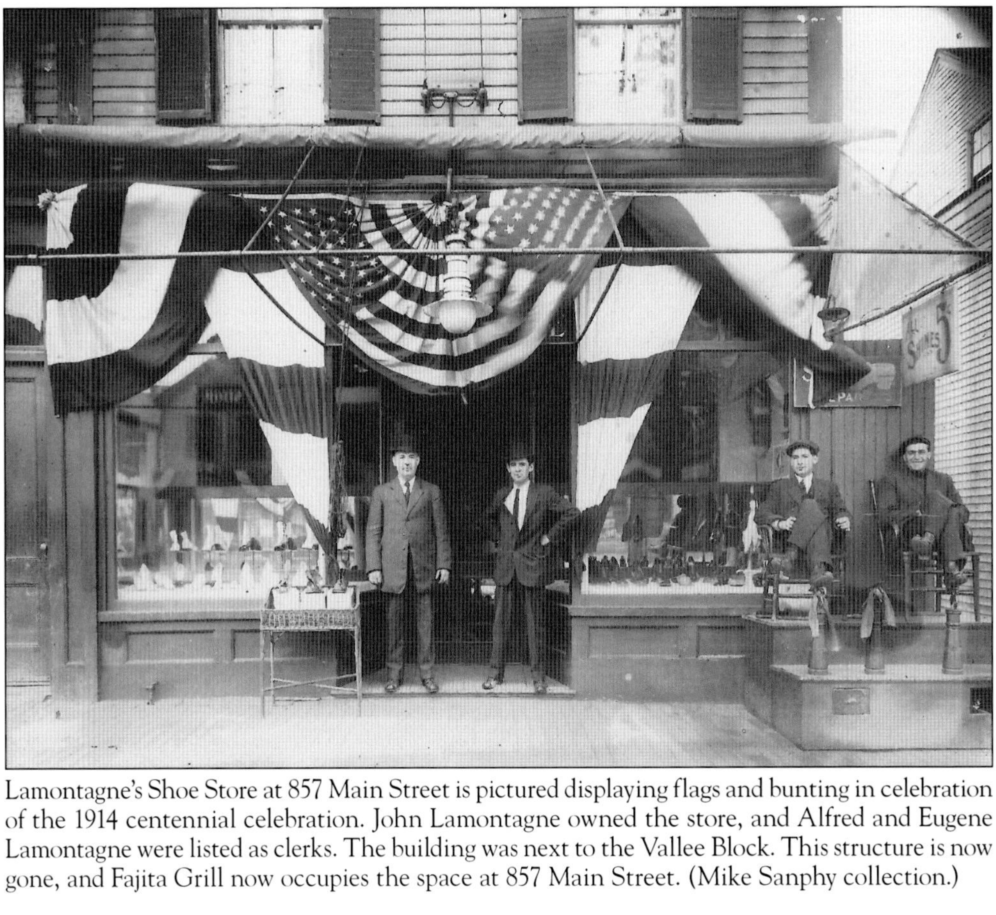

Lamontagne's Shoe Store at 857 Main Street is pictured displaying flags and bunting in celebration of the 1914 centennial celebration. John Lamontagne owned the store, and Alfred and Eugene Lamontagne were listed as clerks. The building was next to the Vallee Block. This structure is now gone, and Fajita Grill now occupies the space at 857 Main Street. (Mike Sanphy collection.)

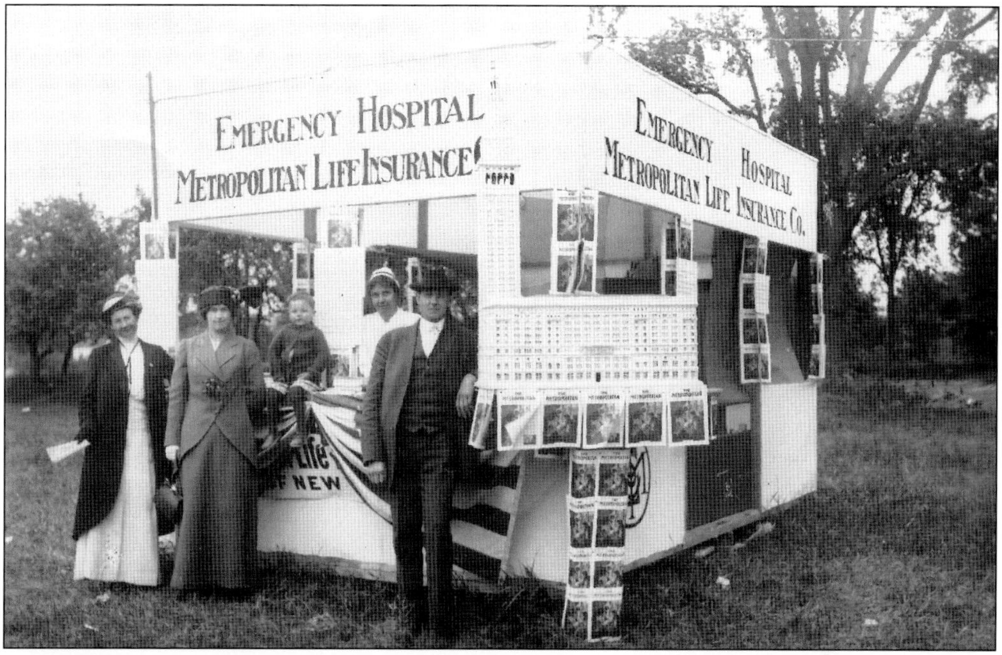

Metropolitan Life Insurance had this booth set up at Riverbank Park during the 1914 centennial celebration parade. (Mike Sanphy collection.)

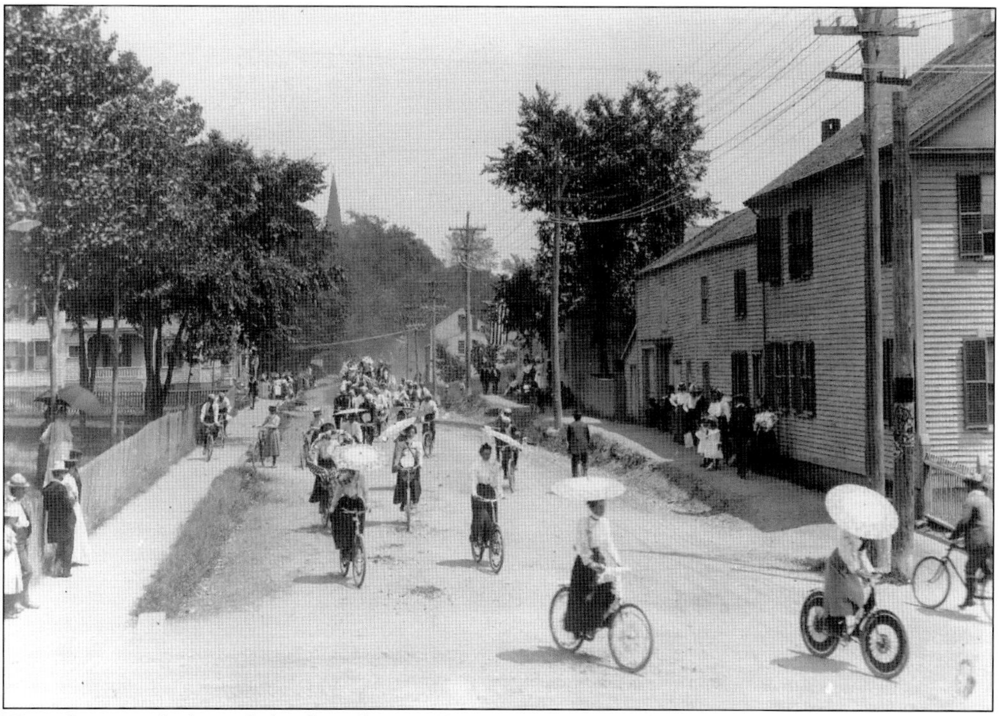

This photograph shows ladies bicycling on Brown Street, at Bridge Street, during a parade in 1899. The steeple in the background is the old St. Hyacinth Church, which was dedicated on August 22, 1879. The house to the right was built in the 1830s as a residence for the agent of the Westbrook Manufacturing Company. The house still stands at 41 Bridge Street. (Mike Sanphy collection.)

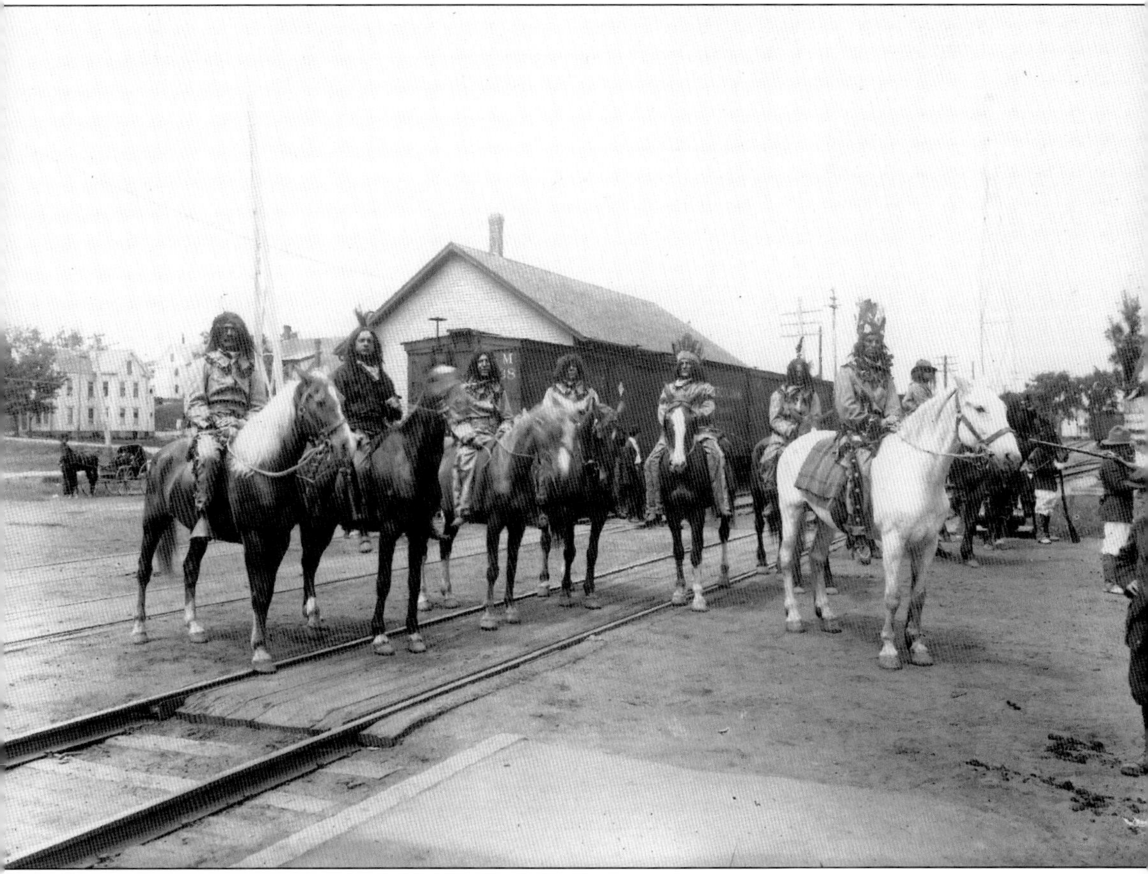

These men are dressed as Indians on horseback during the 1914 centennial parade. These men were possibly members of the Improved Order of Red Men, Pequawket Tribe No. 17 of Westbrook. The group met in Red Man's Hall at 485 Main Street. This organization no longer exists in Westbrook. (Mike Sanphy collection.)

Nine

Berg Family Collection

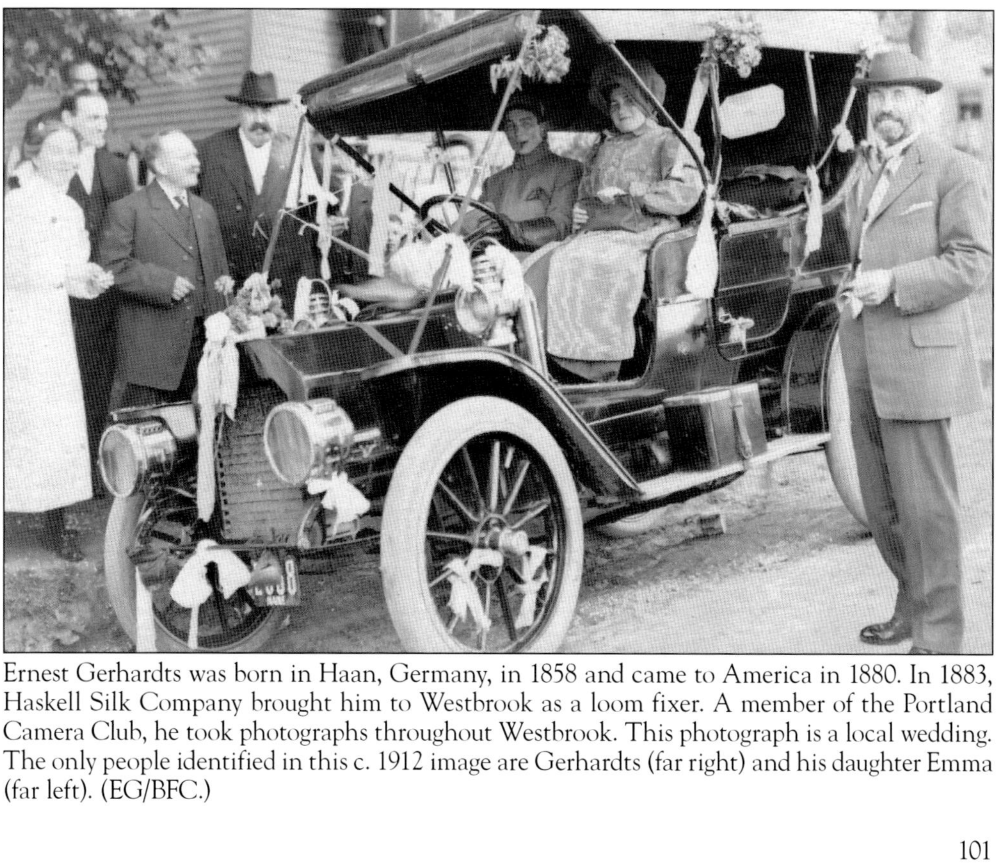

Ernest Gerhardts was born in Haan, Germany, in 1858 and came to America in 1880. In 1883, Haskell Silk Company brought him to Westbrook as a loom fixer. A member of the Portland Camera Club, he took photographs throughout Westbrook. This photograph is a local wedding. The only people identified in this c. 1912 image are Gerhardts (far right) and his daughter Emma (far left). (EG/BFC.)

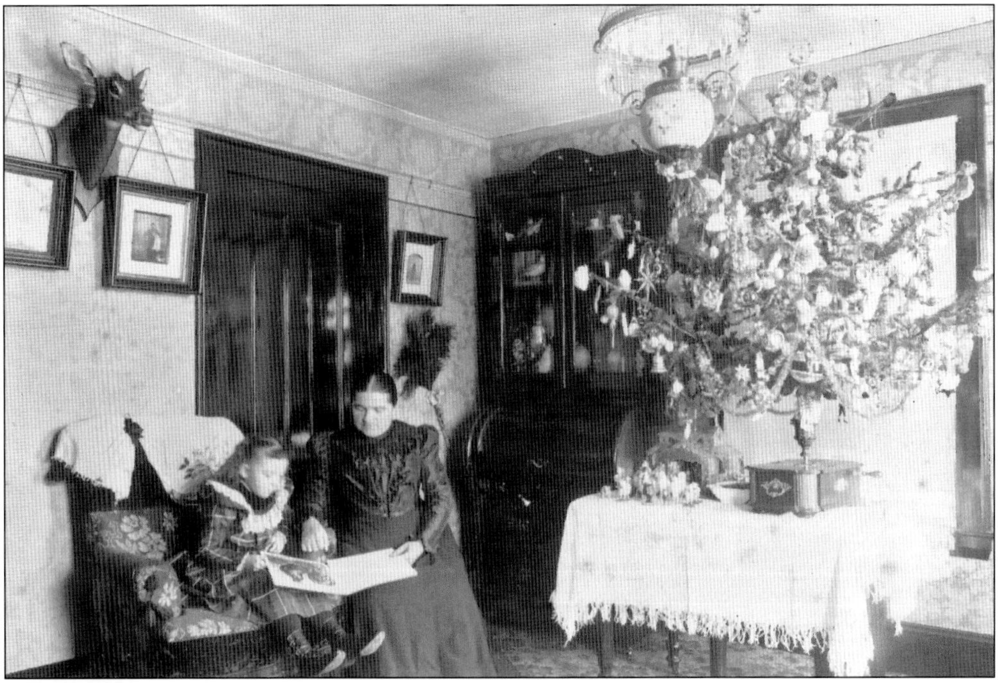

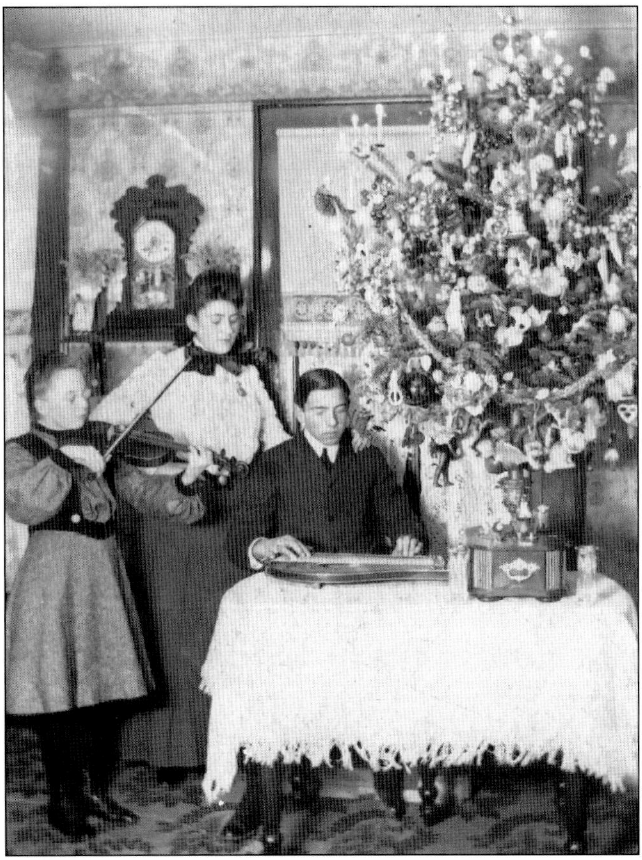

Ernest Gerhardts took many pictures inside his home. This interior photograph shows his wife, Henrietta, reading with their daughter Emma at Christmastime in their Brackett Street home. Their Christmas tree, adorned with over 1,000 ornaments, revolved atop a music box that the Gerhardts brought from Germany. This photograph was taken around 1897. (EG/BFC.)

Emma Gerhardts and her cousin Ernest Theis play music while Ernest's sister Clara looks on in this c. 1905 image. The Theis family came from Germany in 1894 and lived in a separate apartment in the Gerhardts house from 1895 to 1901. Ernest later married Marion Wentworth, daughter of the Bridge Street School principal. He went on to manage the Theis Tire Company. (EG/BFC.)

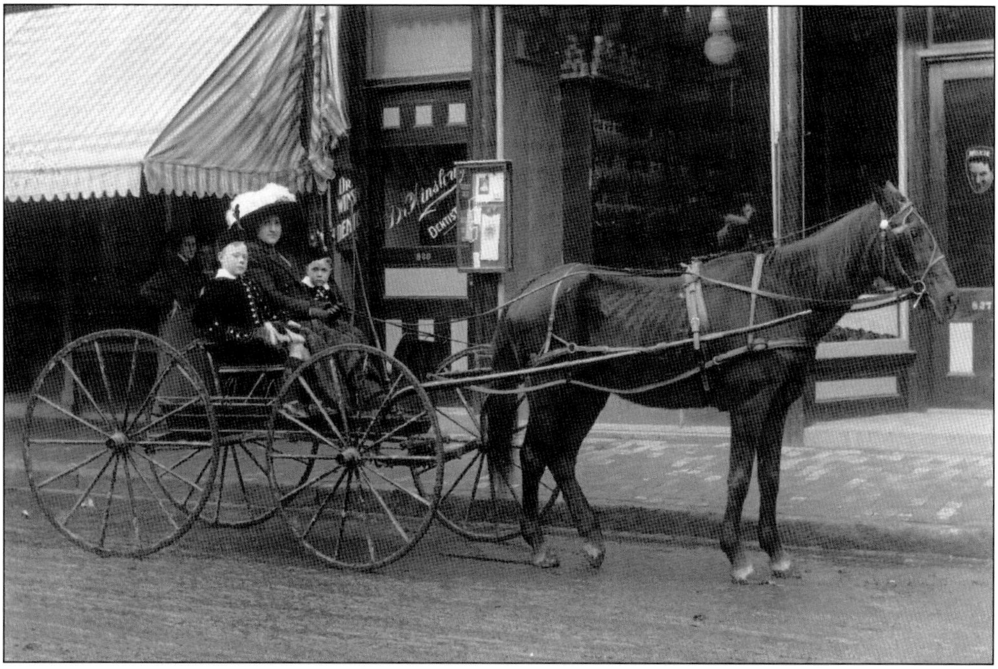

The three unidentified people in this carriage have stopped near the dental office of Dr. Wilson at 839 Main Street. This address was part of the Springer building. Later, Westbrook Hardware was located in this building, as was Parker's Dress Shop. In the 1960s, top-40 radio station WJAB's studios were upstairs, possibly in the former dental office of Dr. Wilson. (EG/BFC.)

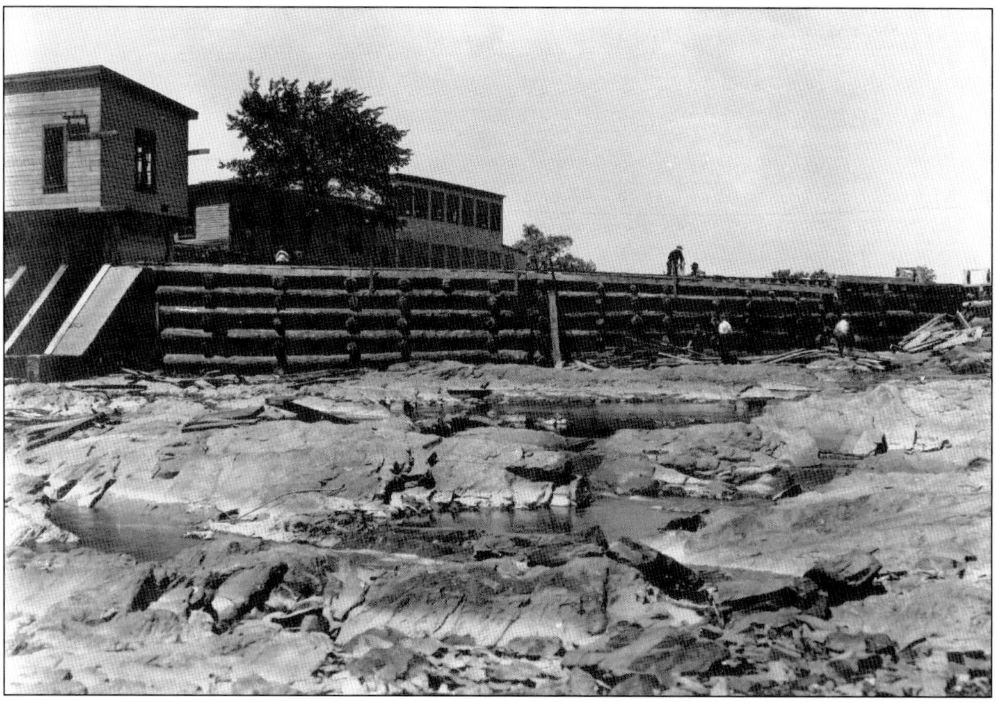

A group of unidentified workers labor at the log dam near the Dana Warp Mill. It is likely that they are cleaning out logs and larger trash during a low water time. (EG/BFC.)

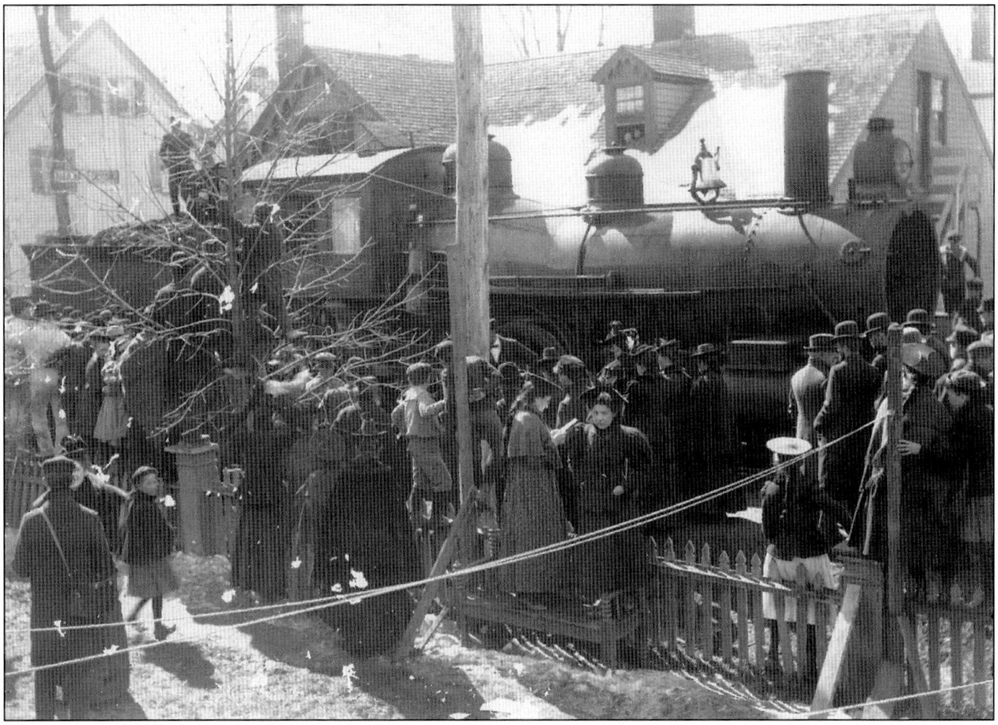

There is no record of why a crowd of over 60 people is gathered around this train. There is no obvious accident, as the other pictures on these pages portray, but there are onlookers in the tree, on the fence and bench, in the widow, and crowded right up against the engine. (EG/BFC.)

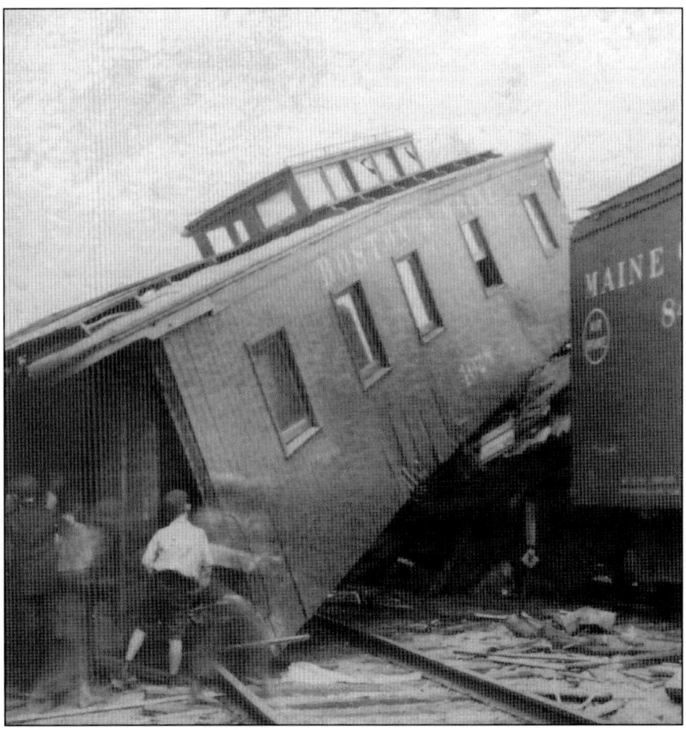

Ernest Gerhardts sometimes used a double-lens camera that allowed his pictures to be viewed on a stereoscope, a turn-of-the-century 3-D viewer. Here, an unidentified boy looks into a derailed railroad car. (EG/BFC.)

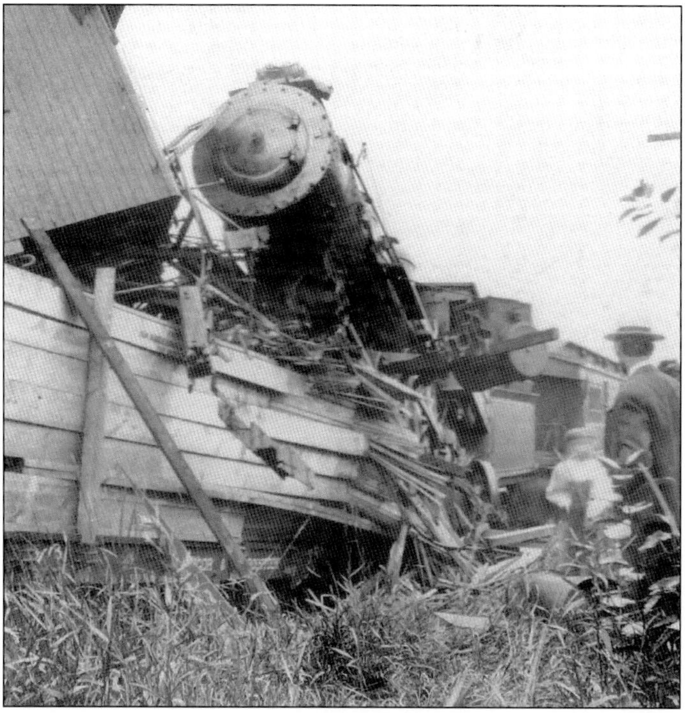

The four pictures on these two pages all involve train accidents. Three of these were taken with Gerhardts's stereoscopic camera, including this picture of a locomotive that has climbed atop of the railcar it hit. (EG/BFC.)

This photograph shows a head-on collision of two locomotives. It is probably the collision that took place between Spring and Church Streets around 1900. (EG/BFC.)

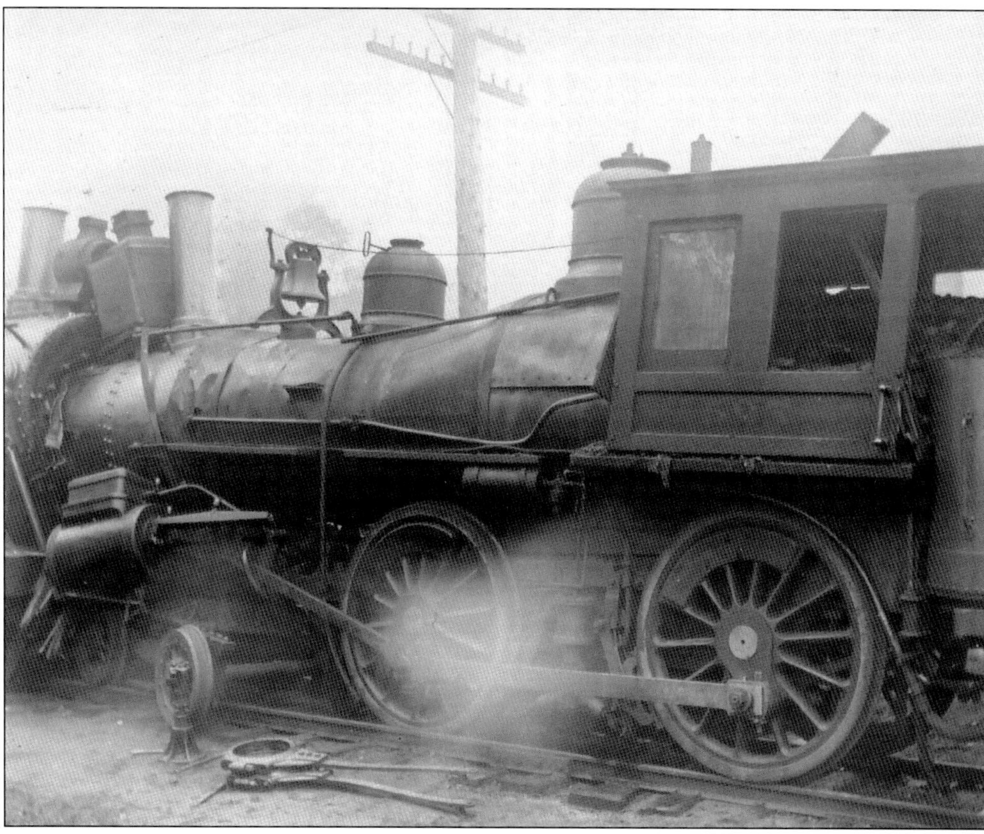

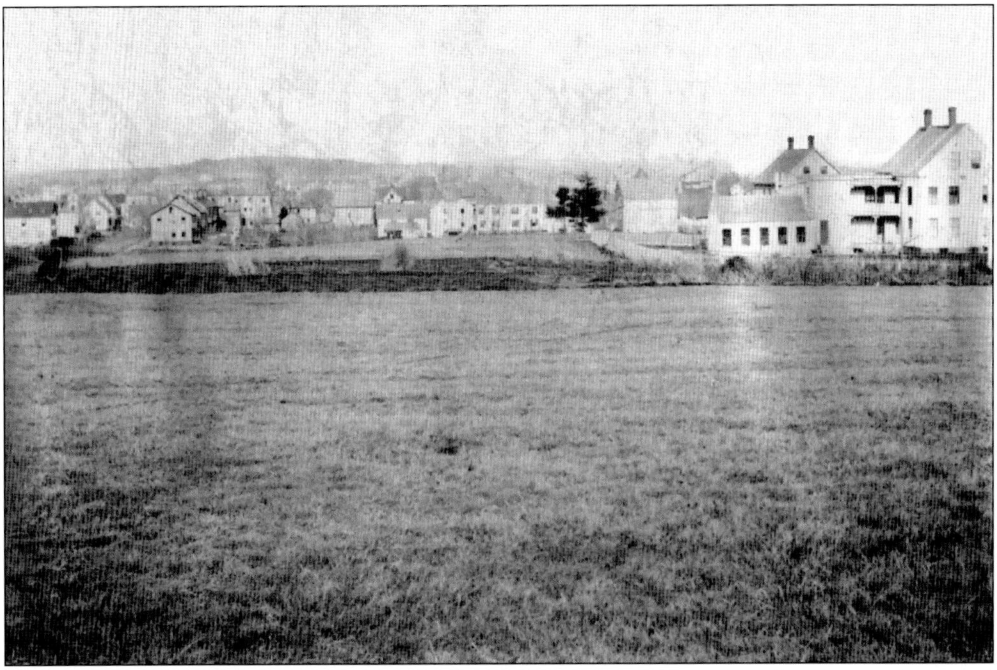

This view looks toward Main Street from the top of the hill between where Brackett and Central Streets now run. On the right is 157 Brackett Street; the last house on the street at that time. Beyond it is 147 Brackett Street and its barn. On the left is Central Street, which then ended near where the old canal used to run. (EG/BFC.)

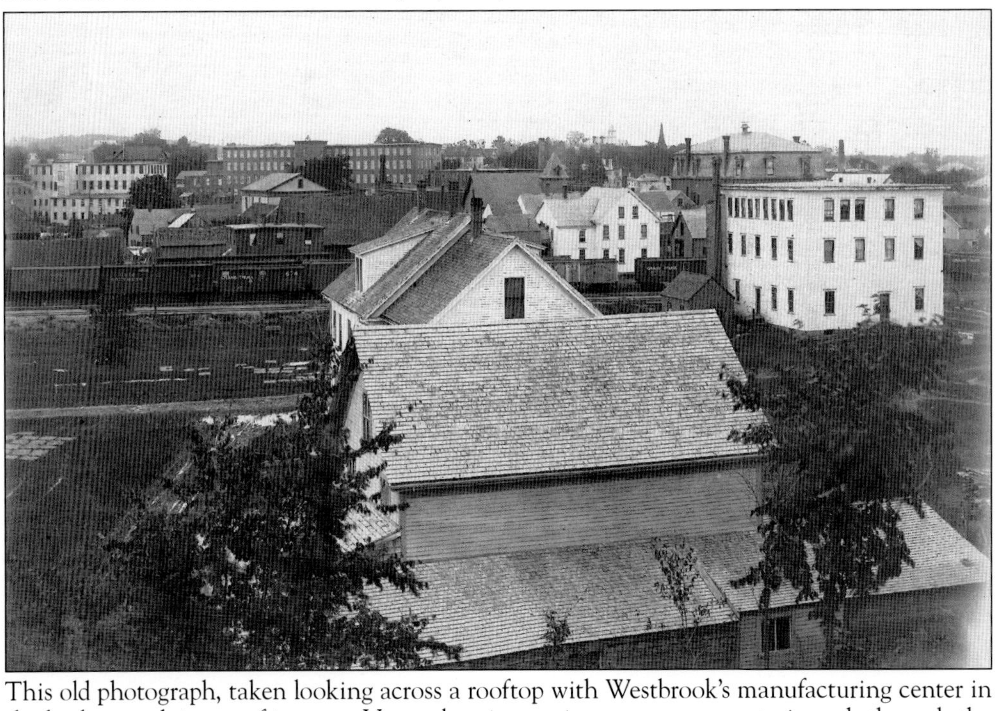

This old photograph, taken looking across a rooftop with Westbrook's manufacturing center in the background, is one of interest. Upon close inspection, one can see a train rush through the scene. (Warren Library collection.)

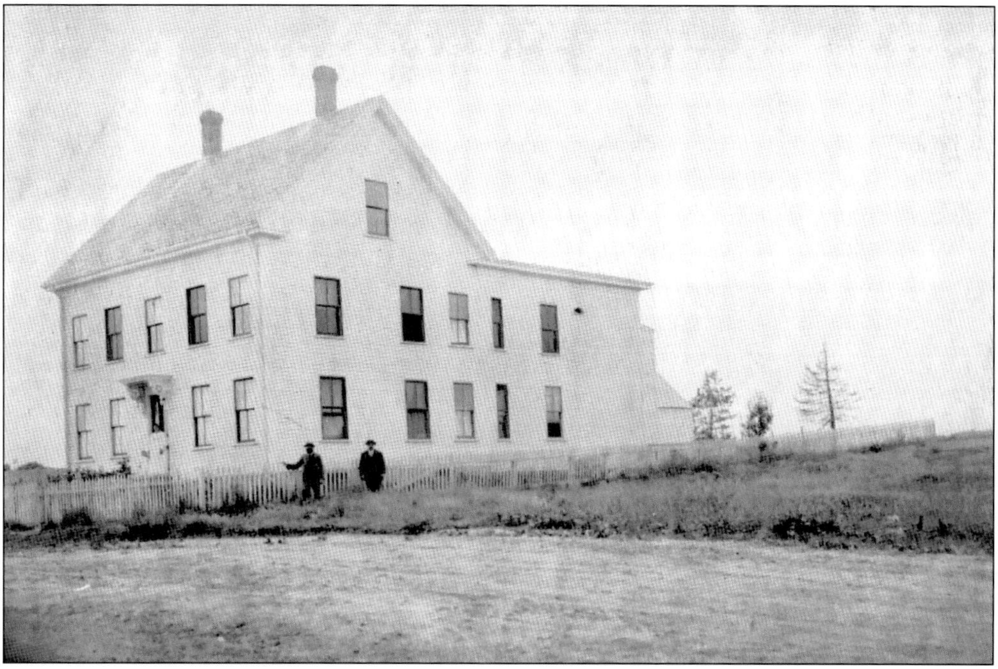

At the top of Brackett Street, Henrietta Gerhardts and her daughter Emma stand at their front door. Ernest Gerhardts (left) and an unidentified friend stand by the northern fence. The house is three years old and stands by itself in a field at the top of the street. (EG/BFC.)

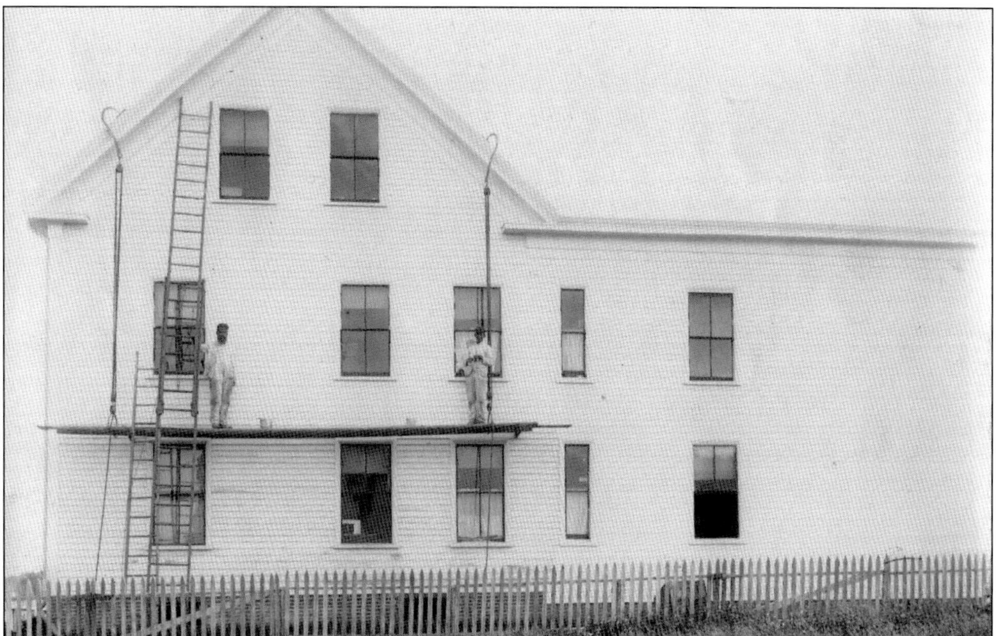

Two unidentified workers put a fresh coat of white paint on the wooden shingles of the Gerhardts' house. Hooks and pulleys hold up their staging. (EG/BFC.)

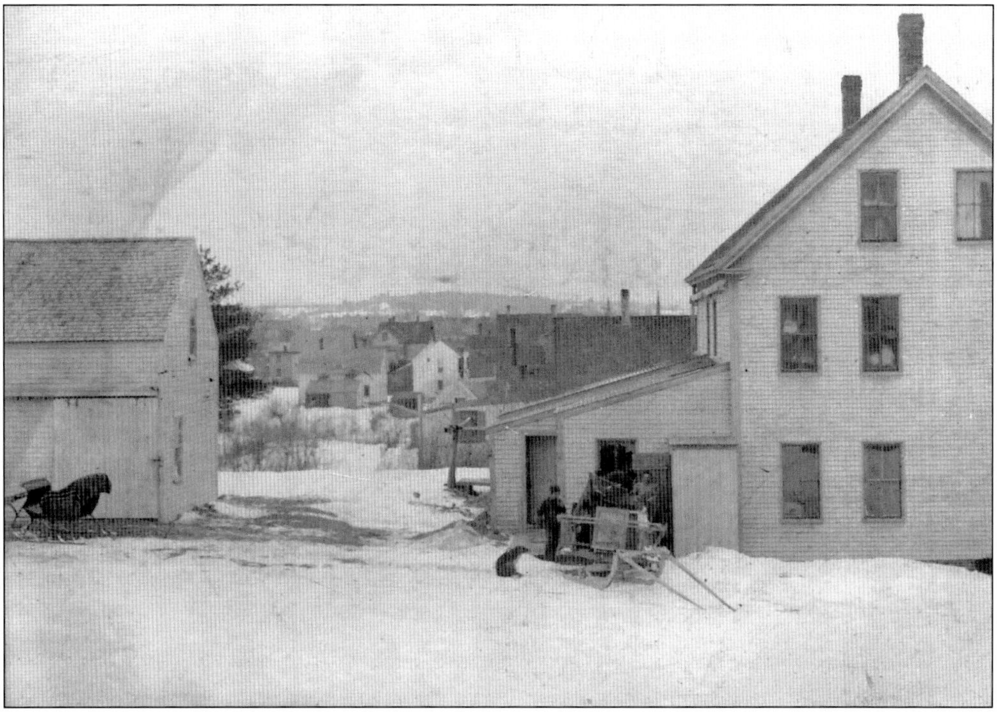

Unidentified workers load a horse-drawn sled at the back of 147 Brackett Street. Farther down the hill are houses on Grant and Central Streets. The hills beyond River Road can be seen toward the horizon. (EG/BFC.)

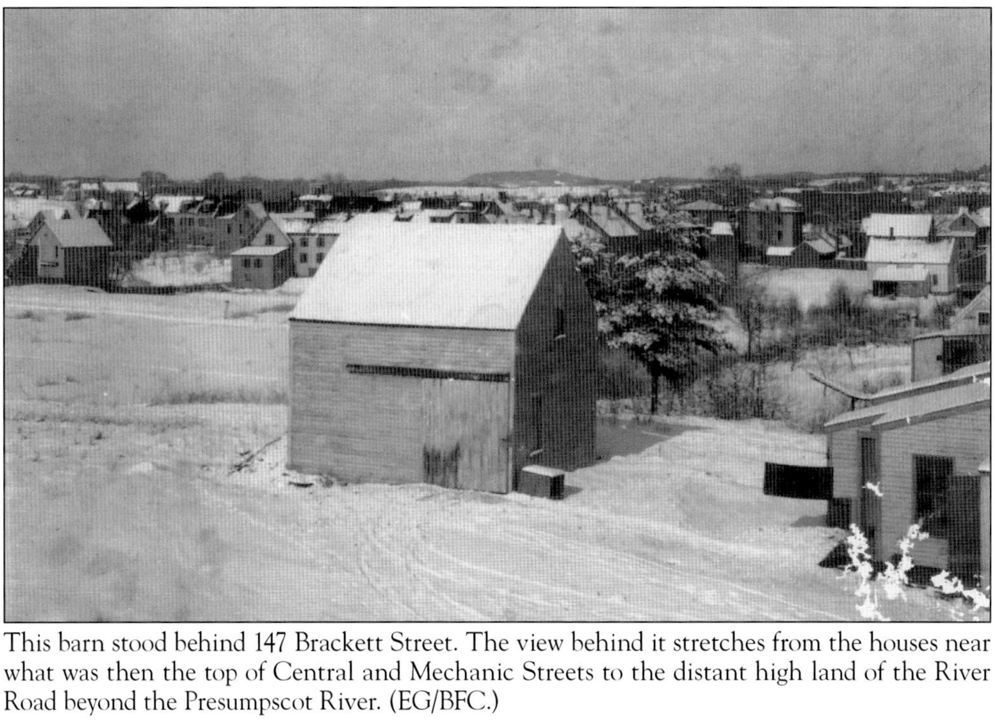

This barn stood behind 147 Brackett Street. The view behind it stretches from the houses near what was then the top of Central and Mechanic Streets to the distant high land of the River Road beyond the Presumpscot River. (EG/BFC.)

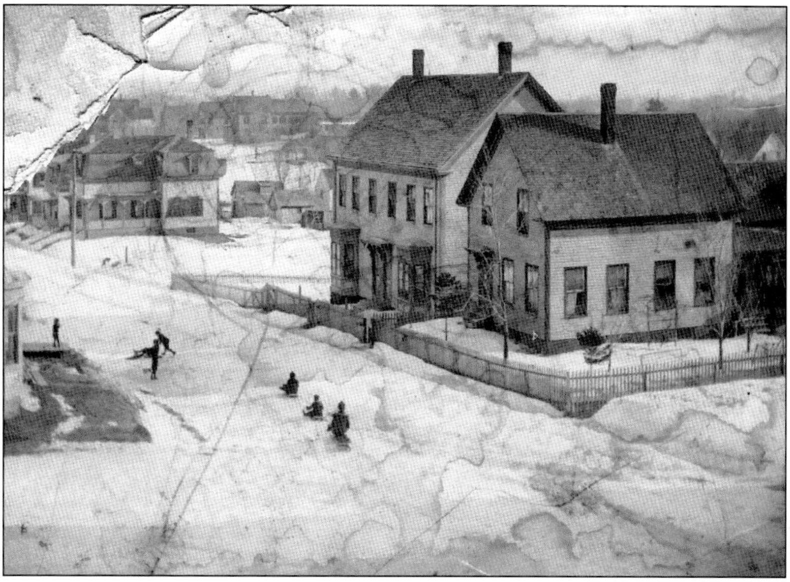

Children sled down Brackett Street. Pennell Street begins just beyond the far corner of the picket fence. Beyond the sheds on Pennell Street, a bit of the snow-covered Beaver Pond and the houses at the top of Church Street are visible. This image was captured around 1900. (EG/BFC.)

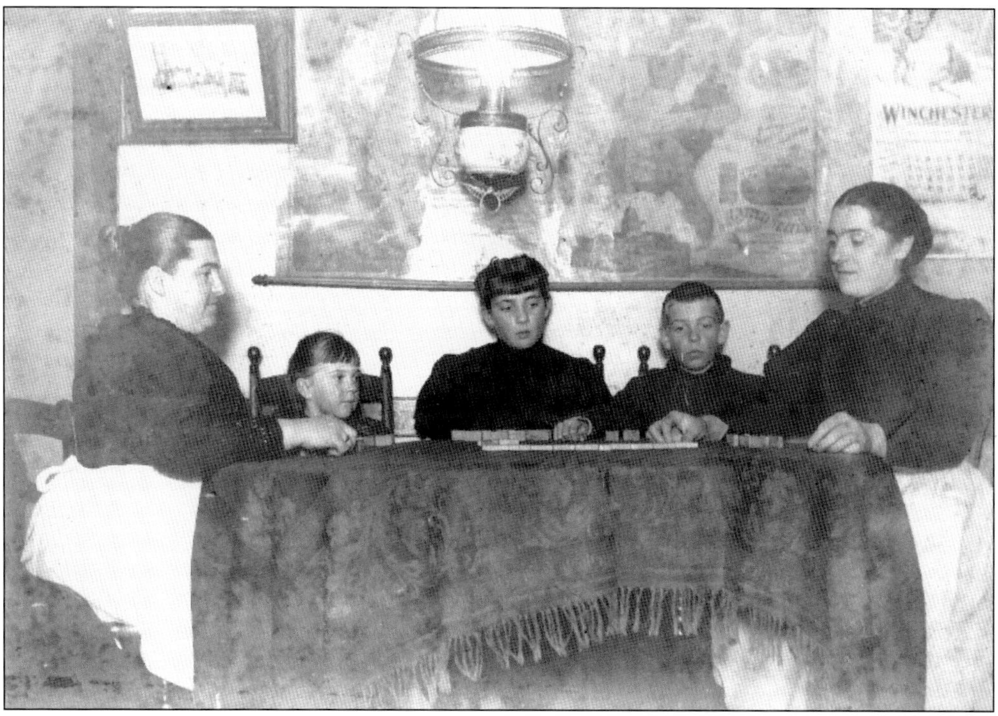

The family plays dominoes at the kitchen table. Henrietta Gerhardts and her daughter Emma are on the left, followed by Marion Theis, Ernest Theis, and their mother Emma Theis, who is Henrietta's sister. An oil lamp hangs over the table, and a large map of the United States hangs on the wall. The Winchester calendar is for the year 1898. (EG/BFC.)

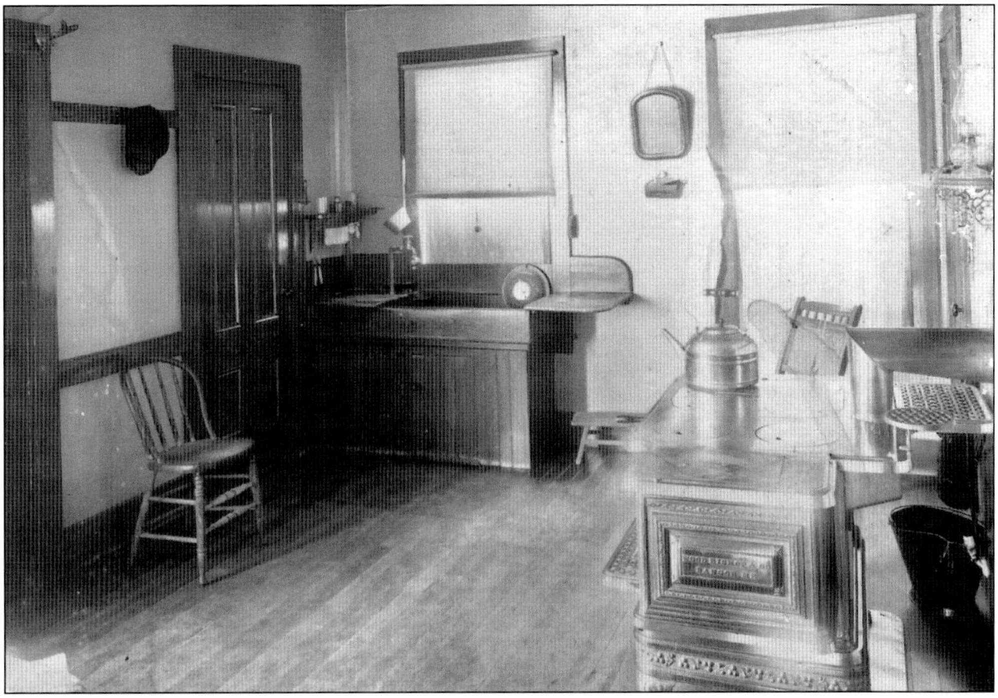

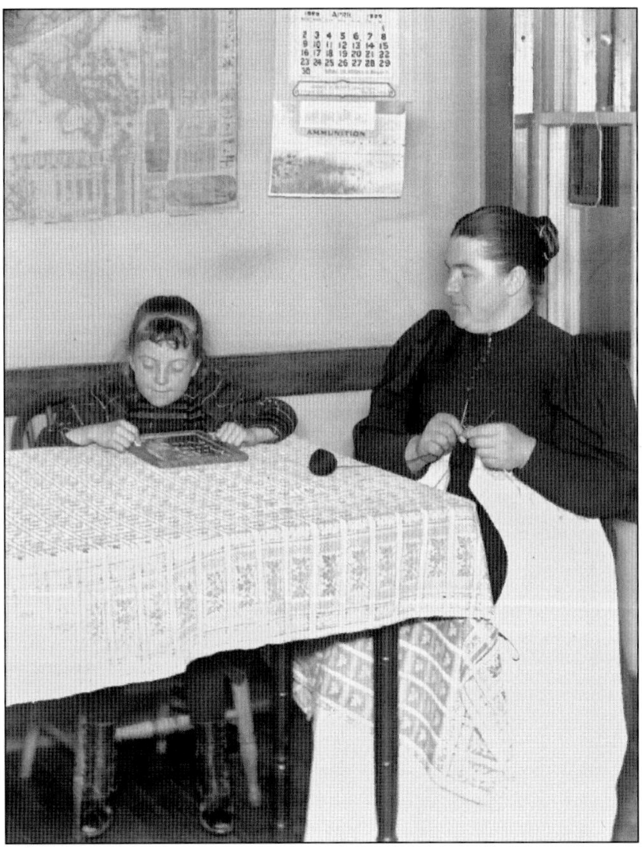

This modern kitchen in 1898 included cold running water. Electricity was still in the future, so the small metal match dispenser beneath the mirror is for lighting lamps as well as the stove. (EG/BFC.)

Six-year-old Emma Gerhardts does math on a slate as her mother, Henrietta, supervises while she does her needlework. The calendar shows it to be April 1899. (EG/BFC.)

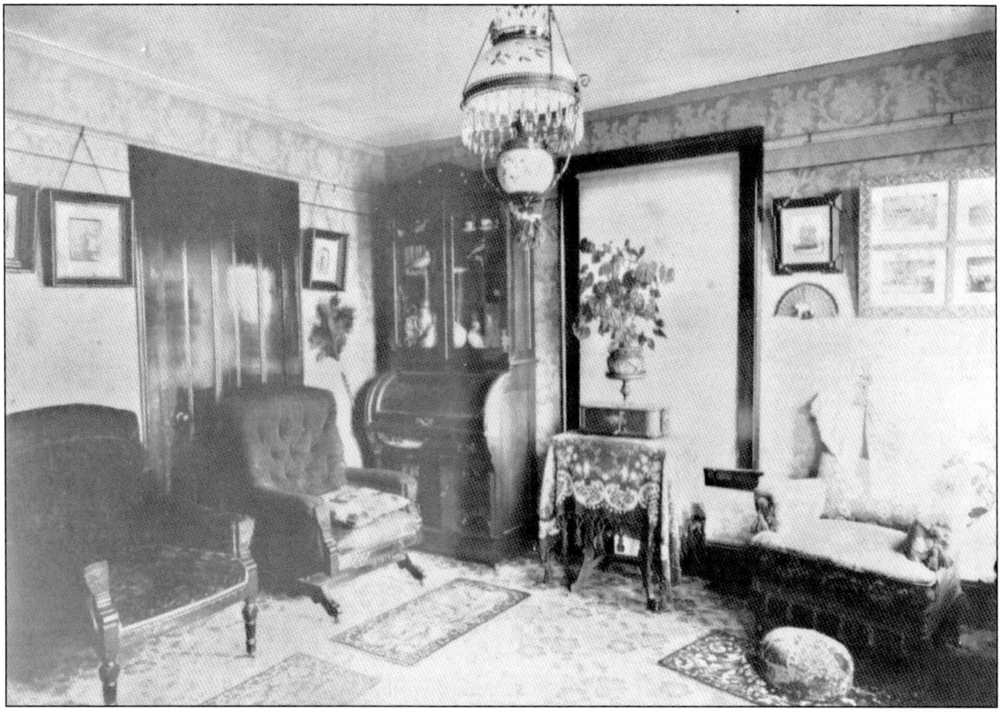

This picture, probably taken in 1898, shows the Gerhardts' parlor. A gaslight hangs in the center of the room. The music box that held the Christmas tree now holds a plant pot. The oak secretary contains a variety of stuffed birds, and framed pictures hang from a track that runs around the upper walls of the room. (EG/BFC.)

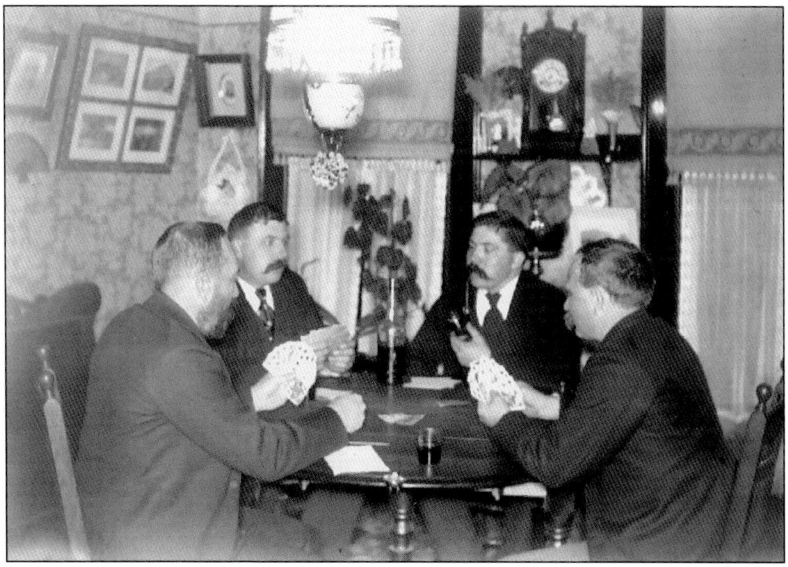

Four gentlemen enjoy a game of cards. The players are, from left to right, Ernest Gerhardts, Fritz Schmalt, an unidentified gentleman with a pipe, and Fritz Theis. (EG/BFC.)

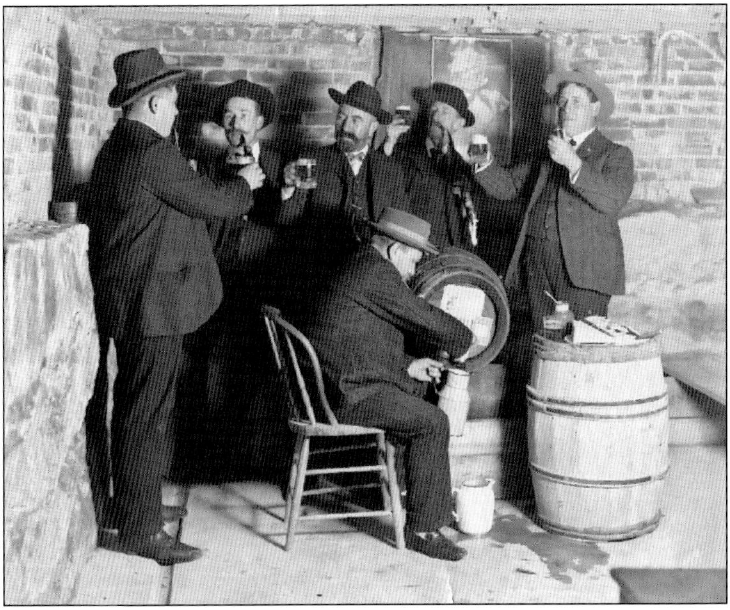

Ernest Gerhardt (standing, center) lifts a glass with an unidentified group of friends. His brother-in-law Fritz Theis taps the keg. (EG/BFC.)

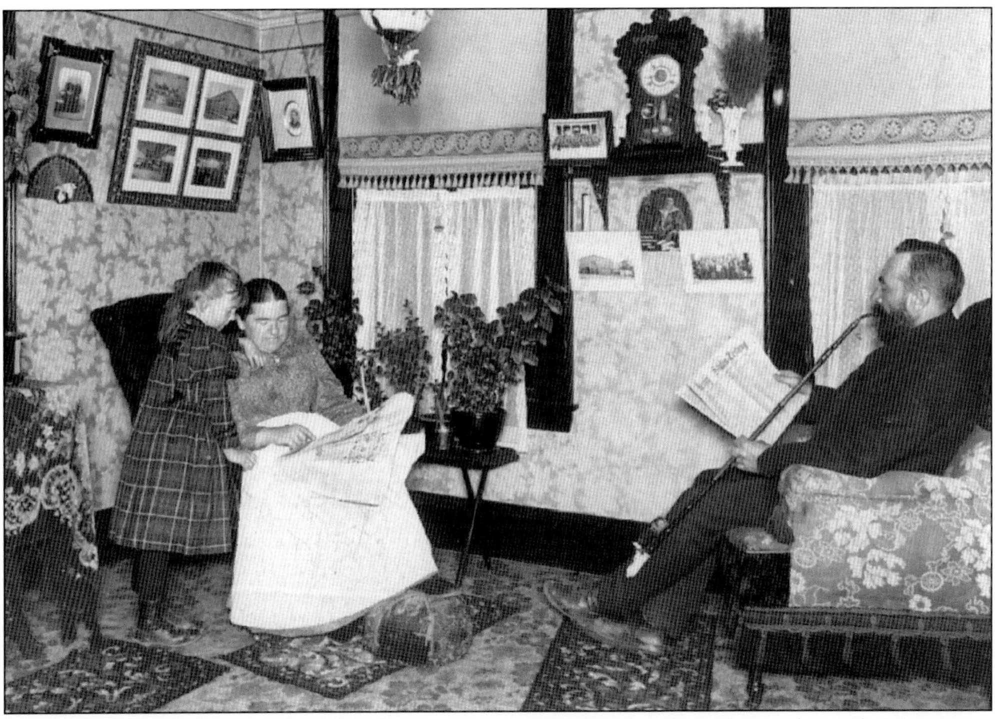

Ernest Gerhardts photographed this domestic scene with his daughter Emma; his wife, Henrietta; and himself at home in their parlor. He is smoking his German long pipe and reading a German newspaper. The large picture frame over his daughter's head displays four photographs of the Haskell Silk Company mill plant, where he worked. (EG/BFC.)

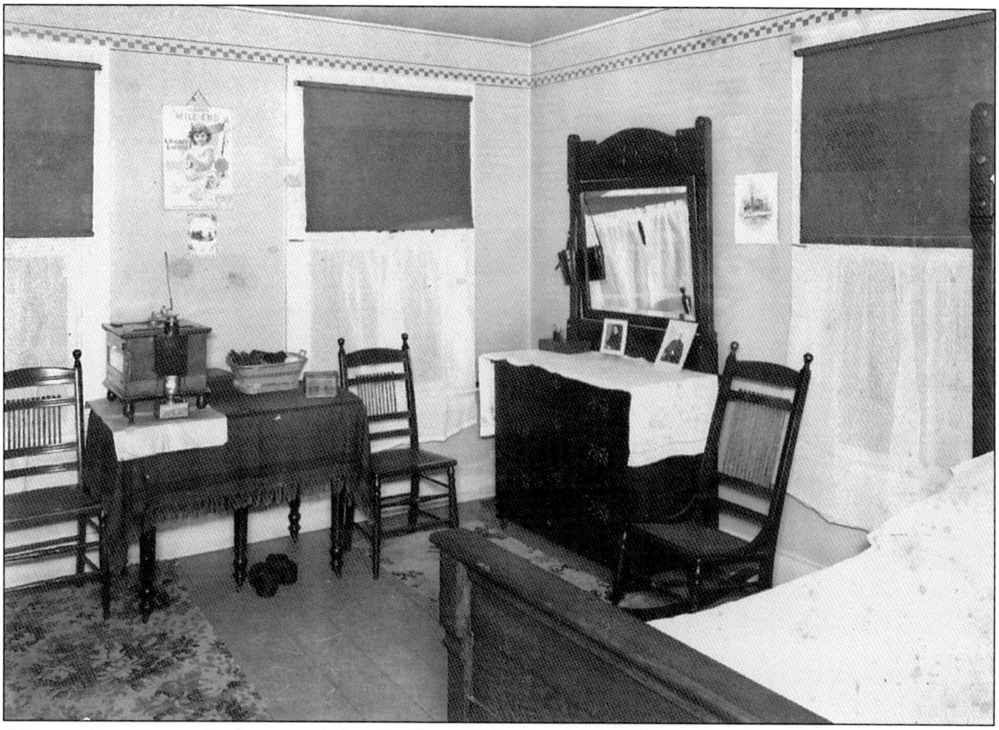

This is the master bedroom of the Gerhardts' house in 1898. It is unknown what the cabinet on the table is, but it appears to be some type of machine. The picture was taken before the house had electricity. The table also holds Henrietta's crochet supplies. Above the table hangs a poster for Clark's "Mile-end" Crochet Cotton, so it is possible this machine relates to her needlework. (EG/BFC.)

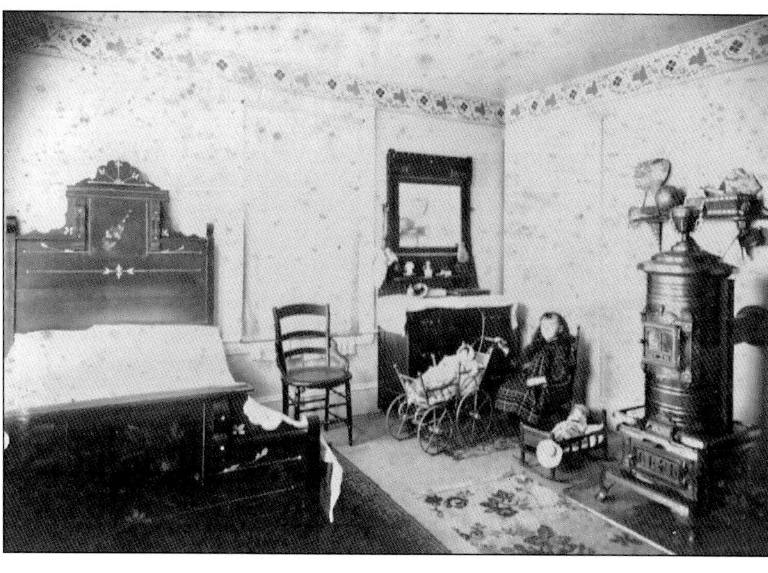

Here is the room of Ernest's daughter Emma, who was five years old in 1898. She poses with her dolls in their doll-sized perambulator and crib. (EG/BFC.)

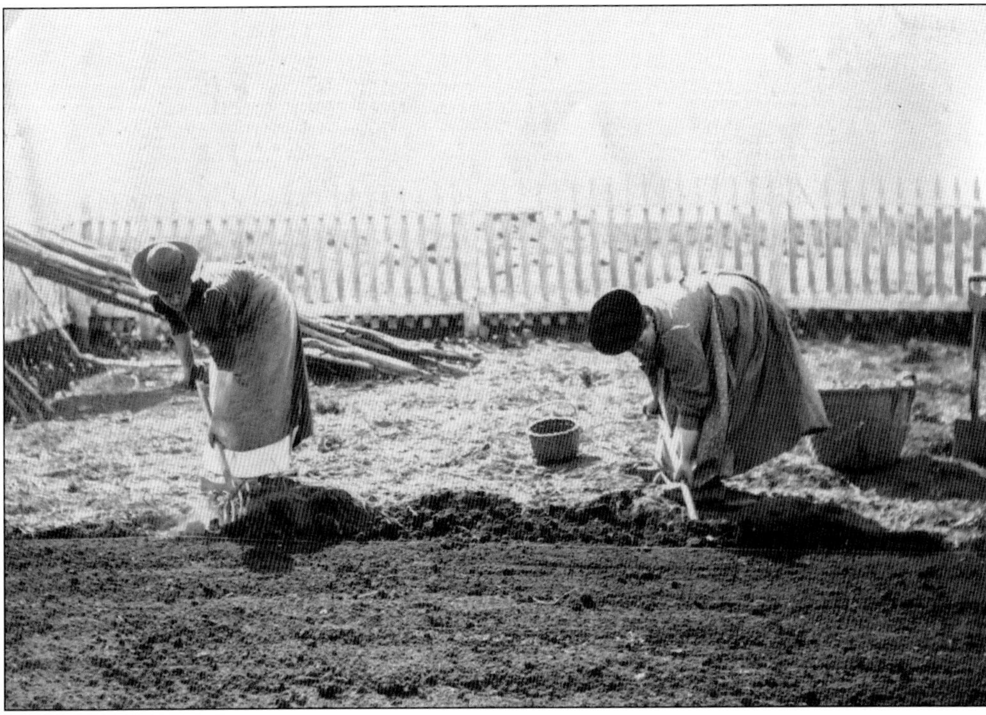

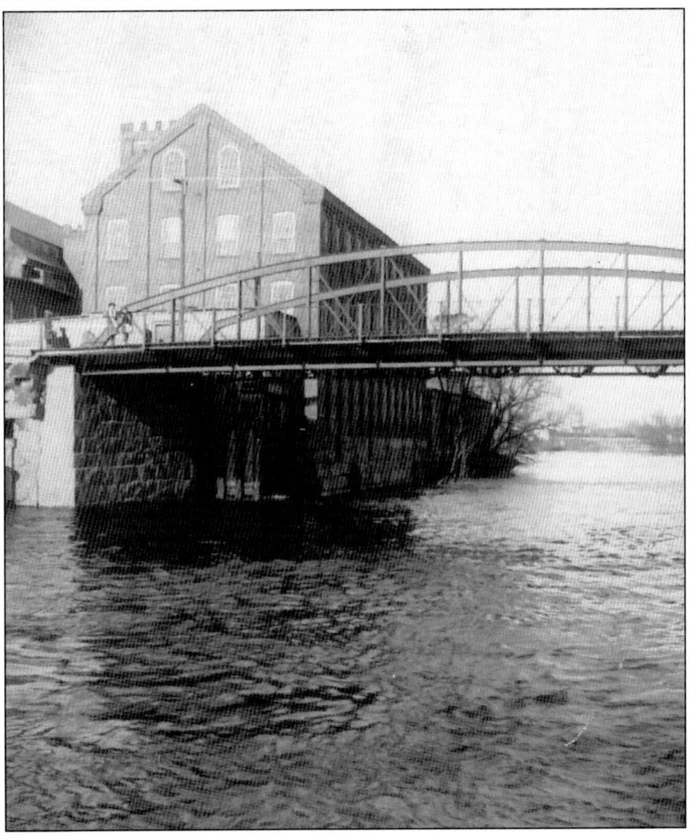

Two sisters, Emma (Schmalt) Theis and her older sister Henrietta (Schmalt) Gerhardts, work side by side in the garden. For six years, Emma and her family lived in a separate apartment in the Gerhardts' house. In 1901, they moved to 128 Brackett Street on the corner of Brackett and Pennell Streets. The garden at 157 Brackett Street continues to produce food in 2013. (EG/BFC.)

The iron bridge on Bridge Street was built in 1871. It was the second iron bridge to cross the Presumpscot River here. The Westbrook Manufacturing Company is just beyond the bridge in this view taken from upstream. (EG/BFC.)

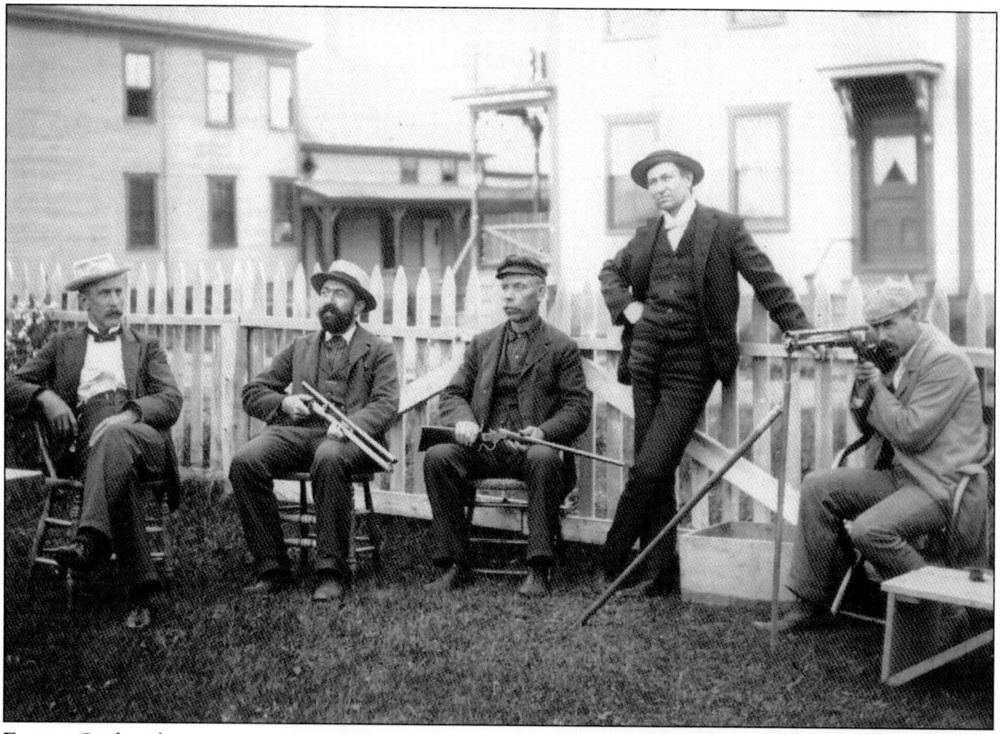

Ernest Gerhardts (second from left) and four unidentified friends do some target shooting in the Gerhardts' yard. Brackett Street runs behind the fence at their back. When this picture was taken, there were probably not any other houses this far up the hill between Brackett and Saco Streets. (EG/BFC.)

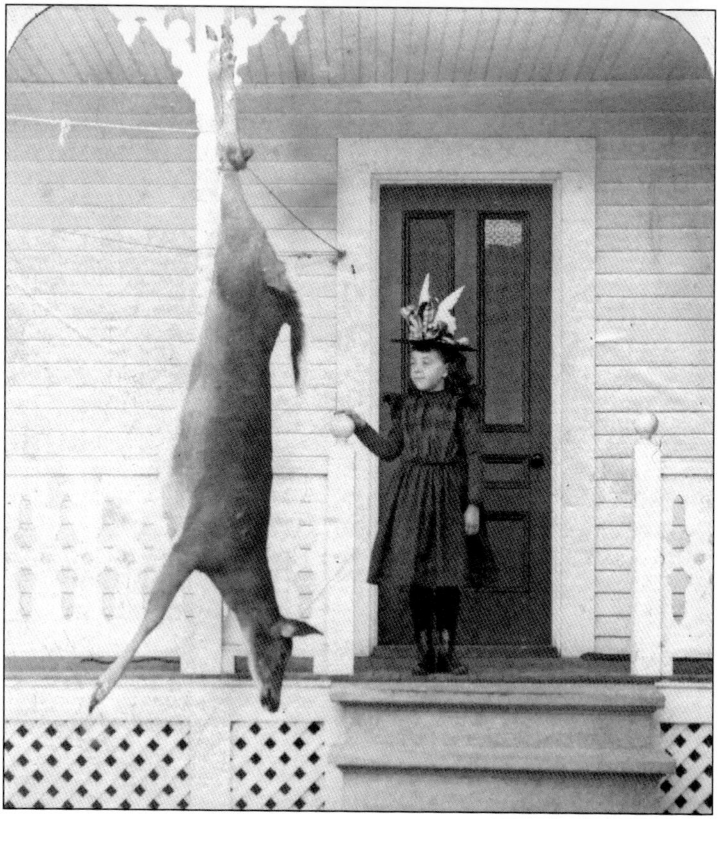

Emma Gerhardts, wearing a very fashionable hat, looks at the deer her father brought back from a successful hunting outing about 1903. (EG/BFC.)

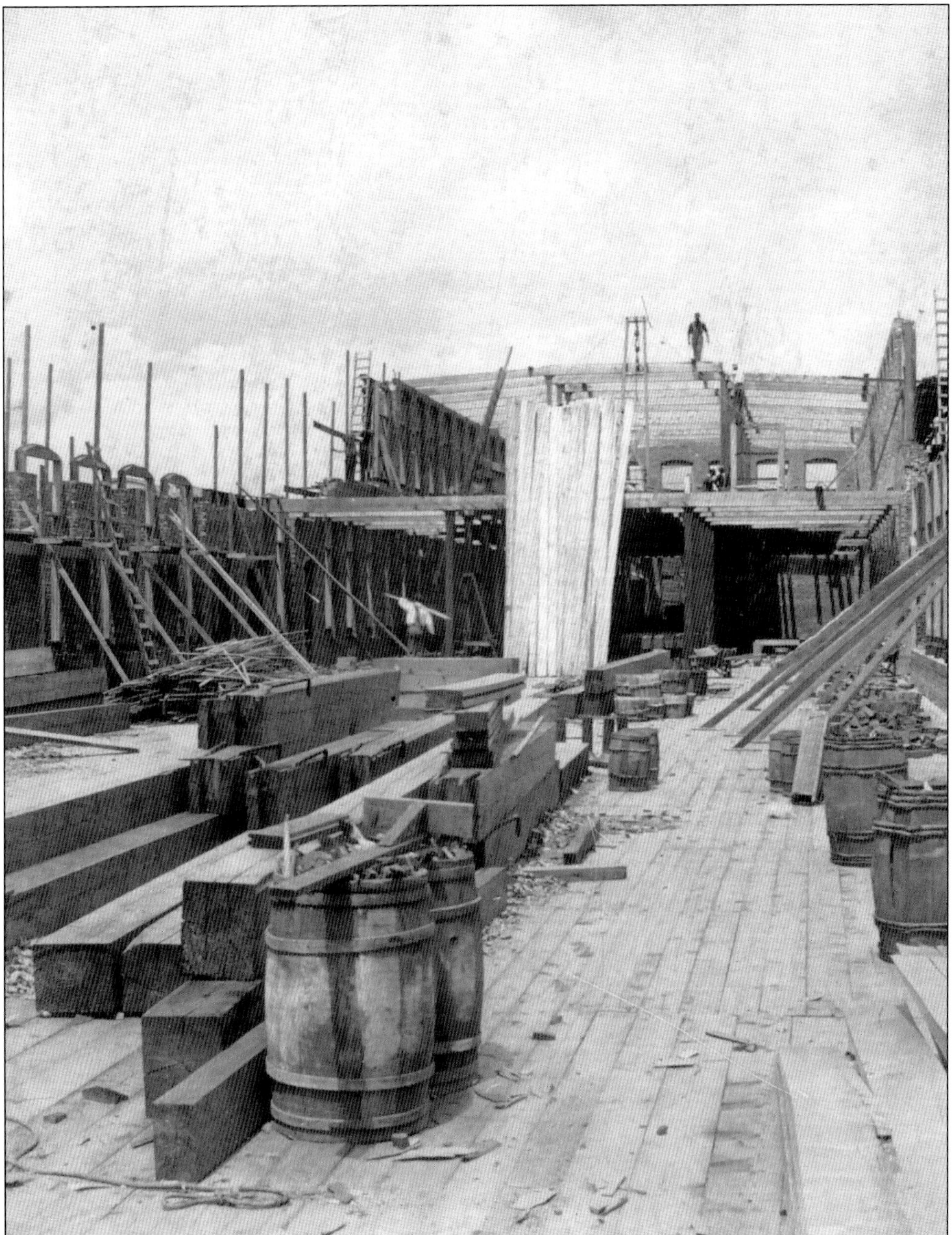

After several smaller expansions, the thriving Haskell Silk Company of Westbrook built a brand new facility on Lincoln Street. Work began in 1901 and was completed the next year. Here, the two-story main building, 55 feet by 330 feet, is shown under construction. (EG/BFC.)

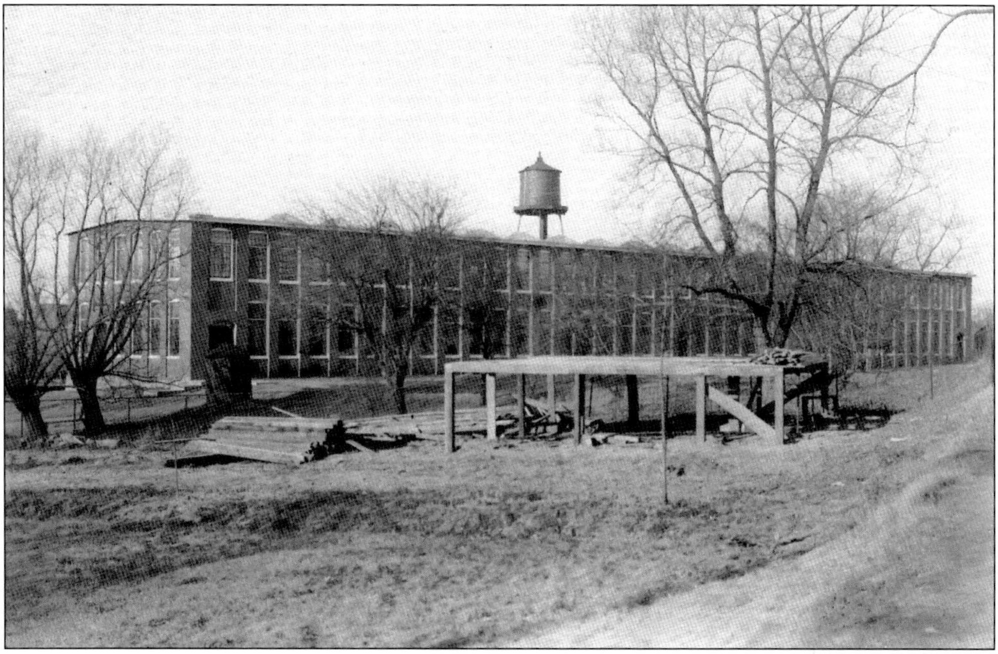

In this photograph, the new Haskell Silk Company plant on Lincoln Street nears completion. Once opened, the new plant was able to double the output of the old. Then, in the early decades of the 20th century, rayon and other synthetic fibers were introduced as less expensive alternatives to silk. Demand for silk dropped, and Haskell Silk Company closed in 1933. This building was later used by the Sebago Moc Company. It now houses riverfront loft condominiums. (EG/BFC.)

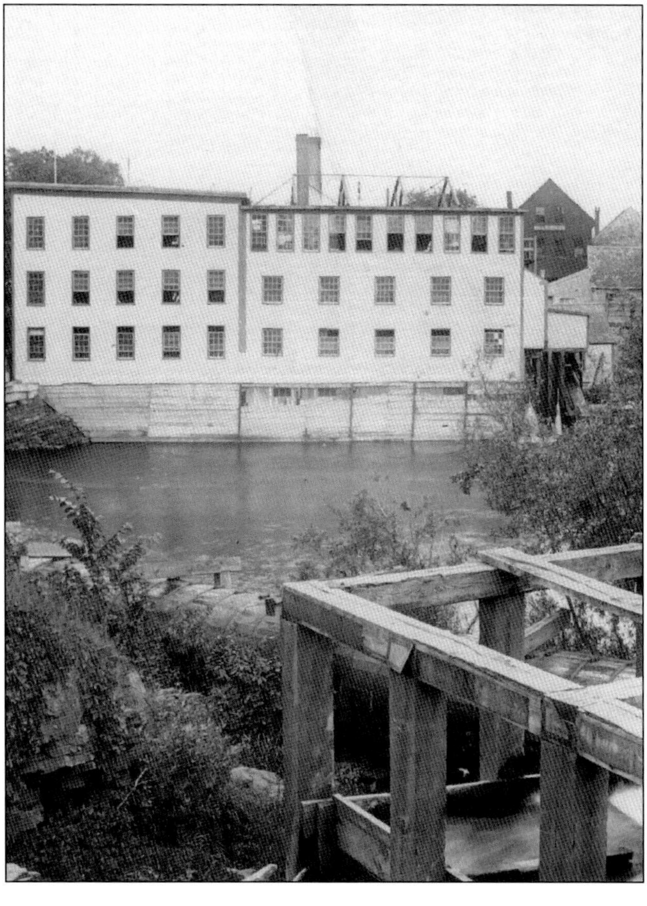

Haskell Silk Company had been expanding for years before its decision to build a new structure. This picture shows the old Haskell Silk Company mill plant, which was located right in the center of town on the west side of Bridge Street. To the left is a three-story expansion added to the front of the original mill. (EG/BFC.)

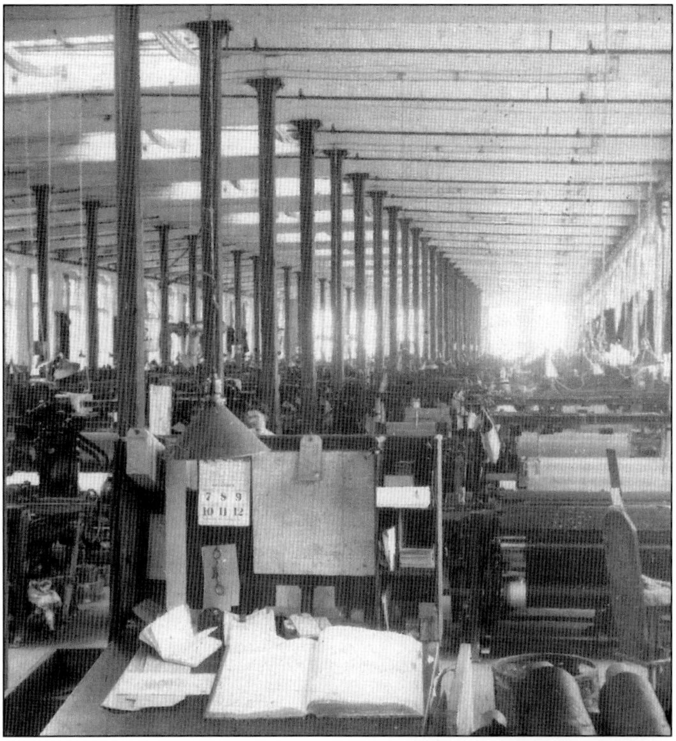

In 1883, Ernest Gerhardts came to Westbrook as a loom fixer for the Haskell Silk Company. Over the years, he advanced and became manager of the second floor at the new Haskell Silk Company building. In November 1904, he brought his camera to work and took this picture of his desk in the spacious new site. (EG/BFC.)

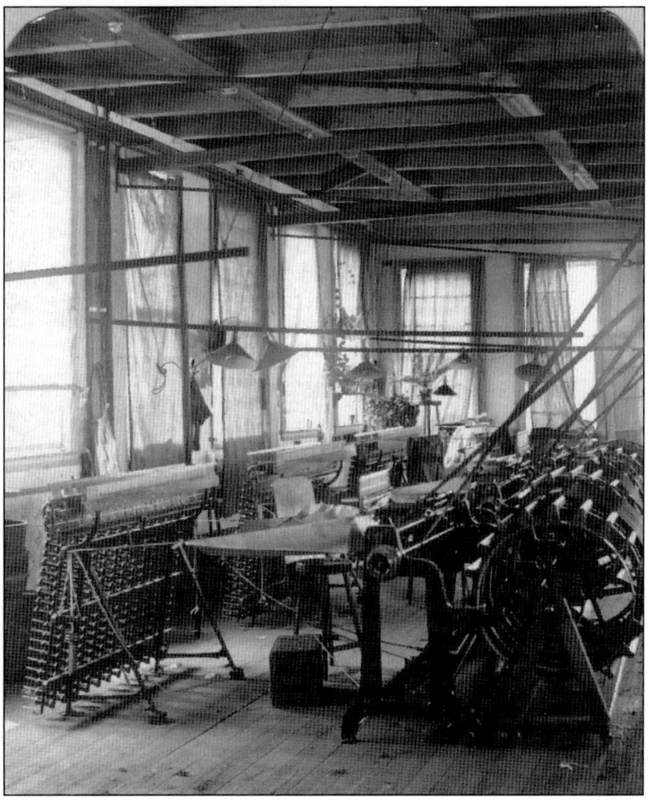

There are plants in the windows, even a potted fern, in this interior shot of the old Haskell Silk Company mill plant. There are also multiple electric lights. The Haskell Silk Company was an early adopter of electric lighting and had its own dynamos to generate electricity. The story is told that the company had to negotiate with its fire insurance company, which preferred gaslights, as they were less of a fire hazard. (EG/BFC.)

Women tend the machines in this interior shot of the old Haskell Silk Company mill. Ernest Gerhardts took most of these interior shots with a stereoscopic camera. Viewing the double image through a stereoscope conveys the real depth of this work space. (EG/BFC.)

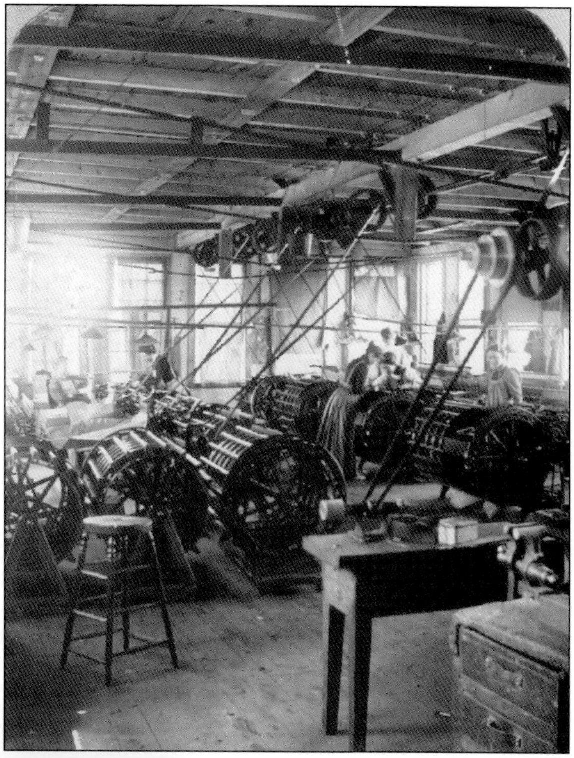

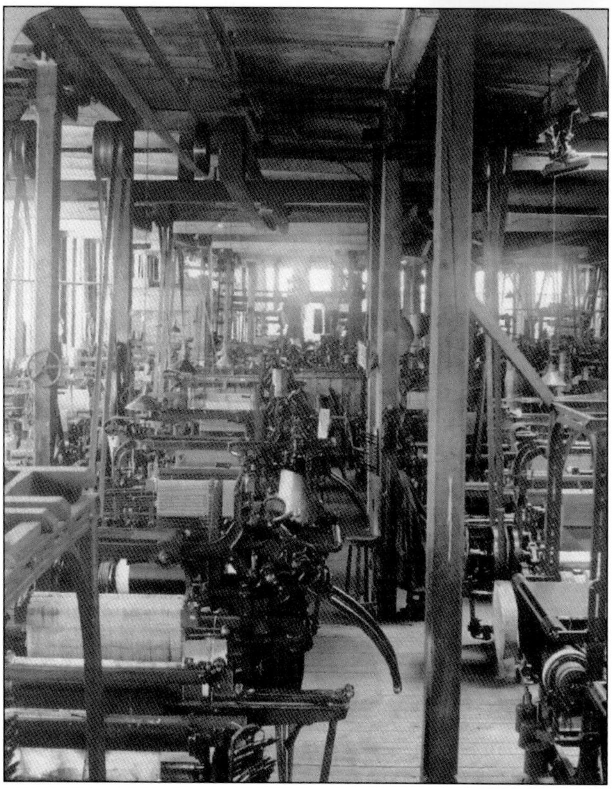

There was no one on the floor and the machines were quiet when Gerhardts took this picture inside the old Haskell Silk Company mill plant. (EG/BFC.)

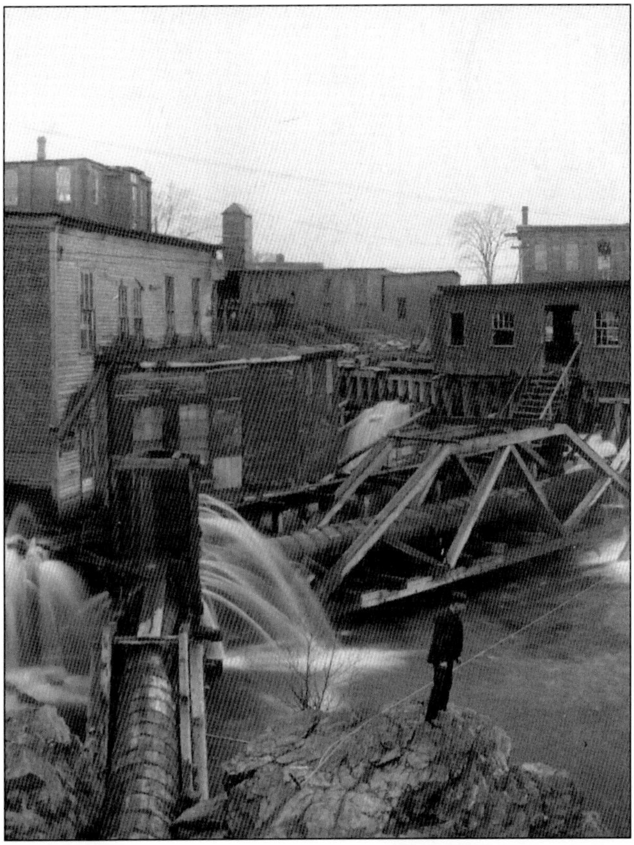

An unidentified man looks down at the Presumpscot River behind the original Haskell Silk Company mill plant. The back of this photograph says only "back of old silk mill." (EG/BFC.)

This once fashionable house had fallen into disrepair by the time this photograph was taken. Its location is uncertain, but it was probably on one of the streets between Church and Saco. Neither the house nor the train tracks exist today, both of their locations crossed daily by thousands on William Clarke Drive. (EG/BFC.)

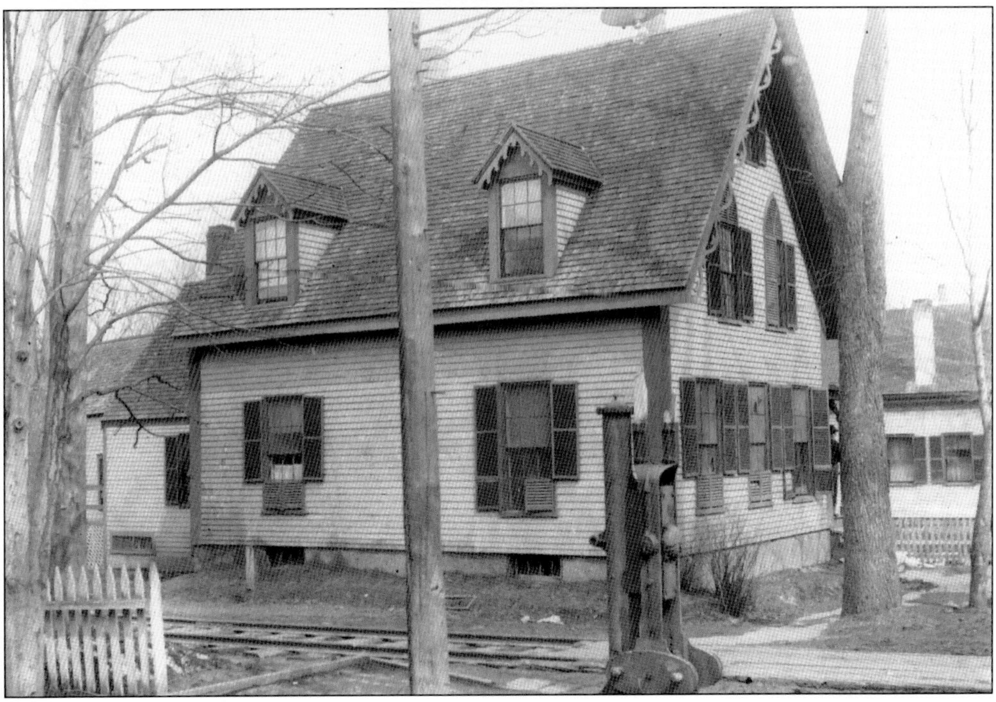

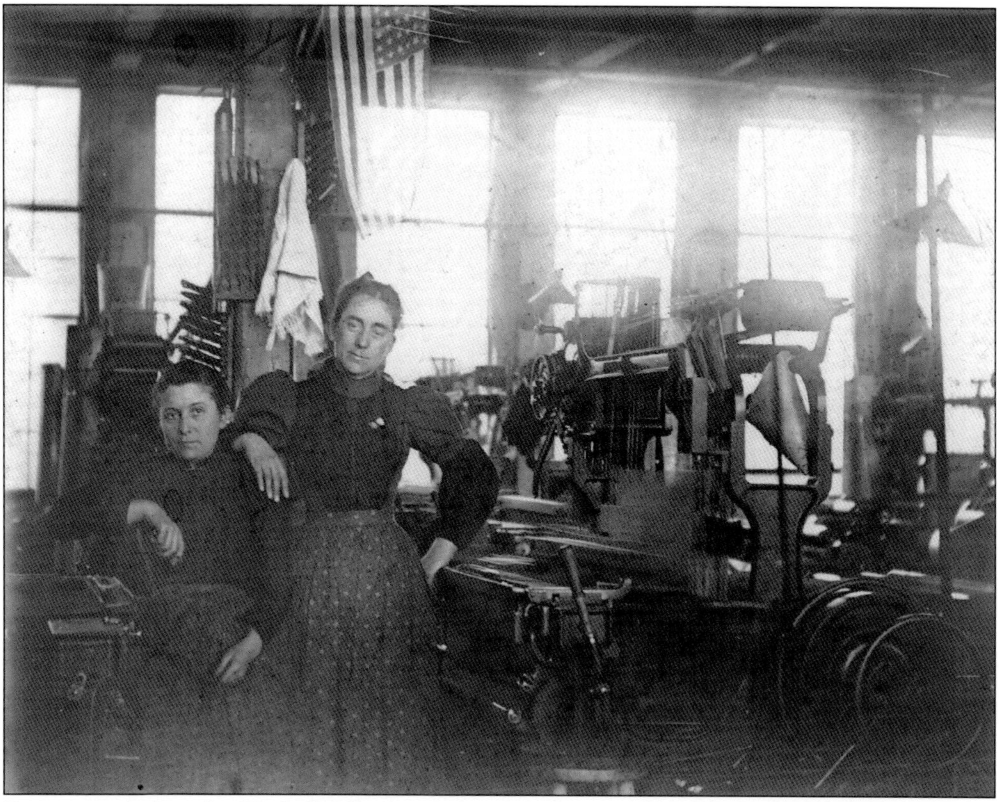

Some time before the Haskell Silk Company moved out of the old building on Bridge Street, Ernest Gerhardts took photographs of some of the machinery and the people who were working there. The pictures on these two pages show some of these Westbrook silk workers around 1900. (EG/BFC.)

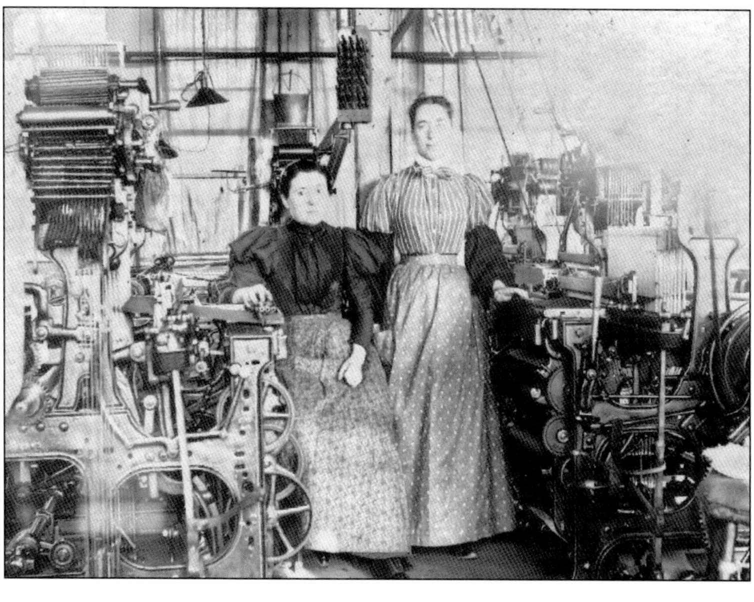

The workers in all four pictures on this page and the next are unidentified. Here, two women pose next to their machines. (EG/BFC.)

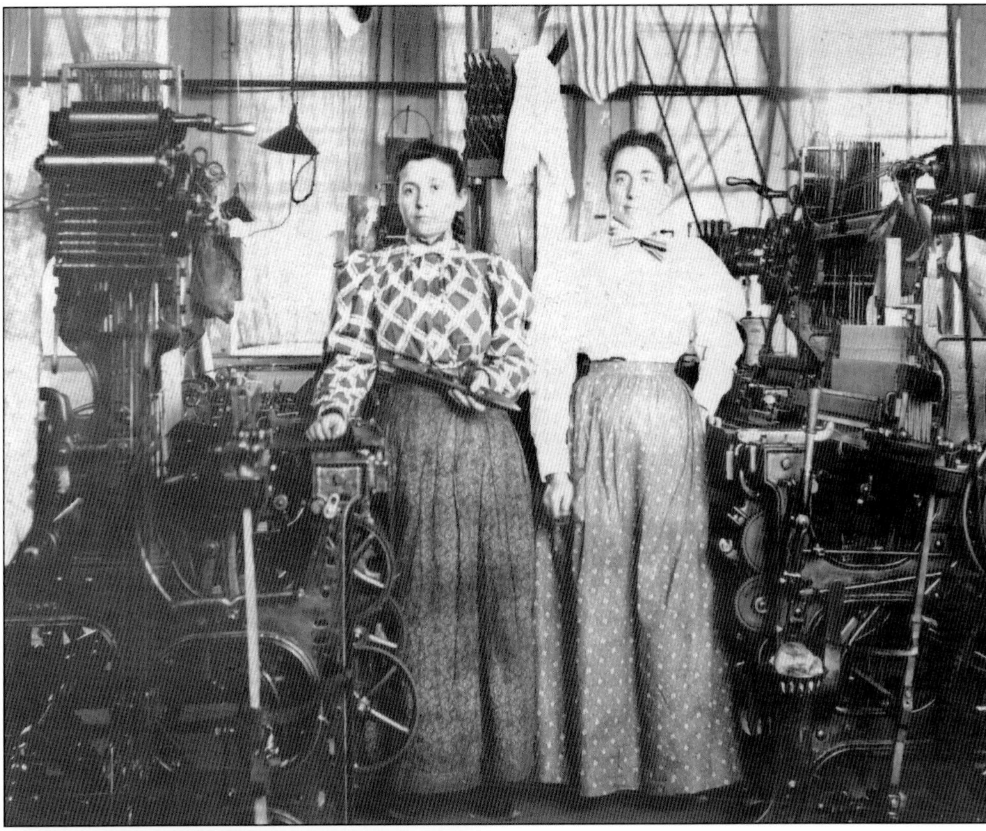

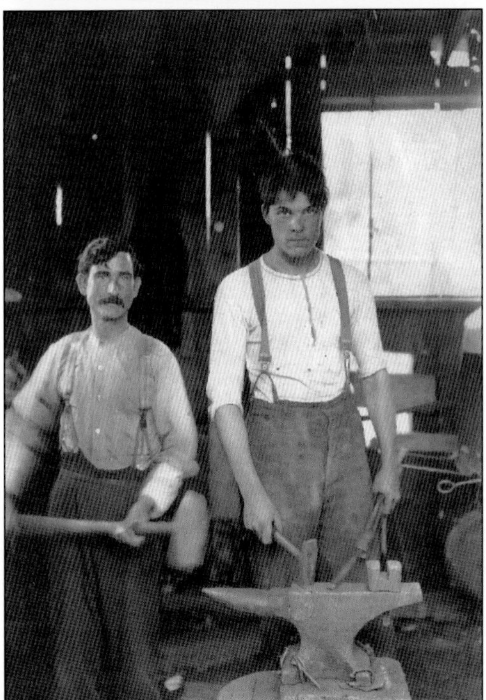

Pictured around 1900, these two unidentified women also worked in the old Haskell Silk Company mill plant. (EG/BFC.)

In the Haskell Silk Company mill plant, two unidentified millworkers stand with a sledgehammer and anvil. (EG/BFC.)

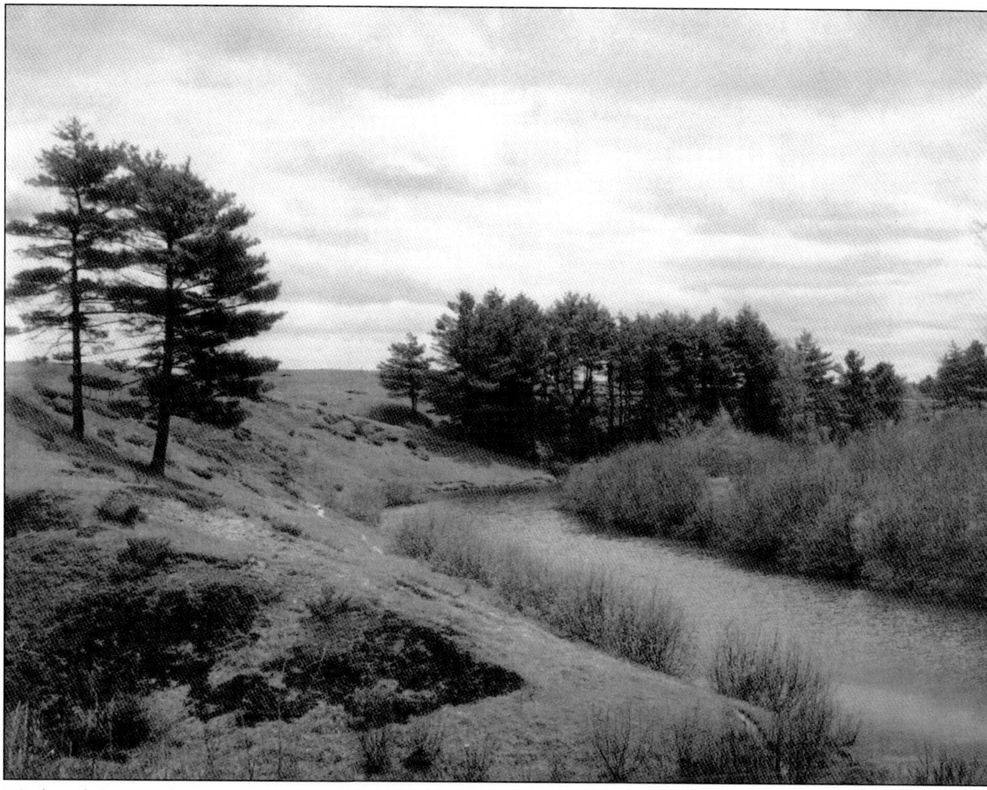

“Solitude” was the name Ernest Gerhardts gave this picture when he entered it into a Portland Camera Club competition. It shows a bend in the Stroudwater River to the west of Spring Street, in back of the farm that was once Bill Clarke’s Blue Spruce Dairy. The image won a local prize, and in 1905, it was published in *Photo Era* magazine. (EG/BFC.)

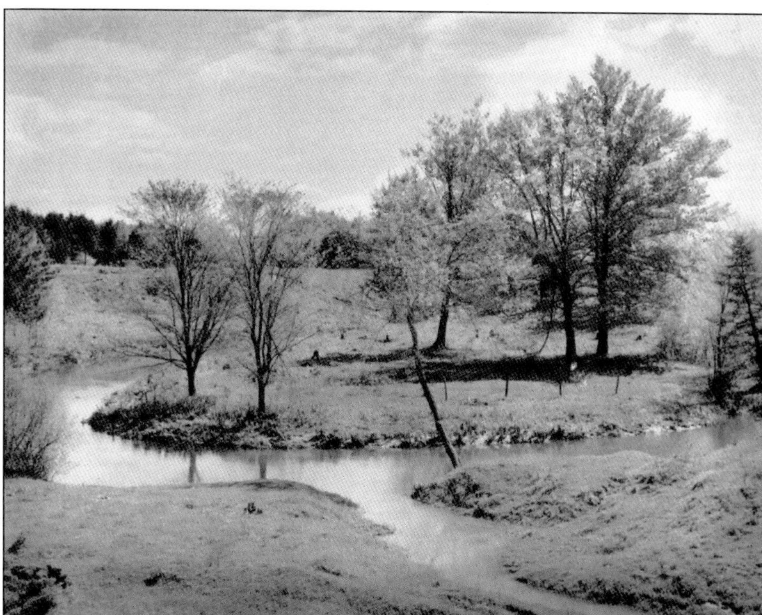

Gerhardts named this second entry, “Where We Meet.” Also taken on the Stroudwater River behind the Clarke farm, it shows a stream joining the river. (EG/BFC.)

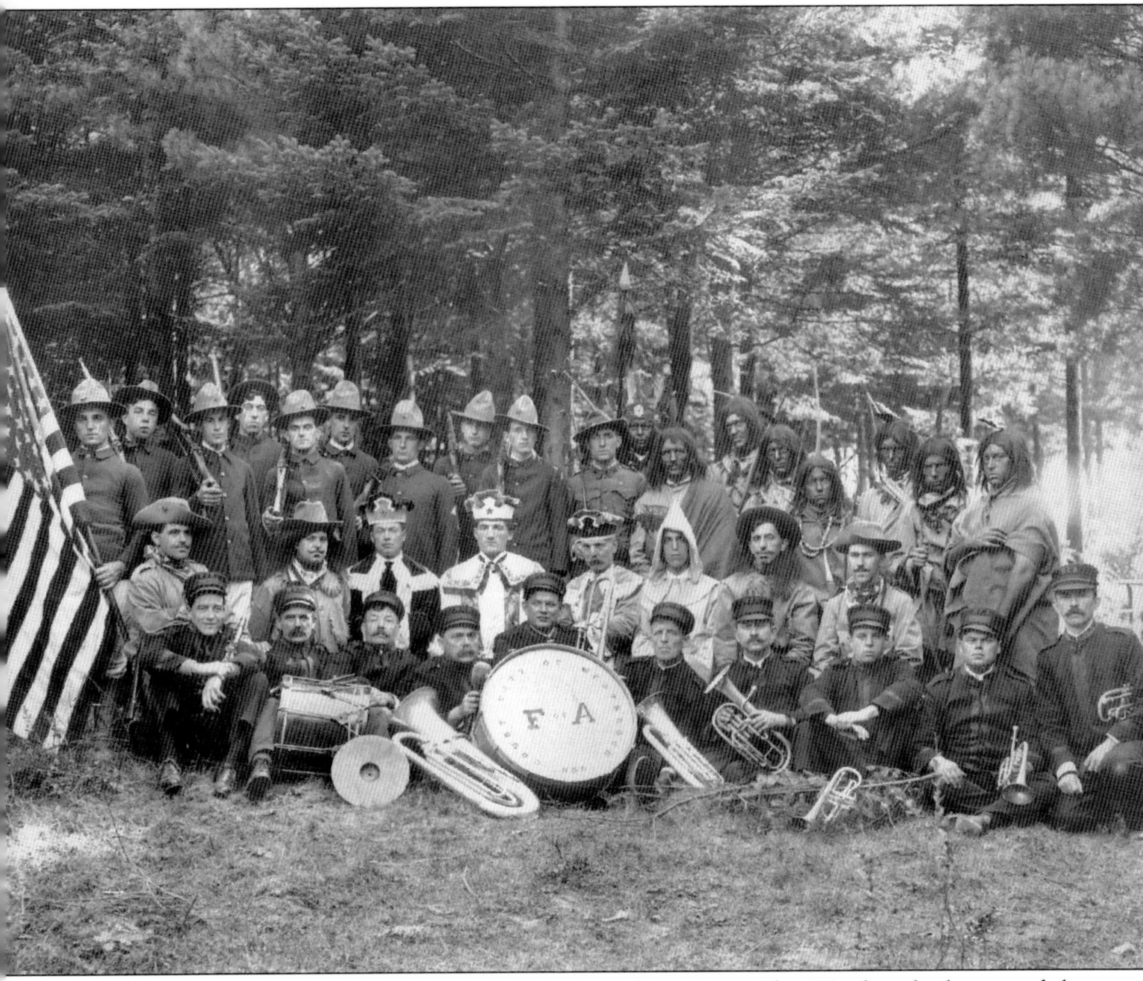

The "F of A" on this drum stands for Foresters of America. The Westbrook chapter of this national fraternal benefit society was organized on June 8, 1900. Their meeting place was on the top floor of the Warren Block. Charter members included Joseph Lebel, Amede Rousseau, Joseph Sampson, A.C. Gouzie, Dr. Adjutor Couturier, Joseph Guimond, Oliver Giguere, Henry G. Rocheleau, Augustin Sicard, and Thomas Welch. Starting with a small group, the membership grew to 130 by 1950. (EG/BFC.)

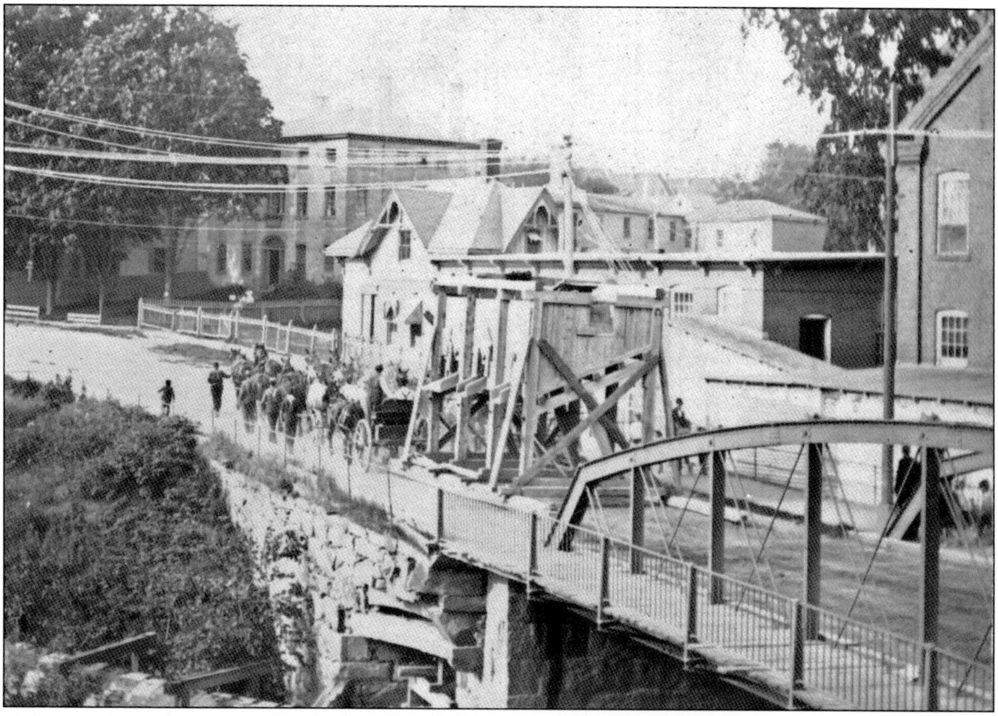

At least a dozen horses are hitched to the skid that is transporting machinery across the iron bridge on Bridge Street from the old Haskell Silk Company mill plant to the new one. (EG/BFC.)

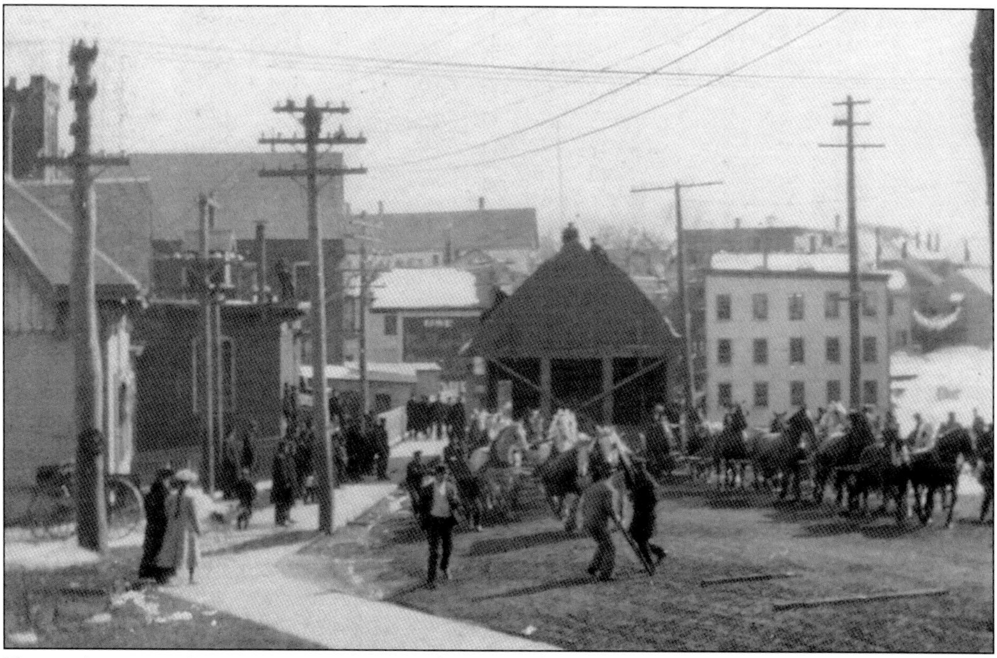

Twenty horses and as many men strain as they start the incline up Bridge Street after crossing the iron bridge with their large and heavy load. It is possible that the freight is from the old Haskell Silk Company mill plant, the white building at right, destined for the new plant on Lincoln Street. (EG/BFC.)

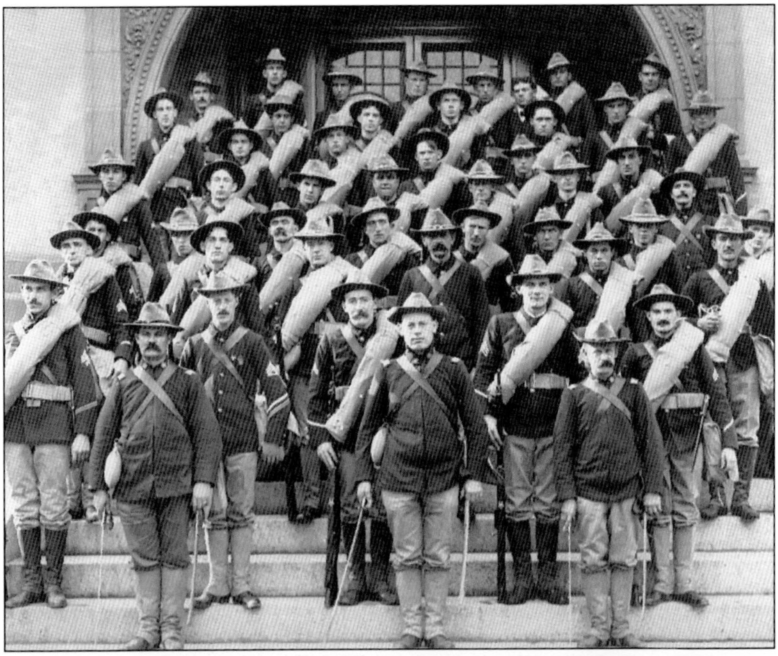

Company M of the Maine National Guard stands for a photograph on the steps of the Walker Memorial Library. (EG/BFC.)

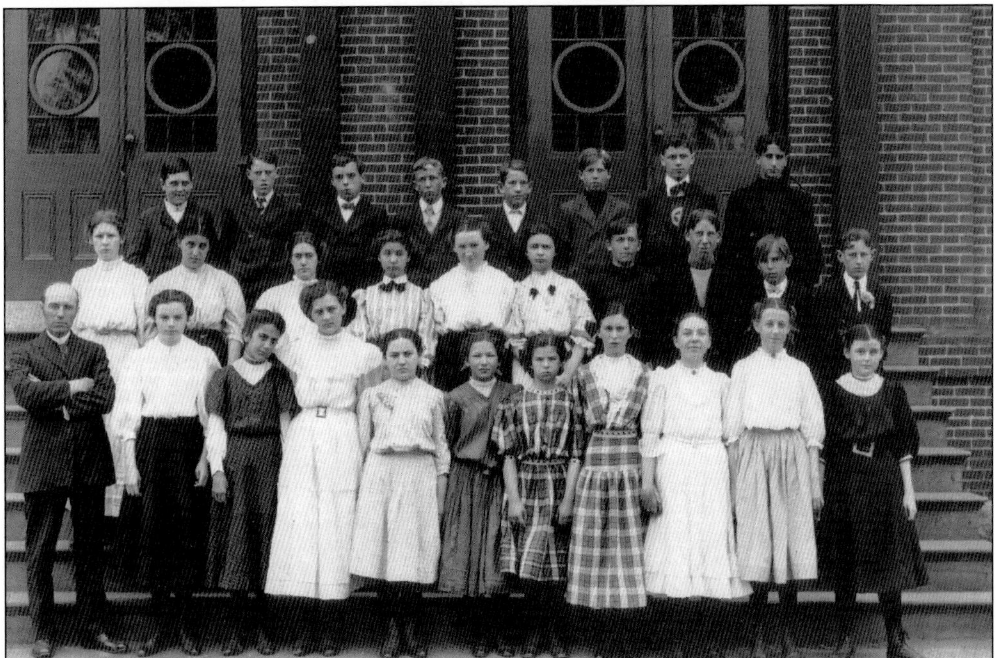

This photograph was taken at Bridge Street School in 1907. From left to right are (first row) Principal Charles Wentworth, Julia Doherty, Edna Blake, Mary Barnes, Emma Reny, Ruth Northon, Ruth Scates, Emma Taylor, Emma Gerhardts, Julia Burke, and Elizabeth ?; (second row) Jennie McAloney, Edith Sharon, Josephine Letarte, Caroline Jordan, Pearl McLean, Winnifred Sturgis, Harold Sinclair, Ira Gemmell, Harold Pride, and Leroy Welch; (third row) Milburn McAloney, Erlon Mosher, Clifford Ward, Everett Sinclair, Robert Parkhurst, Aaron Pride, Lawrence Farrar, and Arthur Arseneault. (EG/BFC.)

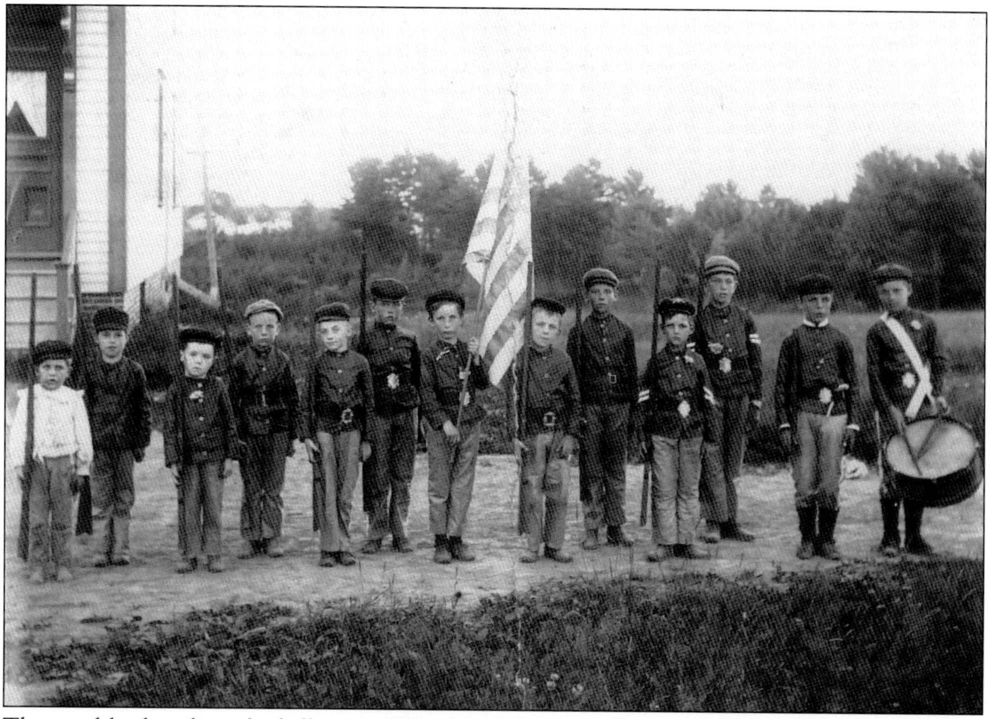

The neighborhood on the hill area of Westbrook between Saco and Spring Streets was known as "Irish Hill." This photograph of the "Irish Hill Gang" was taken on Brackett Street in 1898. Except for the flag bearer and the drummer, each boy holds a wooden practice rifle. (EG/BFC.)

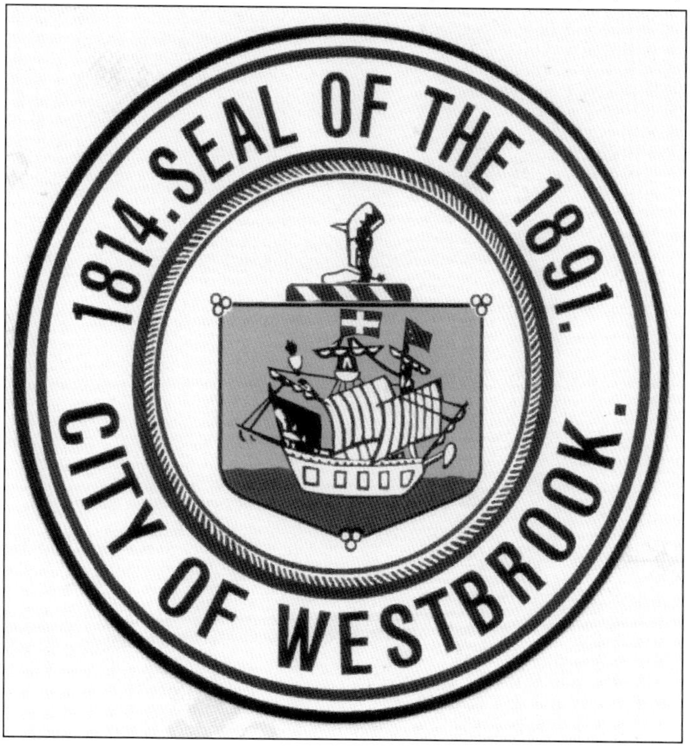

In the center of the city seal is a facsimile of the vessel in which Col. Thomas Westbrook, for whom the city was named, came to Falmouth, bearing the king's permission to select masts for the Royal Navy. Surmounting this is the crest of the Westbrook family, a mailed knee and foot. Around the seal are the words "City of Westbrook," and the dates 1814, the date of the town's incorporation, and 1891, the date of the city's incorporation. The seal was received and adopted on June 4, 1891, by vote of the city government. (Courtesy of the City of Westbrook.)